Creating Cooperation

A volume in the series
CORNELL STUDIES IN POLITICAL ECONOMY
edited by Peter J. Katzenstein

A full list of titles in the series
appears at the end of the book

Creating Cooperation

*How States Develop
Human Capital in Europe*

PEPPER D. CULPEPPER

CORNELL UNIVERSITY PRESS

ITHACA AND LONDON

First published 2003 by Cornell University Press

Printed in the United States of America

Library of Congress Cataloging-in-Publication Data

Culpepper, Pepper D.
  Creating cooperation : how states develop human capital in Europe / Pepper D. Culpepper.
    p. cm.—(Cornell studies in political economy)
Includes bibliographical references and index.
  ISBN 0-8014-4069-6 (cloth : alk. paper)
    1. Occupational training—Europe. 2. Skilled labor—
Europe. 3. Human capital—Europe. I. Title. II. Series.
  HD5715.5.E85 C857 2002
  331.12′5′094—dc21

2002009348

Cornell University Press strives to use environmentally responsible suppliers and materials to the fullest extent possible in the publishing of its books. Such materials include vegetable-based, low-VOC inks and acid-free papers that are recycled, totally chlorine-free, or partly composed of nonwood fibers. For further information, visit our website at www.cornellpress.cornell.edu.

Cloth printing   10 9 8 7 6 5 4 3 2 1

To Mary Louise

Contents

Preface

Surveying the hodgepodge of organizations that supports international cooperation in Europe, a bemused French diplomat reportedly uttered, "It will work in practice, yes. But will it work in theory?" (Fenby 1999, 13). The diplomat would find succor in the literature on cooperation in political science, where the preconditions for cooperation are outlined with Cartesian clarity. Wily individual actors require institutional mechanisms that allow them to monitor one another's behavior and to sanction those who defect. In the absence of such mechanisms, cooperation is likely to fail unless actors are able to draw on an existing repository of social trust to avoid the mutually destructive pursuit of short-term self-interest. Over the last decade, some of the most important studies in political science have described an elegant, if dispiriting, world of two societal equilibria: one in which institutions and social trust already exist and dissuade defectors, and the other in which the absence of either institutions or trust condemns cooperative initiatives to a speedy death by defection.

That, at least, is the theory. The only problem, as the French diplomat noted, is that cooperation sometimes emerges where we least expect to find it. Why? Are there predictable features of public policy that are associated with successful cooperative experiments? Or, instead, are these variations so idiosyncratic that they have nothing more general to tell us about cooperation than that it happens where it happens?

These are the questions that provoked me to write this book. The questions led me to examine the reforms of systems of human capital provision, the success of which depends on securing cooperation among private companies. These reforms were attempted in two societal terrains that, according to our existing theories, should be hostile to the creation of cooperation: the civil society of eastern Germany was supposedly supine after decades of authoritarian rule and French society had been reputedly beaten down by centuries of centralized management from Paris. And in both places, attempts to create private cooperation in the area of skill formation have indeed failed—sometimes. Yet both have also seen surprisingly successful cooperative seedlings take root. This variation, and the reasons behind it, will certainly interest those who study human capital policies or European politics. Those interested in neither training nor Europe, but who do care about the sources of social cooperation, will also find lessons of general significance here. It is with both these audiences in mind that this book has been written.

Throughout the course of this project, I have received a great deal of support. I acknowledge first the kind participation of scores of company representatives from France and Germany. Their anonymity was the condition of their candid discussions with me, and I respect it throughout. But this book could not have been written without their help. Likewise, I thank the associational and governmental actors who agreed to talk to me, often on multiple occasions, about the functioning of their organizations and the development of human capital policies. A complete list of these interviews is provided in the appendices. I am also grateful for the research assistance of Godefroy de Colombe, Jonathan Laurence, Jean Mulot, and Nicolaus Petri and for the administrative support provided by Michael Blackmore.

My greatest academic debts are to the three scholars whose intellectual engagement and personal encouragement sustained this project from beginning to end. Peter Hall read more drafts of this book than anyone else. He provided feedback that was insightful, critical, and copious. The clarity that remains in the final version is the result of innumerable discussions with him that left inchoate, half-formed, or empirically unsupported ideas on the cutting-room floor. Robert Putnam taught me the importance of theory that generates portable expectations and of seeking out a variety of data to try to disconfirm those expectations. Indeed, the book went through an additional set of revisions when he exhorted me to go back, one more time, to the data. David Soskice's theoretical vision inspired this book, and his comments at key junctures have influenced my own explanatory approach. For the high standard set by their own work and their generous support of a project driven by theoretical disagreement with some of that work, I am deeply grateful.

Several scholars read an earlier draft of the manuscript and came to Cambridge to discuss it. The comments and criticism of these scholars— Jeff Frieden, Paul Pierson, Fritz Scharpf, and Eric Verdier—led to substantial improvements in the final version, and I thank them. I am likewise indebted to three anonymous reviewers for their suggestions. Peter Katzenstein read the entire draft and made comments that improved almost every aspect of it, including especially some foundational suggestions for the shape of chapter 1. I would also like to recognize the aid and advice of Stanley Hoffmann and Torben Iversen. Thomas Cusack generously helped me gain access to data sources in France and Germany. Archon Fung and Isabela Mares provided deliberate and rational feedback on multiple chapters. For especially helpful comments on various drafts or on the ideas within them, I am grateful to Lucio Baccaro, Steven Casper, Cary Coglianese, David Finegold, Orfeo Fioretos, Bob Hancké, Nancy Katz, Horst Kern, David Lazer, Mark Moore, Jonas Pontusson, Stephen Silvia, Maurits van der Veen, Karin Wagner, Stewart Wood, and Jean-Pierre Worms.

Many institutions have hosted me in the course of this project. The Center of European Studies and the John F. Kennedy School of Government at Harvard University have been my institutional homes during the writing of the book, and both proved congenial places to work and to reflect on the book's broader implications. Field research took me away from Cambridge for years, and while away I was fortunate to be part of the intellectual communities of the Wissenschaftszentrum Berlin and the Centre de Sociologie des Organisations (CSO) in Paris. After I returned, a sojourn at the American Institute for Contemporary German Studies in Washington, D.C., gave me time to work out some of the policy ramifications of my findings. I thank all the colleagues and friends from these communities who welcomed me into their midst, and I am grateful to the directors of these institutions for their support: David Soskice, Erhard Friedberg, and Jackson Janes.

Generous extramural funding for the project came from the National Science Foundation, the Bourse Chateaubriand, the Social Science Research Council, and the Bosch Foundation. At Harvard, I received financial support from the Center for European Studies, the Department of Government, the Dean's Research Fund of the Kennedy School of Government, and the Weatherhead Center for International Affairs, all of which I acknowledge with gratitude.

Parts of this argument have appeared in print elsewhere, and I thank the following publishers for permission to reprint them in revised form here: Berghahn Books for "Individual Choice, Collective Action, and the Problem of Training Reform: Insights from France and Eastern Germany," in *The German Skills Machine: Sustaining Comparative Advantage in a Global Economy*, edited by P. Culpepper and D. Finegold, 269–325, 1999; Cambridge University Press for "Can the State Create Cooperation?: Problems of Reforming the Labor Supply in France," *Journal of Public Policy* 20(3): 223–45, 2000; and Oxford University Press for "Employers, Public Policy, and the Politics of Decentralized Cooperation in Germany and France," in *Varieties of Capitalism: The Institutional Foundations of Comparative Advantage*, edited by P. Hall and D. Soskice, 275–306, 2001.

Finally, I thank my family for tolerating with good humor the long process of writing this book. My wife, Mary Louise, and the two children who joined us in the course of this adventure, Sophie and Sebastian, are a constant source of joy. My deepest gratitude goes to Mary Louise, who learned two foreign languages and discovered firsthand how labor markets work in two European economies so that I could take the time to finish this research. For this and much more, I dedicate the book to her.

Abbreviations

ACFCI	Assemblée des Chambres françaises de commerce et d'industrie (Peak Association of the French chambers of commerce and industry)
APCM	Assemblée Permanente des Chambres de Métiers (Peak Association of Crafts Chambers)
bac	Baccalauréat (Final Secondary School Certification in France)
BBiG	Berufsbildungsgesetz (German Vocational Training Law of 1969)
BDA	Bundesvereingung der Deutschen Arbeitgeberverbände (Peak Confederation of German Employers' Associations)
BDI	Bundesverband der Deutschen Industrie (Confederation of German Industry and Trade)
BEP	Brevet d'études professionnelles (Diploma of occupational studies)
BiBB	Bundesinstitut für Berufsbildung (Federal Institute for Vocational Training)
BMBW	Bundesministerium für Bildung, Wissenschaft, Forschung und Technologie (German Federal Ministry for Education, Science, Research and Technology)
BTS	Brevet de Technicien Supérieur (Post-Secondary School Technical Training Certificate)
C2T	Centre de Transfert de Technologie du Vimeu (Center for Technology Transfer of the Vimeu)
CAP	Certificat d'Aptitudes Professionnelles (Certificate of Vocational Aptitude)
CBP	Chesapeake Bay Program
CCI	Chambre de Commerce et d'Industrie (Chamber of commerce and industry)
CDU/CSU	Christlich-Demokratische Union/Christlich-Soziale Union (alliance of the Christian Democratic Union and the Christian Social Union)

CEREQ   Centre d'études et de recherche sur l'emploi et les
               qualifications (Center for Studies and Research on
               Qualifications)
CESR   Conseil Économique et Social Régional (Regional
               Economic and Social Council)
CFDT   Confédération française du travail (French
               Confederation of Workers)
CFE-CGC   Confédération française de l'encadrement—
               Confédération générale des cadres (General
               Confederation of Executives and Managers)
CFTC   Confédération française des travailleurs chrétiens
               (French Confederation of Christian Workers)
CGPME   Confédération générale des petites et moyennes
               entreprises (General Confederation of Small and
               Medium-size Enterprises)
CGT   Confédération générale du travail (General
               Confederation of Labor)
CGT-FO   Confédération générale du travail—Force Ouvrière
               (General Confederation of Labor—Labor Force)
CM   Chambre de Métiers (Chamber of crafts)
CMEs   Coordinated Market Economies
CNPF   Conseil national du patronat français (National
               Council of French Employers)
CO   Contrat d'orientation (Guidance contract)
COPIRE   Commission Paritaire Interprofessionelle Régionale
               de l'Emploi (Joint Regional Intersectoral
               Employment Board)
COREF   Comité Régional de l'Emploi, de la Formation
               professionnelle et de la promotion sociale (Regional
               Committee on Employment and Training)
CPC   Commission professionnelle consultative (Joint
               Advisory Board to the Ministry of Education)
CPR   Common Pool Resource
CQ   Contrat de qualification (Qualification contract)
CQP[M]   Certificat de qualification professionelle [de la
               métallurgie] (Certificate of professional training [for
               the metalworking sector])
CTDEC   Centre technique de l'industrie du décolletage
               (Technical Center of the French Bar-Turning
               Industry)
DARES   Direction de l'animation de la Recherche, des Études
               et des Statistiques (Department for research and
               statistics, French Labor Ministry)

DGB	Deutscher Gewerkschaftsbund (German Trade Union Confederation)
DIHT	Deutscher Industrie- und Handelstag (German Association of Chambers of Industry and Commerce)
DM	Deutschmark(s)
DQP	Diversified Quality Production
DUT	Diplôme universitaire de technologie (University diploma of technology)
EU	European Union
FDP	Freie Demokratische Partei (Free Democratic Party)
FEN	Fédération de l'éducation nationale (Federation of National Education Unions)
FFr	French franc(s)
FGMM-CFDT	Fédération générale des mines et de la métallurgie (Metalworking Affiliate of the CFDT)
FIM	Fédération des industries mécaniques (Peak Trade Association of the French Mechanical Industries)
Five-Year Law	Five-Year Law on Work, Employment, and Professional Training of 1993
FM-CFTC	Fédération de la métallurgie (Metalworking Affiliate of the CFTC)
FM-FO	Fédération de la métallurgie (Metalworking Affiliate of the CGT-FO)
FNE	Fonds national pour l'emploi (National employment fund)
FO	Force ouvrière (Name by which CGT-FO is customarily known)
FTM-CGT	Fédération des travailleurs de la métallurgie-CGT (Metalworking Affiliate of the CGT)
Gesamtmetall	Gesamtverband der Metallindustriellen Arbeitgeberverbände (Peak Association of Metalworking Employers' Associations)
GIOst	Gemeinschaftsinitiative Ost
HWK	Handwerk (craft sector)
IAB	Institut für Arbeitsmarkt- und Berufsforschung (German Institute for Labor Market & Job Research)
IG Metall	Industriegewerkschaft Metall (Metalworkers' Union)
IHK	Industrie- und Handelskammer (Chamber of Industry and Commerce)
INSEE	Institut national des statistiques et des études économiques (National Institute for Statistics and Economic Research)
LAB	Landesausschuß für Berufsbildung

LMEs	Liberal Market Economics
LVSA/VMESA	Federation of Employers' Associations in Saxony-Anhalt/Metal Workers' Association of Saxony-Anhalt, Magdeburg
MWSA	Saxon-Anhalt Ministry for Economy
OECD	Organization for Economic Cooperation and Development
OPCAREG	Organisme Paritaire Collecteur Agréé Régional (French Regional Training Fund)
OREF	Observatoire Régional de l'Emploi et de la Formation (French Regional Observatory for Employment and Training)
OSHA	Occupational Safety and Health Administration
PRDF	Plan régional de développement des formations professionnelles (Regional Plan for the Development of Vocational Training)
RPR	Rassemblement pour la République (Rally for the Republic, French Gaullist Party)
RTP	Regional Technology Plan
SME	Small or medium-size enterprise
SNDEC	Syndicat national du décolletage (National Association of the Bar-Turning Industry)
SPD	Sozialdemokratische Partei Deutschlands (German Social Democratic Party)
SSWA	Sächsisches Staatsministerium für Wirtschaft und Arbeit (Saxon Ministry for Employment and Work)
Treuhand	Treuhandanstalt (German Federal Privatization Agency)
UDF	Union pour la démocratie française (Union for French Democracy, French Center-Right Party)
UFAs	Unités de Formation par Alternance
UIMM	Union des industries minières et métallurgiques (Union of Employers' Associations in the French Mining and Metal-Working Industries)
VAS	Vereinigung der Arbeitgeberverbände in Sachsen (Saxon Federation of Employers' Associations)
VME	Verband der Metall- und Elektroindustrie in Berlin und Brandenburg (Metal Working Employers' Association of Berlin and Brandenburg)
VSME	Verband der Sächsischen Metall- und Elektroindustrie (Saxon Metal Working Employers' Association)
WDA	Welsh Development Agency

Creating Cooperation

CHAPTER ONE

The Political Problem of Decentralized Cooperation

Anyone who drives a car quickly becomes conversant with a complex set of mutual expectations that vary from one place to another: the rules of the road in Berlin differ substantially from those in Boston. These mutual expectations are not principally determined by laws dictating speed limits or the side of the road on which we drive. Instead, they are the product of a history of past interactions with other drivers on similar roads. These past histories give us common expectations about how fast we should drive on a given road, regardless of the posted speed limit, or about the way other drivers will react when a traffic signal turns yellow. Changing the speed limit is, therefore, a fruitless way to try to turn Boston drivers into Berliners, as every Boston driver knows.

This is a book about how states try to solve the problem of changing mutual expectations in order to create cooperation. In other words, how can states provoke institutional change? Reforming governments are often able to pass laws that establish new regulations, new incentives, or new formal organizations for implementing policy. But such legislative action is frequently of little import in effecting institutional change. Democratic governments have difficulty directing the process of institutional change because laws are only one of the many sets of rules, both formal and informal, that structure human interaction. Durably transforming the mutual expectations of actors who are embedded within established patterns of interaction is a difficult thing for governments to do.

Nevertheless, governments often want to achieve goals that require private actors to change the way in which they interact with one another because doing so would produce positive social benefits. The challenges posed by cooperative dilemmas have been well documented in classic studies of democratic performance (Putnam 1993) and common-pool resource dilemmas (Ostrom 1990). Such dilemmas are also prevalent in the contemporary economic policy problems of the advanced capitalist democracies (Scharpf 1991, 1997). Some of these problems flow from the faded allure of Keynesian deficit spending as the principal tool of government intervention in the economy. Since the 1980s, policy-makers have increasingly transferred their interventionist energy to the supply side of the economy, realizing that they can most effectively influence economic outcomes by improving the productivity of labor and of capital, the core factors of production (Boix 1998; Garrett 1997; Garrett and Lange 1991). Such policies often aim to promote firm-level adjustment to changes in the international economy (Hall 1999). Yet convincing firms to change their behavior requires governments to design public policy that can solve private problems of coordination and cooperation; in other words, it is like trying to turn Boston drivers into Berliners.

The empirical case on which this book focuses is that of company investment in general skills. Throughout the industrialized world, a particularly attractive strategy to governments of all partisan hues has been to enhance the skills of the workforce, which allows governments both to respond to company demands for skilled workers and to enable individual citizens to benefit from increased returns to their human capital (Crouch, Finegold, and Sako 1999). Companies are then able to compete more successfully in international markets, and workers are able to contribute to and profit from these gains, helping governments simultaneously to reach their political and their economic objectives. The German dual system of apprenticeship training has attracted considerable attention among academics and policy-makers because it somehow persuades companies to make substantial investments in the general skills of their workers (OECD 1994; Acemoglu and Pischke 1998).[1] In theory, companies should be loath to invest in general skills because they lack the means to guarantee a return on their investment. After receiving their apprenticeship training, workers can be poached by other firms that offer them a higher wage (Becker 1964). However, comparative research demonstrates that there are significant gains to workers and to firms when companies can be persuaded to make an investment in firm-based general-skills training (Lynch 1994).

In western Germany, the training system is maintained through a combination of public labor market regulation and private employer coordination, which together clarify the expectations of employers and of employees about the likely training investments of other firms in the

---

[1] General skills are capacities that are transferable, and therefore of use, to many companies, whereas firm-specific skills are of use only to a single company (Becker 1964). In practice, the skills imparted through in-firm training programs, as in the German dual system, often combine general and specific skills. While purely general skills can be conferred through exclusively school-based education, the combination of general and specific skills imparted through firm-based training programs has been shown to overcome the problems of market failure in general skill provision and to produce durable increases in firm productivity and in worker wages (Lynch 1994).

economy (Soskice 1994; Acemoglu and Pischke 1998; Harhoff and Kane 1997). The regulations of in-firm standards and testing for apprenticeship are supervised by the chambers of industry and commerce, while changes to qualifications are negotiated between unions and employers' associations. Employers' representatives ensure that the skills certified are relevant for the current production needs of their companies. Unions ensure that the skills taught are in fact of general character—which is to say, useful to many employers—rather than being narrowly firm-specific (Streeck et al. 1987; Münch 1991).

When such a system of combined state regulation and private interest governance already exists, companies have a past history from which they can reasonably make predictions about what other firms will do. This matters because the calculus of some companies about which strategy to pursue is influenced by what they think other companies will do: companies may find it attractive to make significant investments in firm-based general training if enough other firms also do so. Other things being equal, the potential attractiveness of apprenticeship-style training increases as the likelihood increases of hiring a "lemon"—that is, an apprentice who has individual weaknesses that led his or her initial employer not to retain him or her (Soskice 1994). If many companies in the economy are already investing heavily in training apprentices and retaining those they train, those employers that forgo youth training in general skills face a problem: there will be a high proportion of lemons among their applicants. Given the costs of search and replacement in a highly regulated labor market, this can be expensive (Wagner 1999). The training decision of a given company is therefore at least partially dependent on its expectations about what other companies will do.

The problem of a reform that tries to establish a training system like the one in western Germany is that there is no history of prior cooperation that can help companies know what other companies are likely to do in the face of the reforms. Thus, companies are uncertain about how other companies will respond to the reforms; they are uncertain how new institutions, created to support more in-firm youth training, will function; and they are uncertain whether, in fact, in-firm training can deliver the benefits ascribed to it by government policy-makers. A comparison of government strategies to encourage company investment in general skills through vocational training is, therefore, one of the best ways to consider the problem of how to secure decentralized cooperation among private actors.

During the 1990s, governments in both France and in eastern Germany tried to convince private companies to cooperate with one another in the provision of general skills. A decade later, both these reform efforts are generally regarded as failures. Governments in both economies had great difficulty in encouraging companies to make an uncovered investment in the general skills of their workers. Many companies ignored the reforms altogether, despite extensive government campaigns to persuade firms to consider youth training contracts as a viable way to secure future skilled labor. Others took government subsidies and hired young trainees, but failed to invest heavily in the costs of training them. These companies used the youth merely as cheap, temporary labor, to be replaced by other cheap laborers at the end of their training contracts. Yet there was a minority of companies in both France and in eastern Germany that were convinced to hire apprentices, to invest heavily in their training in skills that are both general and certifiable, and then to hire them afterward in work contracts. They made this investment decision with the knowledge that other companies in the economy had not chosen to train in youth contracts and thus with the awareness of the potential threat of their workers' being poached by these other, nontraining firms. Success was not evenly distributed throughout France and eastern Germany but was instead concentrated in a few areas. These are regions in which companies were convinced of the potential value of the vocational training reforms. What differentiates them from the other, failed regions and what lessons they offer for other reforms involving decentralized cooperation are the questions with which this book is centrally concerned.

A NEW CONCEPTION OF POLICY-MAKING

What is the problem faced by national and regional governments when they pass laws in order to change firm-level vocational training practices? These reforms decentralize powers to regional governments, and they also delegate certain prerogatives to private-sector organizations, so the fate of the reforms depends in part on the successful performance of these new institutions. Yet the success of the reforms is ultimately determined by the ability of public- and private-sector actors, working through the new institutions, to convince companies on the ground to change their training behavior in a coordinated fashion. What the state is doing in reforms like these is creating incentives and constraints—subsidies and fines—to induce changes in company choices. But at the same time, it is trying to construct institutions that facilitate the emergence of co-ordinated action among companies.

This, I argue, constitutes a fundamentally distinct problem of policy-making, one predicated on the pervasiveness of uncertainty and a corresponding need for mechanisms to devise a coordinated response by social actors in the face of this uncertainty. In studies of the political process, it is too often assumed that the problems of governments that want to influence social behavior are either legislative or executive. The shelves of political scientists sag under the weight of books explaining how legislative institutions influence the successful building of winning coalitions or how regulatory agencies are (or are not) constrained to execute faithfully the intent of the legislature. Rather than assuming that the principal challenge of policy-making always lies in passing laws or administering laws, this book examines a class of policies in which the most difficult problem is getting private actors to cooperate with one another after a law premised on such cooperation has been adopted. This problem, which I call the problem of decentralized cooperation, is clearly apparent in reforms that attempt to convince companies to invest in the provision of general skills.

There are definite advantages for a given company in having more highly skilled workers. But investing in the general skills of workers is risky because workers can be hired away by competitor companies before the original training company is able to recoup its investment in those skills. The possibility of such poaching limits the willingness of any company to invest in general skills, unless it knows that many other companies will also make such an investment. How any company decides to respond to changes in the regulatory framework therefore depends jointly on that company's perception of the gains from changing its behavior and a calculus of how that company believes others will respond to changes in the policy framework.

This confronts policy-makers with serious problems of coordination under uncertainty. It is well established in the literature on the economics of transition that the uncertainty of the benefits from a reform—even when that reform will clearly improve the future income of a majority of the population—can be sufficient to block the adoption of such a policy (Rodrik 1996; Fernandez and Rodrik 1991). Scholars in this literature worry about the adoption of such policies because they assume that the important politics of reform takes place in the democratic process of choosing a set of framework laws. Thus, the dilemma frequently addressed is whether governments making the transition to a market economy should adopt shock therapy or a more gradualist set of policies (Dewatripont and Roland 1995). When the adjustment to the incentives established by laws can be assumed, this is the correct problem to emphasize. But when, as in the cases of reform studied in this book, the problem of uncertainty extends to knowing how other actors will respond to the reform *after it has been passed*, the character of the problem changes. Actors not only need a way to estimate how well new political institutions and new practices will work, but they also need a mechanism to help coordinate their expectations about what other actors are likely to do. Faced with the fact of a reform premised on securing decentralized cooperation, how do companies decide how to respond to a new set of policy incentives?

While this is in some sense a problem of implementation, the existing literature on policy implementation does not explicitly consider problems of decentralized cooperation. One strand of that literature is directly informed by a command-and-control perspective on state action. The problem of implementation, as this literature has seen it, is how to keep the discretion of street-level bureaucrats within narrow enough bounds that the goals of lawmakers can be put into practice. Having a clear causal theory underlying policy and structuring delivery to minimize veto points are therefore seen as key variables in determining the success of the implementation of a given policy (Pressman and Wildavsky 1973; Mazmanian and Sabatier 1983; McCubbins and Schwartz 1984). Human capital reforms premised on eliciting firm-level cooperation, however, cannot be solved simply by ensuring that laws are administered faithfully. Individual companies will look to what other companies are likely to do, rather than how state agencies will react. Their voluntary investment in general skills cannot be ensured by public decree.

Just as command-and-control regulation fails to capture the problem of decentralized cooperation, so too does the bottom-up perspective of implementation in neocorporatist polities. This work stresses the importance of studying "policy problems as defined and addressed by relevant social actors" (Hjern and Hull 1982, 105), particularly employers' associations and unions. These studies highlight the role of the social partners in helping to administer public policy, and at that level of generality they clearly foreshadow some of the claims made in this book. However, the underlying conception of the policy problem in this research is different than that of decentralized cooperation, and it is different in a consequential way for how states can succeed in solving it. Human capital reforms attempt to elicit private cooperation, and not merely to connect local actors with available public resources, whether informational or financial (Hjern and Porter 1981; Mayntz 1983; Hull and Hjern 1987; cf. Ergas 1987). Subsequent work in this vein on actor-centered institutionalism continues to demonstrate how the organizing capacity and strategic choices of collective actors may thwart the ability of governments to achieve their policy goals (Scharpf 1997). However, the goal of persuading individual companies to cooperate with one another (rather than with the state) is still conspicuously absent in this literature, whereas it is a defining feature of situations of decentralized cooperation.

Problems of decentralized cooperation are defined by three salient characteristics: the existence of strategic interaction, the potential exis-

tence of multiple equilibria, and the presence of causal uncertainty.[2]
These were the central problems faced by French and eastern German
policy-makers trying to reform their vocational training systems, and
they arise increasingly in other areas of policy-making, as I discuss in the
final chapter.[3] Strategic interaction refers to the commonplace observa-
tion that individuals can only assess the returns to their action by considering how other individuals will respond to the changed policy
framework. Depending on how others respond, there may be several
possible outcomes that are Pareto-improving; this is a common situation
of multiple equilibria (Calvert 1995; Scharpf 1997). In a world of
perfect communication and perfect information about the disposition
of other actors, these are not particularly difficult problems to solve. But
in the real world that governments inhabit, uncertainty is a principal
barrier to achieving one of these welfare-improving changes in
individual behavior.

The Destabilizing Effects of Uncertainty
In the absence of uncertainty, policy problems involving pure coordination are easily solved: if a better outcome can be assured through
coordination and everyone knows with certainty the returns facing everyone else, it does not make sense for us not to coordinate our actions with
other social actors (and the others know this). Yet the uncertainty
involved in many sorts of reforms is in fact substantial. This uncertainty
springs from the inability to gauge the performance of new institutions,
the actions of other players, or the causal consequences of what we will
gain if we do change our behavior.

New institutions, or institutions being called on to play new functions,
do not have an established track record of providing these goods. Thus,
even if they are technically capable of providing the goods in question,
such as the information circulation that is required for fine-tuning a new
training program, the institutions have not established a pattern of
having done it before, so actors may attach a lower probability to their

[2] Throughout this book, I refer in general to problems of coordination as well as to
the specific cooperative structure of the decision individual firms face in making a training investment. Coordination problems require that actors come to similar expectations
about an iterated interaction, given multiple potential equilibria. For companies, the
problem of decentralized cooperation requires a cooperative move in a given interaction—forgoing the possible immediate gains to defection in view of the long-term benefits to mutual cooperation. Achieving this cooperation over repeated interactions is itself
a coordination problem (Calvert 1995).

[3] Scholz and Gray (1997), for example, have noted similar problems of the command-
and-control model in accounting for the role played by the Occupational Safety and
Health Administration (OSHA) in the United States.

capability than they would in a situation in which they have seen the institutions function normally.[4] The ultimate government trump card in such reforms—sanctioning—is hobbled by the fact that a new sort of behavior is being called for and thus a new set of responses is being designated as sanctionable. There is going to be some uncertainty about what exactly constitutes defection and what constitutes cooperation—on the parts of both the potential sanctioner and of the sanctionee—in this new realm of coordinated action.[5] In times of reform, not only do new institutions lack the credibility to monitor deviations from cooperation, but the nature of sanctionable behavior is itself uncertain. It is clear what the government is urging actors to do, but if most of the concerned actors are not persuaded that others will be persuaded that the institutions will work as advertised then sanctions have to apply to a majority of the population. In such a situation, sanctions lose their reputational sting—because everybody is doing it, so the reputational loss is not high, and because any sort of sanctioning authority faces an implausibly difficult task. When everyone defects, it is very hard to mete out sanctions to the whole population. Thus, the very uncertainty created by governments trying to change the political economic equilibrium drastically reduces the credibility of the institutions that will be called on to facilitate that reform.

These effects compound the difficulty of estimating how other actors will respond to the reform. Alone, the uncertainty caused by imperfect information may not be the death knell of cooperation; indeed, it can under certain conditions foster its emergence, if time horizons are long enough (Kreps et al. 1982; Kreps 1990; Bendor 1993). But the problems of the credibility of new institutions engender a destabilizing second-order effect of backward induction: actors not only experience the results of uncertainty themselves, but they also know that other actors are experiencing the same uncertainty and that other actors are therefore less likely to engage in cooperative action. To the extent that the fruits of cooperation can only be reaped if a sufficient number of actors adopt the same cooperative strategy, the fact that actors think that others are less likely to participate in the new arrangements makes it less likely that they will participate.

---

[4] Riker and Weimer (1995) make a similar point in discussing the problems of credibility of a new institution—private property rights—in the postsocialist states of central and eastern Europe.

[5] Consider the case of sanctions as stigma, which is certainly consistent with a norm of generalized reciprocity and is also alluded to by Finegold and Soskice (1988). It is simply not credible in a situation of reform that behavior that has not previously been considered out of bounds instantaneously become the subject of social stigma.

Finally, and most important, the attempt to convince actors to co-ordinate around a new equilibrium point creates uncertainty about whether the causal mechanisms that supposedly generate the high payoff to cooperation actually do deliver that outcome. In the case of vocational training, for example, does high-level investment in appren-tices actually produce a higher long-term payoff than not training? Iida (1993) has called this "analytic uncertainty" to distinguish it from the more familiar problem of strategic uncertainty, which pertains to uncer-tainty about the attributes of other actors. This is fundamentally a cog-nitive problem. Analytic uncertainty refers to the misapprehension of one's own payoff matrix, as well as the opponent's payoff, because the causal mechanisms of the new system are not clear or well understood. A reform of the political economy often asks players to move to a mutu-ally beneficial pattern of cooperation when the actors are skeptical that the causal model of policy-makers accurately predicts the payoff they (the actors) will receive. If the causal mechanisms underlying one's own payoff matrix are uncertain, then there is a problem of "pure learning" about the real causal mechanisms at work in the world (Iida 1993).[6] Problems of decentralized cooperation require that private actors acquire information about the world before altering their past patterns of strategic interaction. How, in the presence of this uncertainty, might actors be convinced to cooperate with each other?

THE POSSIBILITY OF COOPERATION: RATIONALIST VERSUS
CONSTRUCTIVIST EXPLANATIONS

Under what conditions will individual actors ever cooperate with one another? This is a fundamental question in political science. Inter-national relations theorists consider the preconditions of international cooperation, scholars in comparative and American politics ask how political institutions can facilitate socially beneficial collective action, and political theorists since Hobbes have questioned how individual interests can be reconciled with the public good.[7] Cutting across these

---

[6] Iida (1993) discusses the case of international monetary policy coordination to illus-trate how uncertainty about the causal mechanisms (i.e., different models) of the macro-economy yields different perceptions of the payoff matrix. Analytic uncertainty is most extreme when complexity is high and cognitive familiarity with the logic of the new model is low. Human capital policies, for example, pose problems of lower complexity than macroeconomic policy-making, but there is a similar uncertainty at the company level about whether or not new patterns of skill investment will yield the returns promised by governments, which is generated by the unfamiliarity of the microlevel decision-makers with the new logic.

[7] Although these questions are debated across the social sciences, the confrontation between rationalism and constructivism has been particularly prominent in international relations theory, where it is perhaps the central debate in the field (Katzenstein, Keohane,

debates is a common polarity of views on the way actors develop common expectations about how others will act. On the one side stand proponents of rational choice with the concept of credible commitments: the idea that cooperation requires the development of institutions through which actors with stable preferences can state their intentions, monitor whether their behavior corresponds to these stated intentions, and sanction noncompliance (Keohane 1984; Williamson 1985; North 1990). Institutions to facilitate credible commitments are necessary, in this view, for cooperation to emerge. Much rational choice theory therefore predicts failure for attempts to create cooperation ex nihilo, when neither markets nor hierarchies are up to the job. On the other side of this divide stand constructivists, who point out that cooperation happens all the time, even under unlikely (for rationalists) preconditions. This is possible, according to the constructivists, because individual preferences are ultimately the product of collective understandings: "Agents themselves are on-going effects of interaction, both caused and constituted by it" (Wendt 1999, 316). The constant reconstruction of these self-understandings can lead to a redefinition of how actors with apparently divergent preferences identify their own interests. When cooperation is the dependent variable, this is a theoretically important difference. If preferences are ultimately subject to continual redefinition, then "the possibilities for change may be greater than if, say, a 'prisoner's dilemma' is treated as an unchangeable fact about some aspect of world politics" (Fearon and Wendt 2002, 64). Charles Sabel (1994: 159) holds the logical extreme of constructivist argumentation when he argues that there are no necessary or sufficient conditions for cooperation to emerge.

For purposes of explaining the empirical success or failure of cooperation and the formation of common knowledge, there are several key differences between these two approaches.[8] The first is ontological: rationalists start from the presumption of individualism, whereas con-

---

and Krasner 1998, 674–82). There are risks in adopting this terminology for debates in comparative politics, where scholars have written about the social construction of ethnic identity as a rationalist process (Fearon and Laitin 2000). However, this a discussion of wide import; little is gained, and much generality would be lost, by using different terminologies for the same phenomena across different subfields. See also Finnemore and Sikkink (2001) for a discussion of constructivism in international relations and comparative politics.

[8] This is not the place for a comprehensive comparison of rationalism and constructivism. International relations theorists have been particularly active in considering such differences; see Fearon and Wendt (2002), Finnemore and Sikkink (2001), and Fierke and Nicholson (2001).

structivists start from a holist ontology. This point of departure leads to a methodological divergence over the preferred unit of analysis. Rationalists show how individual units (say, companies) have defined preferences. The choices of these individual actors about whether or not to cooperate flow from these fundamental preferences, usually assuming a world where actors are rational and guileful (Williamson 1985, 47). For constructivists—even those who study companies in a market economy—individual understandings of preferences are jointly constructed, so the operative unit of analysis is often the network of linked actors. The strategic choices of these actors are, as Granovetter has influentially phrased it, "embedded in concrete, ongoing systems of social relations. . . . [In business relations,] prisoner's dilemmas are often obviated by the strength of personal relations, and this strength is a property not of the transactors, but of their concrete relations" (1985, 487–91).[9]

Varieties of Capitalism versus Deliberative Association
This ontological divergence conditions two other clear distinctions between rationalist and constructivist approaches to explaining cooperation: how information circulates and how institutions change. In this section I contrast these two dimensions of rationalism and constructivism, drawing examples from two literatures in comparative politics. The first literature, popularly known under the rubric varieties of capitalism, uses the assumptions and mechanisms of rational choice theory

---

[9] A network theory need not be constructivist. Social capital theory, as adumbrated by Putnam (1993, 2000) and Coleman (1990), is a rationalist theory of networks. Social capital theory sees informal social networks as a set of institutions for circulating information and developing the norms of reciprocity that allow the civic community to prosper. In the community rich in social capital, dense but cross-cutting social ties circulate information to establish common knowledge. The widespread existence of norms of generalized reciprocity fosters cooperative behavior by limiting the propensity to exploit the cooperative overtures of others. Once you defect in the social-capital-rich community, those playing with you will defect in the future—at least until you return to the cooperative path—which means you cannot benefit from future cooperation (Axelrod 1984). Social capital research has blossomed over the last decade, but questions of operationalization of its causal role make it difficult to put it to a definitive test. In this research I opted for a relatively crude strategy using the primary measure of social capital adopted by Putnam (1993, 90) in his landmark study of regional reform in Italy: the density of secondary associations. The argument runs that the higher the density of local voluntary associations, the better positioned a community is to resolve its disputes in a collectively beneficial and mutually satisfactory way (Putnam 1993; Skocpol and Fiorina 1999). This proposition is not borne out in my data—regional success in creating decentralized cooperation does not correlate with the density of secondary associations. There may be other ways, not reflected in these data on associations, that networks and norms of reciprocity influence the securing of decentralized cooperation.

to explain how actors in a political economy coordinate their actions with one another (Hall and Soskice 2001; cf. Kitschelt et al. 1999, Iversen 1999). The second, which Stark and Bruszt (1998) call deliberative association, draws on constructivist theory to show the ways in which interests and identities are constituted (and reconstituted) through ongoing processes of negotiation among private and public actors (cf. Sabel 1994; Herrigel 1996; Bluhm 1999). Although the two differ significantly in many respects, both rely on the development of institutions for monitoring and sanctioning, although rationalists are more explicit in their recourse to these institutions to stabilize cooperation.

The varieties of capitalism framework of Hall and Soskice (2001) is premised on the existence of distinctive institutions by which actors in different sorts of political economies can make credible commitments to one another. In liberal market economies (LMEs) such as the United States, the market is the principal mechanism by which economic actors coordinate their expectations. The coordinated market economy (CME)—here, Germany is the classic case—depends on organizations and rules to structure interactions among actors and to clarify mutual expectations; in other words, to produce nonmarket coordination. This solution to the problem of coordination relies, inter alia, on employers' associations and unions to circulate information, to resolve conflicts of interest and negotiate changes to formal rules, and to identify and sanction those actors behaving noncooperatively.[10]

In the CME, the role of information circulation provided by employers' associations is of fundamental importance in clarifying mutual expectations among companies. What sort of information is exchanged through an employers' association in the varieties of capitalism framework? It is, in a word, *private information*: that is, information that is available to some actors and not to others. This information often has a bearing on the cooperative choices of individual actors. It is in this sense strategic. The association serves as a central clearinghouse of information about strategic behavior as well as an intermediary among firms, allowing them to signal their intentions to one another. Its ability to play this role is theoretically distinct from any sanctioning ability it may have.

----

[10] Formal employers' associations are one of several institutions through which firms attempt to coordinate their activities; other such institutions include networks of cross-shareholding or long-term relational contracting (Hall and Soskice 2001, 8–15). Although I use formal employers' associations to illustrate the various functions through which credible commitments are created in the varieties of capitalism approach, other institutions may also fulfill these same functions. In Germany, it is in fact true that coordination is provided primarily by employers' associations and unions (Hall and Soskice 2001, 34).

In other words, it serves as a vessel for firms to communicate with one another using cheap talk (which is what game theorists call unenforceable communications). The association adds here its status as a reliable and impartial transmitter of signals among companies. As argued by Randall Calvert, "communication is central to any institution that would allow the participants to realize the available gains from coordination. Moreover, *private* communication is critical, as is the role of the trusted intermediary who can make suggestions and carry credible information" (1995, 256). This is the informational role played by employers' associations in CMEs.

Constructivists in political economy are uniformly more concerned with problems of *local information* and its circulation than are rationalists (Cohen and Rogers 1992, 426). Local information is, of course, just a type of private information, in that it is asymmetrically held. Yet, whereas the private information held by actors in the varieties of capitalism framework is primarily strategic, constructivists observe that actors on the ground have a better sense of how the economy really works than do actors at the center, and, of course, the exact details of this functioning vary from one place to another, depending on local contexts. Thus, policy-makers hoping to secure cooperation "must acquire situated knowledge—intimate, deeply proprietary knowledge—of present best practices and already-present futures" (Stark and Bruszt 1998, 123). Local information is so important in this view because mutual understandings are constantly being revised in light of the empirical experiences that local actors are undergoing as they simultaneously negotiate with, monitor, and learn from one another (Sabel 1991, 1994). Their interaction and experimentation creates a base of useful knowledge, and the most successful networks in promoting the conditions for economic growth are those in which actors use their network capacity to circulate this information (Saxenian 1994; Locke 1995).

Monitoring and sanctioning play roles in both sorts of theories, but they are especially central to rationalism. Institutions for monitoring allow some actors to know whether other actors have done what they said they would do; and they allow this information to become common knowledge (Ostrom 1990, 125). Institutions for monitoring are standard features of arms control regimes and of common-pool resource dilemmas, where the operative dictum is "trust but verify." In the LME, generally accepted accounting practices and routine auditing allow balance sheets to serve as effective monitoring devices for financial markets. By way of contrast, the financial systems in CMEs depend on the functioning of institutions of network reputational monitoring to deliver private information about the operations of a firm (Hall and

Soskice 2001, 10; cf. Deeg 1999, 102–22). Such institutions provide the information to actors necessary to maintain confidence in the likely behavior of actors with whom they are trying to coordinate.

Sanctions, if credible, actually change the payoff matrices of actors by making defection a more costly (and therefore less attractive) alternative to cooperation. Elinor Ostrom's (1990, 1998) work on common pool resources, using both experimental and field research, has shown particularly convincingly how graduated sanctioning mechanisms can remind actors of the cost of noncooperation without immediately ostracizing them from the community of potential cooperators. For a state interested in eliciting societal cooperation where it has not existed previously, such a graduated sanctioning mechanism seems well suited to the necessarily incremental process of change. In the varieties of capitalism literature, David Soskice asserts that employers' associations "have significant informal sanctioning ability" (1994, 34). Associations can use this capacity to punish those firms that do not behave cooperatively in apprentice training by withdrawing from them other benefits they enjoy (cf. Finegold and Soskice 1988, 48; Hall and Soskice 2001, 47).

The focus of the constructivist approach, in which identities and interests are viewed as being mutually constitutive of one another, in no way undermines the necessity of monitoring and sanctioning. "While social relations may indeed often be a necessary condition for trust and trustworthy behavior, they are not sufficient to guarantee these and may even provide occasion and means for malfeasance and conflict on a scale larger than in their absence" (Granovetter 1985, 491). In this respect, constructivists in comparative politics depart somewhat from constructivists in international relations, where there is a stronger emphasis on sociological work emphasizing norms of appropriateness rather than norms of consequences—asking "how should a person like me act?" instead of "what will happen to me if I defect?" (March and Olsen 1989).[11] Granovetter's (1985) critique of oversocialized conceptions of action heavily influences theorists of comparative politics and political economy, who are well aware that wariness is the order of the day, even among companies that collaborate with one another. Institutions of mutual monitoring, in this view, provide suspicious actors an opportunity to keep an eye on one another as well as an opportunity for information exchange (Sabel 1994). Even the strongest partisans of the role of deliberative associations in democratic politics stress that this scheme only works in areas where such networks have effective sanctioning power to deter noncooperation (Cohen and Rogers 1992). On this

---

[11] Fearon and Wendt (2002, 60–62), however, downplay the differences between constructivists and rationalists on this score, even in international relations.

score, the differences between rationalist and constructivist approaches
are minor.

The two literatures have, however, strongly divergent analyses of the
character of institutional change. Rationalist analysis is at its best when
it can provide a convincing account of the way in which existing institutions create credible commitments among social actors, such that they
are willing to cooperate with one another. Peter Hall and David Soskice
(2001), for example, show how the institutional frameworks of liberal
and coordinated market economies are strongly self-reinforcing. Moreover, the dynamics of self-interested politics further reinforces these
equilibria: both voters and producer groups have incentives to preserve
their respective comparative institutional advantages (Iversen and
Soskice 2001; Wood 2001; Hall and Soskice 2001, 63). These political
and institutional dynamics explain why such equilibria are resistant to
the various exogenous shocks that buffet them. The corollary of this
tenet is that those political economies that do not already possess a high-
skill equilibrium—such as France and eastern Germany—will find it
extremely difficult to establish one.

Yet the strength of equilibrium analysis is stability, not change. How
does change happen? The most promising avenue of change for rationalist models is through a tipping, or cascade, model (Schelling 1978).
Such models have been used by Susanne Lohmann (1994) to explain
the dynamics of collective protest in eastern Germany and by David
Laitin (1998) to explain how ethnic identities change. Tipping models
speak directly to the problem of creating cooperation because they
explain how people will act based on how they think others will act.
Lohmann's (1994) example of the Leipzig protests that helped bring
down the Berlin Wall nicely illustrates the mechanism. In spite of widespread disaffection with the political and material deprivations of life in
the German Democratic Republic, no individual wanted to protest
alone. When individuals saw others participating in protest, however,
they used this information to reevaluate their likely individual costs (in
terms of arrest or worse) and benefits (in terms of triggering regime
change). In such a situation, once one unusually large turnout occurs,
it may trigger such a reevaluation among a substantial number of other
individuals, who will in the next round further affect a third set of individuals, and so on. The great merit of the tipping model is the ability to
show how an apparent equilibrium, once shaken by exogenous changes,
can change radically (see chap. 2). The problem with a tipping model,
and with change more generally in rationalist models, is that the mechanisms by which the first individual is convinced to act are often murky
and post hoc, such that "great social shifts seem impossible at one point
but inevitable at another" (Laitin 1998, 55). When the tipping point is

not specified a priori in an equilibrium model, this raises questions about how we can usefully derive falsifiable predictions from it.

In the elegant world of rationalist equilibrium, institutional change is often constrained by individual actors pursuing their self-interested logic to socially suboptimal outcomes. The constructivist view starts from the premise that those individual interests themselves are constituted through ongoing interaction with other actors. Such an assumption does not deny the difficulties of coordinating in a situation of multiple potential equilibria or of eliciting cooperation when defection would yield higher payoffs. Instead, it simply introduces the idea that strategic interaction—that is, choosing a course of action when the outcome of your action depends on what others do—is a process characterized by multiple sorts of uncertainty. Actors in this view are not merely uncertain about the sort of people with whom they are interacting; they may also be unclear about what game they are playing and consequently how they should understand their own stakes in the game. Thus, the framework of deliberative association suggests a decidedly more soluble problem of institutional change than does the rationalist approach. Vicious circles of socially suboptimal mutual defection are not immutable because the nature of interests is always subject to negotiation and open to reinterpretation. However, this can also be analytically unsatisfying: Is it true that, when social actors try to cooperate, "we can never know the outcome of their efforts at cooperation in advance," as Sabel argues (1994, 159)? This indeterminacy is unsettling, particularly for public policy-makers who are trying to figure out how to get out of socially suboptimal traps of mutual defection.

TOWARD SYNTHESIS? DISCUSSION, DELIBERATION, AND THE ROLE
OF PUBLIC POLICY

One of the most interesting points of tangency between these two approaches to explaining social change is their dispute over the nature of deliberation and discussion. This dispute boils down to a simple question: Does collective discussion simply allow actors to pursue their own interests more efficiently, or does it in fact change the way they define their individual interests? For rationalists, deliberation is all about improving the efficiency of collective decision-making by bringing to light information that would otherwise not have been incorporated into collective discussions: "discussion might then be a means for lessening the impact of bounded rationality, the fact that our imaginations and calculating abilities are limited and fallible. So, faced with a complex problem, individuals might wish to pool their limited capabilities through discussion and so increase the odds of making a good choice" (Fearon 1998, 49). The rationalist conception is, above all, technical;

discussion improves the information available to all actors such that they can jointly devise a better solution than any one of them could develop individually. For constructivists, though, stressing only its informational qualities leaves out the most important feature of deliberation: changing individual preferences by reasoned recourse to commonly accepted norms of fairness (Mansbridge 1992; Cohen 1997, 74).[12] Beyond producing technically improved solutions, deliberation transforms individual understandings of self-interest: "discussion is precisely the process by which parties come to reinterpret themselves and their relation to each other by elaborating a common understanding of the world" (Sabel 1994, 138). In the constructivist view, individuals do not merely develop a better way to do what they wanted to do anyway. The process of their joint discussion significantly influences what they want to achieve. This difference over the nature and benefits of discussion and deliberation has significant consequences for the sorts of institutions that public policy should encourage, as we shall see later.

In the varieties of capitalism framework, deliberative institutions are an important element of the coordinated market economy. The ability to deliberate presupposes "institutions that encourage the relevant actors to engage in collective discussions and reach agreements with each other" (Hall and Soskice 2001, 11). Actors use these institutions to serve three functions. First, deliberation increases their ability to assume common knowledge, giving each of them additional information on how the other actors are likely to respond to a new set of challenges. Second, it provides a forum to evaluate the risks and rewards associated with a given course of action, and then to negotiate how these costs and benefits will be distributed. Thus, when multiple welfare-improving equilibria are possible, a capacity to deliberate allows actors to resolve disputes about which solution will be chosen (Scharpf 1997). Finally, deliberative capacity enables actors to overcome problems of bounded rationality, particularly when faced with new situations. In other words, it gives actors a collective capacity to puzzle through problems that are complex (Fearon 1998, 49–52). In a world economy where rapid change is a constant, this capacity can be extremely useful in devising effective responses to volatile conditions of competition.

The varieties of capitalism approach equates deliberation with discussion—as iterative information exchanges that can overcome problems of asymmetrically distributed information and problems of bounded rationality. In contrast, the constructivist view sees deliberation as public reasoning, not simply public discussion (Cohen 1998). Thus,

---

[12] A discussion with Archon Fung prompted this formulation, although he bears no culpability for it.

preferences are not fixed, as in the rationalist account, prior to a discussion within a network or a polity. Instead, those prior preferences may change through the exercise of practical reason, that is, having to justify jointly made choices in terms of reasons viewed as legitimate by the other members of the group (Cohen 1998, 198–201). To be clear, this conception admits that deliberating actors may well have divergent preferences. What they are constructing, through the act of conversation, is a contingent joint identity based on potentially common interests. "As relations become discursive in the sense just described, firms can assess continuously through direct experience whether particular partners are able to advance a joint program or not, and whether, if they are, the result could be a fusion of identities that creates enduring mutual interests" (Sabel 1994, 146). This seemingly abstract process is attributed to concrete examples of small firms in parts of Germany by Gary Herrigel[13] and to Czech social actors by David Stark and László Bruszt.[14] In such cases, networks can promote reasoning on the basis of common, jointly constructed interests, thereby facilitating coordination on Pareto-superior equilibrium points.

What discrepant views of public policy flow from this discussion of discussion? For the varieties of capitalism approach, common knowledge is only likely to emerge through the laborious establishment and maintenance of coordinating institutions that make credible commitments and common knowledge possible. "Because they have little experience of such coordination to underpin the requisite common knowledge, LMEs will find it difficult to develop non-market coordination of the sort common in CMEs, even when the relevant institutions can be put into place" (Hall and Soskice 2001, 63). Thus, the fundamental role of public policy at time t is to maximize the existing modes of coordination in the economy, not to try to build new ones. "It follows that economic policies will be effective only if they are *incentive compatible*, namely

---

[13] "To understand how groups of independent producers could act together to create institutions for their collective benefit, one has to appreciate the decentralized, interconnected, and fundamentally regional character of production in these districts. . . . [E]ach producer understood itself as a specialist among specialists, all of whom together were engaged in the production of the output of an industry. What mattered was that the industry remain competitive, that it had the capacity to continuously acquire new technologies, product ideas, and engineering skills. For individual producers, this was a collective, industrial, regional problem, not an individual one" (Herrigel 1996, 51–52).

[14] "Thus, institutionalized deliberations made it possible for the trade unions to shift their time horizons as, for example, when Vladimir Petrus, who led the Czech Trade Union Chamber from 1992 to 1994, explicitly acknowledged the government's reform strategy as 'the key to prosperity that could make the union's *long-term objectives* realizable.' At the same time that tripartite structures moderated trade union demands, they moderated the policies of the government and altered its time horizons as well" (Stark and Bruszt 1998, 186).

complementary to the coordinating capacities embedded in the existing political economy (Wood 1997). In liberal market economies, where coordination is secured primarily through market mechanisms, better economic performance may demand policies that sharpen market competition, while coordinated market economies may benefit more from policies that reinforce the capacities of actors for non-market coordination" (Hall and Soskice 2001, 46). In this framework, then, the role of the state is to facilitate nonmarket coordination in political economies where such mechanisms already exist and function. Where they do not, as in France and eastern Germany, the prognosis is equally clear. By the very internal logic of the varieties of capitalism approach, building a high-skill equilibrium where mechanisms for coordination do not already exist is a political project likely to fail.

Given the constitutive character of deliberation in constructivist theory, the ways in which public policy can promote cooperation are two: by supporting existing deliberative networks and by promoting the emergence of new institutions to facilitate deliberation. The first entails establishing public institutions that can allow networks to function efficiently, whether they be banks for small-firm finance (Herrigel 1996) or transportation infrastructure in high-tech districts (Saxenian 1994). The second involves prodding actors in a common geographical area— say, within the administrative boundaries of a region—to discuss how their potentially joint interests can be furthered by working together (Sabel 1995). In other words, governments cannot possibly match the information-circulation and deliberative capacities of these networks, but they can respond to identified needs for which the networks turn to public policy-makers. Yet government officials also do not want to be duped. They must develop accountability standards through which lessons based on local experiments can be learned and passed on to other local experimenters while laggards are held accountable for failure to perform up to jointly agreed-on standards (Sabel, Fung, and Karkkainen 1999). States are constrained by the fact that much of the most relevant information for policy-making is not available to them. It resides in actors on the ground and circulates through the networks in which they are embedded. Effective policy-making is thus most likely when governments can embed policy-making in existing social networks (Evans 1995; Stark and Bruszt 1998).

Table 1.1 summarizes the differences in the rationalist and constructivist approaches to explaining the emergence of cooperation.

ASSOCIATIONS AND EMBEDDED POLICY-MAKING

In this book I propose a theoretical course that steers between the treacherous theoretical shoals of rationalist overdeterminacy and con-

Table 1.1 Rationalist and Constructivist Explanations of Cooperation

	Rationalism	Constructivism
Ontology	Individualist	Holist
Nature of private information	Strategic	Local
Institutional change	Tipping	Discursive
Deliberation	Coordinative	Constitutive
Role for public policy	Incentive-compatible	Embedded

structivist indeterminacy. The best way to explain why cooperation succeeds or fails is to use a rationalist ontology to answer the questions asked by constructivists. Constructivists observe that cooperation happens more often than rationalists predict, and they correctly infer that this is because rationalists are missing something about how individuals perceive their own interests. This something is cognitive, not constitutive. The problem of analytic uncertainty, a definitional feature of the politics of decentralized cooperation, requires that actors learn about the nature of causal relationships in the world. This cognitive problem is fully consistent with a rationalist ontology. To solve the problem, however, is a problem of persuasion. States need to gain access to information about the most likely cooperators and develop strategies that allow them to overcome analytic uncertainty. To do so, states need to rely on embedded policy-making, as the constructivists argue.

The approach developed in this book follows the varieties of capitalism literature in its emphasis on the informational and deliberative functions of employers' associations in facilitating coordination (Hall and Soskice 2001). This private information is above all *relational*; that is, it has to do with what companies know about their own propensities to cooperate and how those relate to the propensities of other companies. Although companies may be willing to share this information with one another or with a representative association, they will not willingly share it with the state. Companies distrust the state, and they have good reasons to hide that information from policy-makers if doing so will provide them with potential access to subsidy money (i.e., rents). Technical expertise—of the sort especially stressed in the constructivist literature—is also important in assessing the feasibility of certain reform strategies, although states may well be able to acquire this technical expertise on their own. But relational information will be extremely difficult for governments to acquire, which makes capable private associations the prerequisite to securing decentralized cooperation.

Deliberation is of decisive value in problems of decentralized cooperation, but it is important in the rationalist, not the constructivist, sense. I argue that the capacity of an association to promote collective problem-solving is most important in overcoming problems of bounded rationality, where the process of discussion can "clarify the likely consequences of different policies and suggest entirely new ideas through brainstorming" (Fearon 1998, 49). Deliberation is important not because, as the constructivists would have it, the process of talking about collective decisions persuades actors to reason using arguments grounded solely in norms of fairness on which they commonly agree. Instead it is important because it allows private associations to use their access to private information to fashion creative strategies to help overcome the uncertainties that prevent actors from cooperating with one another. And private associations, when they have these capacities, are far better at fashioning these strategies than are states, a claim shared both by rationalists and constructivists.

There is an important, if unfortunate, terminological distinction to be made here. Attempts by rationalists to commandeer "deliberation" are likely to lead to conceptual confusion. Constructivists and rationalists mean different things when they use the term, and the constructivists got there first. James Fearon recognizes this danger and proposes that the term "discussion" is more appropriate to refer to the informational and coordinative features of rationalist "deliberation." I want to be even more precise, focusing exclusively on the conception that collective discussion is a very effective means of collective problem-solving (not of fundamentally changing preferences by use of practical reason). Hall and Soskice include this problem-solving element in their notion of deliberative capacity, but their more expansive view also includes reference to coordinating capacity and norms of legitimacy. Throughout this book, I denote the collective brainstorming feature of private associations as *dialogic capacity*—that is, the ability of associations to promote extended discussion and to help actors develop collectively solutions they might not have conceived on their own.

But rationalist approaches typically rely too heavily on a credible sanctioning mechanism as the prerequisite of successful cooperation (cf. Ostrom 1998). Given the high degree of uncertainty that is characteristic of situations of reform, sanctioning mechanisms established to enforce new types of behavior will lack credibility because everyone is uncertain what everyone else will do. If sanctions were necessary for reforms premised on securing decentralized cooperation to be implemented successfully, then this uncertainty would condemn almost all of them to failure. And that, of course, is what the static varieties of capitalism framework leads us to expect. It is very difficult to change equilibrium expectations—that is, expectations that individuals have about what other actors believe to be true (Przeworski 1998)—because those beliefs are anchored to a world where existing institutions all serve to reinforce the futility of thinking others will think differently.

It is precisely at this point that the constructivists have something to teach the rationalists about the character of multiple kinds of uncertainty. Problems of decentralized cooperation arise in situations characterized by multiple potential equilibria and high analytic (or cognitive) uncertainty. Ex hypothesi, then, strategic uncertainty is not the only sort of uncertainty that limits their prospective action. The approach developed in this book therefore concentrates on the centrality of information—its circulation, mobilization, and diffusion—in resolving this uncertainty. To solve problems of decentralized cooperation, then, governments must realize that interests in cooperation are distributed heterogeneously throughout the population. The group that the state must concentrate on trying to convince to become durable participants are those actors who waver on the border between participating or not participating in the goal of the policy reform. These waverers are uncertain about the consequences of their choice to change their ways of interacting with other private actors.

Targeting the uncertainty of waverers is, therefore, the fundamental goal of governments trying overcome problems of decentralized cooperation. If the state is poor when it comes to the currency of relational information, it is still rich in the more conventional monetary resources. The state can, through the use of subsidies, insure wavering companies against the possible losses of changing their behavior. As in the case of countries adopting macroeconomic stabilization policies or of individuals trying to solve common-pool resource dilemmas, there is a status quo bias (Fernandez and Rodrik 1991; Ostrom 1990): the uncertain effects of change make even those actors who may gain under the new regime reluctant to endorse change. The threat of loss is what dissuades them from changing their behavior, and transitional subsidies are of crucial importance in convincing them to experiment with alternative strategies. However, the wealth of the state is not infinite, and this is where the importance of relational information enters the equation. Relational information is valuable only when it can be used to discriminate between actors of different propensities to adopt a new set of policies in order to target subsidies on those most likely to coordinate around a new societal equilibrium point.[15] Thus the challenge of decentralized cooperation is for governments to develop conduits linking them to the

---

[15] This point has been well analyzed in Scharpf's discussion of "active implementation" (1983, 111). Implementation is the "persuasive secondary program" of subsidy policies, in which accurately targeted subsidy policies are used to promote social learning among their recipients.

relational information that private associations can provide. Instead of a state apparatus being autonomous, it must be able to tap into the information resources of civil society. What is required, using terminology developed by Peter Evans (1995) and Stark and Bruszt (1998), is embedded policy-making.

Private associations not only deliberate on the basis of relational information; they can also be effective advocates in convincing waverers to experiment with new forms of cooperation. This is an expressly political role: using information to mobilize consent. Whereas sanctioning imposes costs for noncompliance, mobilizing capacity is simply informed advocacy. Associations that have shown the ability to promote discussion over policy choices can be very effective advocates to their uncertain members, even though they may lack the ability to sanction those members.

Decentralized cooperation is a new challenge, one that requires a new response from states. In many areas of economic policy-making in the advanced industrial democracies, the task of regulatory reform is now primarily one of joint problem-solving (Regini 1997b). Just as the effective role of the state in the economy has moved from one of steering through macroeconomic policy to one of facilitating adjustment through the supply side of the economy, the way in which states can be effective in developing policy has changed. The state continues to have a role in providing oversight (against rent-seeking) and political accountability (against poor performance), but the informational advantage of the Weberian state apparatus has seriously diminished. Private organizations have the best access to the relational knowledge necessary to target policies at the most likely participants in reform projects, and states must be able to mobilize that information in order to succeed. (In chap. 2, we consider the dynamics of changing the beliefs of waverers in more detail.)

THE EMPIRICAL STRATEGY
The empirical strategy of this book was born of a sort of natural experiment conducted by governments in France and eastern Germany in the early 1990s, when both adopted sweeping reforms of their vocational education and training systems. At the root of both reforms was the goal of making their training systems work more like that of western Germany, in which companies invest in the provision of certifiable general skills through the apprenticeship system. Both reforms combined in-firm training contracts, paid for by employers, with a certificate of general skills awarded after the training period. A goal of these reforms was thus to convince companies to invest in the provision of general skills, whereas the certification of those skills created a trans-

parent device for allowing other employers to assess the capacities of workers. Policy-makers in eastern Germany and France could mimic the legal arrangements that facilitated this human capital investment, and they could provide additional incentives for firms to train, in the form of subsidies for hiring apprentices. Yet the success of their reforms ultimately depended on persuading companies to choose to invest in training their own young workers rather than using alternative methods to procure the skills needed for production.

The methodology of this study flows from the intellectual question: Why do these reforms succeed or fail in securing decentralized cooperation among companies? To answer the question, we need to know whether companies are cooperating. The prevalent analytical trend in comparative political economy is to acknowledge that companies are important strategic actors and that governments principally influence the course of economic change by convincing companies to choose new strategies of adjustment in the face of international competition (Hall 1999). Yet our methodological tools lag behind our analytical advances, and researchers in mainstream political economy have generally failed to develop techniques to incorporate the study of firm behavior systematically into studies of government economic strategies (cf. Boix 1998; Iversen 1999; Garrett 1997). Some political economists have generated important insights into regional patterns of economic organization by working at the level of the firm (Sabel 1994; Herrigel 1996; Saxenian 1994), but these scholars have seldom constructed multiple subnational samples in order to compare the impact of public policy in different regions and in different countries. In this book, I incorporate detailed firm-level research into a research design animated by questions of significant interest for those concerned with the broader problems of cooperation and policy-making in the hopes of bridging the gap between the firm level and more conventional studies of the impact of public policy on the functioning of the advanced capitalist democracies.

In order to control for many sector-specific characteristics that influence decisions about an investment in vocational training, I concentrate on the single most important sector in both political economies: the metal and electronics sector.[16] In both France and eastern Germany, this sector accounts for the largest single share of manufacturing production and employment, and the companies in this sector compete in export markets as well as being exposed to international competition at home.

---

[16] I refer throughout this study to the metal-and-electronics and metalworking employers interchangeably because they are politically unified in their representation. More details about the exact sorts of metal companies studied, as well as details about how the firm samples were assembled, are presented in chapter 3.

Equally important for a study of the politics that underlie reform, this sector dominates interest representation in these political economies. In Germany, the organizations of employers and of workers in the metal sector are the most powerful members of their respective peak organizations. Moreover, the wage negotiations between Gesamtmetall and the IG Metall serve as benchmarks for agreements in other sectors (Hall 1994). In France, the metal employers are equally hegemonic in the employers' peak confederation (Bunel 1995). Given the centrality of this sector in both political economies, the results of training reforms in the metal industry are of greatest interest for drawing inferences about the overall success of the reforms in changing company behavior.

Why compare training reforms in France and eastern Germany? Three similarities support the value of such a comparison. First, both reforms clearly adopted the western German apprenticeship system as their comparative standard. This similar baseline created substantial commonalities in the structure of the two reforms, and it has the evaluative advantage of providing an empirical benchmark by which we can assess the levels of company investment in apprenticeship training. Second, both national governments devolved important policy-making authority to embryonic regional governments to manage the coordination of training policy, and both reforms established a similar set of organizational structures to ensure that employers' associations and unions could provide institutionalized input to the regional policy-making process. Finally, both major legal projects occurred at about the same time: the eastern German laws in 1991, the French governing law in 1993. Thus, the comparative data I present in chapters 3–5 derive from two reform projects that are roughly the same age and that both took place in similar international economic contexts.

Skeptics will rightly note that France and eastern Germany are hardly two peas in a pod: France is one of the world's leading capitalist economies, whereas eastern Germany is a former state-socialist economy whose institutions have been transplanted from western Germany. From a methodological point of view, how might this difference potentially bias the results that we obtain from the comparison? The principal dependent variable is the cooperation of companies through investment in general skills training. We might expect the results to be biased, calling into question our causal inferences, if there are some unobserved features of these political economies that are correlated with our explanatory variables and with the dependent variable (King, Keohane, and Verba 1994). Comparative research must be particularly attentive to this problem, and throughout this book there is an explicit effort to consider the most important specificities that might be relevant to the results in the two countries (in particular, past histories of apprenticeship training and experience with investment in a market economy). Yet our confidence in the findings is increased by the fact that the primary variation in the successful creation of cooperation occurs within each country rather than across the two countries. Those who argue that the two national cases are not comparable must explain why we observe similar patterns of variation within France and within eastern Germany.

Overview of the Findings

The goal of the reforms was to convince companies to make substantial uncovered investments in youth training contracts. But it is difficult to estimate accurately the net investment made by firms in training because neither the costs nor the benefits are easily measurable (Lynch 1994; von Bardeleben, Beicht, and Fehér 1995; Wagner 1999). Two indicators are particularly useful in predicting rough levels of investment in youth training. The first is the training ratio, which measures youth trainees as a percentage of the labor force. If this proportion is too large, it is indicative of either explosive growth or the practice of using apprentices as a substitute for low-skill labor without investing seriously in them. If it is too low, the firm is either shrinking or not using apprenticeship as a significant source of future skilled workers. Using information about western German patterns of training as well as the goals enunciated by political actors in France and eastern Germany, I have identified a target range for the training ratio for the metal and electronics sector that indicates use of apprenticeship-style training at western German levels. The second indicator is the retention rate—the more money a company invests in training a worker, the more that company will want to keep the worker after the training period in order to reap the return on its investment. A higher retention rate is therefore generally indicative of a higher level of training investment, other things being equal.[17]

To extrapolate the findings from each individual firm to the aggregated level of the employment zone, I have constructed a high-skill training index, which combines these indicators to represent the proportion of firms within a given employment zone whose training practices correspond to those of firms in the western German metal and electronics sector. The employment zone is a subnational jurisdiction defined by governments in both countries on the basis of a coherent local labor market, and as such it was the obviously appropriate unit of analysis for making comparisons both within and across regions in France and in

---

[17] For many firms I have further qualitative information about the level of their investment in training, discussed in chapters 4 and 5. The training ratio and the retention rate are the standard yardsticks I use to compare all firms in the sample.

Table 1.2 Overview of Employment Zones in France and Germany[a]

Employment Zone	Region/State	Polity	High-Skill Training Index (%)[b]	N
Control				
Mayen	Rhineland-Palatinate	West Germany	42	7
Success				
Leipzig	Saxony	East Germany	57	7
Plauen	Saxony	East Germany	40	5
Valley of the Arve	Rhône-Alpes	France	40	5
Failure				
Lyon	Rhône-Alpes	France	25	4
Halle	Saxony-Anhalt	East Germany	20	5
Sangerhausen	Saxony-Anhalt	East Germany	17	6
Vimeu	Picardy	France	14	7
Strasbourg	Alsace	France	11	9
Amiens	Picardy	France	0	4

[a] Source: Interviews conducted in 1995 and 1996 in France and Germany.

[b] Proportion of companies judged to be training according to western German standards, as determined by the training ratio and the retention rate. An employment zone is categorized as successful when its index exceeds 34 percent (cf. Wagner 1999). (See appendix A.)

eastern Germany.[18] I compiled samples of firms in four eastern German and five French employment zones, along with one western German employment zone. Only in zones where at least 34 percent of the firms in my sample manifested these training practices—which is the overall proportion of firms training in the western German metal sector (Wagner 1999)—did I classify the employment zone as having succeeded in establishing high-skill training patterns. The resulting classifications are listed in table 1.2; the western German control zone (Mayen) is in the first row, and the three zones that have been success-

[18] There are 348 employment zones (*zones d'emploi*) in France and 176 (*Arbeitsamts-bezirke*) in Germany (thirty-five in eastern Germany, excluding the western half of Berlin). German zones have on average more than twice the population of the French zones, but this difference has no effect on the ability to compare the two. The median population of my five French employment zones was 340,000, and the median population of my four eastern German zones was 395,000. The firm sample from Strasbourg includes firms located in the adjacent employment zones of Haguenau-Niederbronn, Molsheim-Schirmeck, and Sélestat-Sainte-Marie-aux-Mines, and in all comparisons with the other employment zones I count this as a single zone making up Greater Strasbourg.

ful at generating high levels of training and retention are listed first: Leipzig, Plauen, and the Valley of the Arve. In the majority of the employment zones that I studied, the attempted reforms and the subsidies used to promote them failed to convince firms to move to a high level of investment in youth training contracts.

How can we explain the variation in these outcomes? Why do we observe success in Leipzig but failure in the neighboring zone of Halle? What has enabled the Valley of the Arve to overcome the conditions that subvert the emergence of cooperation elsewhere in France? The rest of the book takes up these questions.

Roadmap of the Book

Chapter 2 begins where any inquiry into cooperation must, with an analysis of why actors might have an interest in cooperating with one another. Accordingly, I examine the stakes for different types of companies in investing in general skills. The analysis demonstrates that the strategic situations facing small and large companies in the two political economies differ dramatically. In both political economies, it is among the small- and medium-size enterprises (SMEs) that we are likely to find the companies that are waverers. In the second part of the chapter I develop the explanatory framework of relational information at length, focusing on the inability of states to procure information about waverers without the assistance of private organizations.

The next three chapters constitute the empirical heart of the study. Chapter 3 examines in detail the training behavior of companies in eastern Germany and France, while chapters 4 and 5 build on this detailed evidence to assess the politics of human capital development in the two countries. Chapter 3 provides an overview of the empirical results of the reforms, confirming the interest analysis of chapter 2. Large firms in eastern Germany energetically engaged in promoting cooperation: they invested in the training of their own apprentices as well as assisting SMEs to invest in transferable skills training. Large firms in France, on the contrary, had no interest in providing such training in general skills, and it showed in their behavior. In practical terms, they were not investing in such training contracts; in theoretical terms, they were shirking. The SMEs in both countries, however, manifested substantial uncertainty about the individual benefits they might reap from cooperating in general skills investment. Their uncertainty was both strategic and cognitive. Despite this universally perceived uncertainty, however, there was variation in the actual training behavior of SMEs in both countries, some making investments consistent with high-level general skills training and others not. Moreover, the successes were geographically concentrated.

Explaining this variation is the task of chapters 4–5, which ask the questions: What are the capacities of employers' associations in these two political economies? Do governments develop their human capital policies through embedded or through autonomous policy-making? And do the answers to the two previous questions explain where cooperation emerges and where it does not in eastern Germany and in France? As chapter 4 demonstrates, the transfer of employer and labor union organizational capacities to eastern Germany was, overall, a great success. Across the new federal states of eastern Germany, these organizations were capable of fulfilling the tasks of private interest governance delegated to them in the western German system. Yet, as I show in the second part of the chapter, not all state governments developed institutional conduits to the information held by private-sector actors. The government of Saxony relied heavily on the input of employers' groups in the making of state policies for encouraging cooperation in vocational training, whereas the government of Saxony-Anhalt instead made policy in remarkable isolation from employers and unions. The different information sets of the two governments led to distinct policy strategies in the two states, and, of the two, the Saxon policy proved far more effective at mobilizing companies to experiment with decentralized cooperation.

Chapter 5 turns to the justly maligned organizational capacities of French employers. The lack of coordinating capacity exhibited by these associations engendered many of the dysfunctions that followed the French reform. A succession of laws attempted to build up the French regions as the center of French youth training policy, but the incapacity of employers' associations to provide the private information necessary for the regions to assume that role de facto crippled regional policy-making. Instead of designing policies aimed at promoting heavier firm investment in general skills, the regions were compelled to limit their policy-making to areas over which they had access to good information. This was true even in the region that had most aggressively sought to develop a distinctive regional policy based on private-interest governance, Rhône-Alpes. The only case of success that we observe in France occurred in the Valley of the Arve, where an employers' association succeeded in using private information to direct public, indiscriminate subsidies at the most likely cooperators. It was the particular strategy of the association in the Arve that enabled the area to post one of the few success stories of the French training reforms.

The final chapter zooms out from the particular cases of French and German reforms to consider the broader implications of these findings for cooperation and for policy-making more generally. States challenged by problems of decentralized cooperation are most likely to succeed when they can develop conduits to private information. Building organizations that have such capacity is difficult, but it appears to have a substantial payoff for states that want to promote institutional change. Harnessing relational information gives policy-makers the best chance to develop policies that enable private actors to overcome the twin hurdles of strategic and analytic uncertainty. Many of the goals pursued by advanced industrial states, such as preserving the environment and promoting private innovation, are likely to present states with problems of decentralized cooperation. How these states respond depends on the associational structure of the political economy. Governments in CMEs must promote private problem-solving while limiting rent-seeking. LMEs, typically more wary about giving private interests a formal role in the policy-making process, are forced to consider how private information can best be mobilized for the public interest in a way that is both legitimate and effective. As problems of decentralized cooperation are increasingly likely to arise across the industrialized world, these lessons have much to teach both those who make policy and those who study the politics behind it.

CHAPTER TWO

Relational Information and Embedded Policy-Making

Why do reforms premised on securing decentralized cooperation some-times succeed? The reasons they should fail, which were enumerated in chapter 1, are compelling. Actors fear that a cooperative move will be exploited; they lack a history of common knowledge from which to esti-mate how others will respond to incentives to cooperate; and they are uncertain that the Pareto-improvement preached by politicians accu-rately describes the new payoffs. In the presence of these numerous pit-falls, how can states succeed in securing decentralized cooperation?

Policy-makers in eastern Germany and France widely believed by 1990 that the western German apprenticeship system was worthy of emulation. French politicians had long appreciated the virtues of the German system in producing highly skilled workers, and the problem of youth unemployment had moved this issue to the center of the eco-nomic policy programs of successive French governments in the 1980s. In eastern Germany, the crumbling of the Berlin Wall in 1989 was fol-lowed by the equally sudden collapse of the inefficient manufacturing sectors of the eastern German economy. The western German appren-ticeship model seemed to provide a means through which the produc-tivity of the eastern German workforce could be improved to enable eastern German companies to compete successfully in international and domestic markets. Governments in both systems wanted to copy the high-skill equilibrium that western Germany had created, in which com-panies invested in the provision of general skills though apprenticeship training and then capitalized on their skill advantages to compete on the basis of continuous incremental innovations (Finegold and Soskice 1988; Streeck, 1992). It seemed like a great plan.

The general failure of this plan, after a decade of reform, should not obscure the more interesting fact that both France and eastern Germany witnessed pockets of success. To explain why, I start with a set of assump-tions about the individual calculus of cooperation of companies con-sidering whether or not to cooperate with the goals of the reforms. This chapter first explores the different interests of firms of different sizes in the two countries. I then consider how the heterogeneity within each general size category of firms influenced the dynamics of changing their expectations. Finally, I examine analytic uncertainty as a cognitive issue and how such uncertainty can be overcome. Taken together, these assumptions form the basis of a rationalist explanatory framework that stresses the importance of relational information, the dialogic capacity of private associations, and embedded policy-making in securing decentralized cooperation.

THE INTERESTS OF COMPANIES

Cooperation presumes the existence of courses of strategic interaction that can be mutually beneficial. Creating cooperation is only possible in a situation in which mutual restraint can provide improved joint payoffs. To understand the politics of creating cooperation in any given situation, we have to start with an analysis of the interests of different actors.

How can we characterize the strategic situation that confronted companies in eastern Germany and France after the adoption of the training reforms aimed at promoting company investment in the provision of general skills? Public policy-makers and history presented the firms with a set of skill certification options. These firms had to decide simultaneously which product market strategy to pursue and which human capital development choice they would make. These were choices they had to make without knowing what other companies would choose to do because this was a situation of disequilibrium—the potential skill provision options available to every company had been altered by the reforms of public policy, and each firm did not know how to predict what the others would do.

In this section I present a stylized ordering of the preferences of companies that portrays the general strategic situation they encountered as a result of reforms of the vocational education and training in France and eastern Germany. Among companies in a given sector of the economy, the most prominent difference in training preferences was a function of their size: large firms in France had different interests from large firms in eastern Germany, and both had different interests from SMEs.[1] This was because the political and economic resources of large firms gave them a wider array of possible choices than was available to small firms.

For both small and large firms, the choice to be made about skill development is a function of the product market strategy a given firm

---

[1] Empirical studies both of the political representation of employers (Silvia 1997; Bunel 1995) and the political economy of employers' interests (Hancké 2001; Bluhm 1999) have repeatedly stressed that size is one of the principal cleavages among employers in France and Germany.

adopts. This insight has been well developed in the literature on the varieties of capitalism, which stresses that the political preferences of companies are in large measure determined by their skill requirements (Hall and Soskice 2001). Thus, a product market strategy based on incremental innovation—also called diversified quality production (DQP) (Streeck 1992)—requires that the workforce possess a high level of general and industry-specific skills (knowledge of machinery not specific to one company). Such a strategy also demands a set of firm-specific skills relevant to the organization of production at a particular company (Soskice 1994; Estevez-Abe, Iversen, and Soskice 2001). The base of high-level general skills allows the company to delegate to its workers a significant level of autonomy in deciding the best approach to solve a given problem of production, so that these workers are capable of managing a quick retooling to adjust to changes in the demands of markets. This, not coincidentally, is the mix of skills that the dual training system in western Germany has been tailored to provide companies in the manufacturing sectors. It is not a skill set that was widely held by workers in eastern German or French firms in 1990, both of which relied to a greater extent on semiskilled workers and a Fordist organization of production (Hitchens, Wagner, Birnie 1993, Boyer 1995).

Thus, the differences in preferences about training investments among firms of different sizes are a function of the production strategy those firms want to pursue. Organizing work to maximize the advantage of a product market strategy based on DQP is costly when the workplace is not currently organized that way. Company managers deciding how to respond to the training reforms in France and eastern Germany had to weigh the potential benefits of investing in apprenticeship training and organizing the workplace on a DQP model against the risks of losing skilled workers to other firms, which would make it impossible to pursue a DQP strategy. Their political preferences about training policies flowed from their evaluation of this trade-off.

Eastern German Large Firms

The majority of privatized large firms in eastern Germany were quickly bought by western German conglomerates (Carlin and Mayer 1995), a fact that profoundly conditioned the choices of these companies with respect to investments in human capital development. When German policy-makers and the social partners agreed to extend the western German model of codetermination and highly regulated labor markets to eastern Germany, this constraint compelled large firms in eastern Germany to invest in the technology necessary to pursue the same DQP strategy of incremental innovation followed by western German large companies. Because the western German regulatory framework made it very difficult for these companies to try to compete in highly price-sensitive markets (e.g., by slashing labor costs), the large privatized companies clearly preferred the DQP product market strategy. Moreover, because they were owned by western German corporations, they had easy access to the capital necessary to invest in reorganizing the workplace to optimize the use of highly skilled workers. The only uncertainty facing eastern German large firms was what other companies would do in the area of training, given the post-transition disequilibrium.

If large companies could not attract the labor necessary to conduct a DQP strategy, they would lose their investment in organizing production this way. They had to reorganize their plant, which was costly, and they had to pursue a (less desirable) strategy of competing in price-sensitive markets. These costs were more substantial than the costs of investment in any one round of apprentices.

Consider the situation of a hypothetical eastern German large firm (firm EGL). If firm EGL hires apprentices and trains them in general skills, and no other firm hires apprentices, then the other large firms will be able to poach the trainees from firm EGL. Thus, firm EGL will be constrained to abandon its DQP production profile, losing the sunk costs of its investment in the technology to do so, because it cannot hire the skilled workers necessary to execute that strategy; it will also lose its investment in the general skills of its apprentices. This is the firm's worst outcome (Z). If firm EGL does not train apprentices, and no other firms train apprentices, then it also loses its investment in the DQP strategy because there are no workers with the requisite skills available to implement this product market strategy. But firm EGL does not lose the investment in training apprentices, so this outcome (Y) is preferable to Z.

The other two choices available to firm EGL are to train, given that everyone else trains (W), or not to train and instead to poach workers from others, given that everyone else trains (X). Firm EGL prefers both W and X to either Y or Z, because both W and X allow EGL to pursue a DQP strategy of production. Large firms depend heavily on group work, and they prefer having their own apprentices to poaching apprentices from elsewhere because of the importance of ensuring the fit of individual workers within the company culture (Wagner 1999). Firm EGL therefore prefers W to X because it would rather have its own trainees than poach trainees from another large firm, who might turn out to be not as well adapted to group work in firm EGL.

Firm EGL thus has the following preference ordering: W > X > Y > Z. This is the configuration of a classic assurance game (cf. Scharpf 1997). In an assurance game, no actor has an incentive to defect (choose options X or Y), as long as that actor knows that other actors are likely to cooperate. The socially optimal choice (W) is also the individually optimal choice. Firm EGL wants to avoid outcome Z, in which it trains and nobody else does. But EGL would rather train its own apprentices, if it can be sure that the other members of the large firm population will do the same. EGL knows that other large firms prefer DQP to a cost-competitive strategy, and the other large firms know this too. In this situation, all that is required in order for eastern German large firms to coordinate their choice on outcome W—which is the best outcome for each one of them—is to have a credible source of information that other large firms are likely to choose the same outcome (cf. Calvert 1995). Because there are obvious gains from coordinated action for the large firms in eastern Germany, large firms have a collective interest in trying to establish and reinforce the credibility of the new eastern German employers' association. Doing so gives them the coordinating capacity necessary to pursue their preferred production strategy.[2]

Because of their heavy reliance on a DQP production strategy, we also expect large firms in eastern Germany to have had a vested interest in the transfer of the western German training system to eastern Germany. That system, which is based on the voluntary investment of companies in training, concedes to employers and unions the right to bargain directly over skill certifications with little interference by the state (Streeck et al. 1987). The state concedes that control to the social partners in implicit exchange for the ability of companies to provide sufficient apprenticeship places to young job seekers. At times of crisis, when it appears that the voluntary places offered by companies are not sufficient to absorb youth on the labor market, the German government often threatens to impose a training levy on all firms (cf. Wonneberger 1994). Such a threat carries with it a challenge to employer control of the system, and the loss of this control is resisted by German employers (Wood 1997). Large companies in eastern Germany had, therefore, a strong self-interest—tied to their desire to retain control over the training system—to see that the number of apprenticeship places offered by companies could accommodate the demands of youth in the labor market. Yet large German employers only provided a small minority of the apprenticeship places, even in the western German labor market. Large companies therefore had an incentive to ensure that SMEs were also investing in apprenticeship training, to ensure the political viability of the system.

---

[2] Even though actors could benefit from an institution that solves collective action problems, no individual actor has an incentive to provide the collective capacity (Bates 1988). However, eastern German large firms were already endowed with an organizational capacity, thanks to the existence of the western German association that piloted the institutional transfer. This solved their problem of institutional provision.

French Large Firms

French large firms differed from their eastern German counterparts in two very significant respects. First, the skill certification options with which the government confronted them were not identical. Second, the regulatory environment facing French large firms, including the presence of weak unions, did not compel them to pursue a DQP strategy, and so they had not made the investments necessary to maximize productivity under DQP (Boyer 1995; Regini 1997a). To move to a different productive strategy would therefore require them to pay the additional costs of optimizing their plant layout to exploit the increased general capacities of their shop-floor workers. As a result of these two differences, the preferences of French large firms in the face of government reforms looked rather different from those of their eastern German counterparts.

Eastern German large firms had no credible alternative source of skilled labor besides the apprenticeship system. French large firms, in contrast, could draw on the general education system, on apprenticeship, or on the qualification contract (CQ). First introduced as a legal instrument to promote in-firm training in general skills in 1984, the CQ was an important measure by which the French government attempted to adopt a certification similar to the western German apprenticeship contract (see chap. 3). The CQ was by law negotiated by the social partners, but in actual fact employers dominated the process of defining the requirements of the certification (Charraud 1995). In order to develop a CQ, companies required extensive assistance from the employers' association. Large employers, by virtue of their power within the association, were able to use the CQ to develop an almost completely firm-specific qualification that was subsidized by the state (Charraud, Personnaz, and Venau 1996).

Imagine the situation of the hypothetical French large firm FL. The government has passed a series of reforms asking FL to invest heavily in the provision of general skills through youth training contracts. Any move by firm FL to invest in these contracts will impose two types of costs on it: direct training costs and the indirect costs of investing in its production facilities to move to a DQP strategy so that it can use these new workforce capacities efficiently. If firm FL invests in this sort of training and no other firm does, it will lose its trainees through poaching and it will have sunk worthless investments into changing to a DQP strategy. This outcome (Z) is its worst possible result. But if FL trains and every other large firm also trains, firm FL will still have to invest in changing its production strategy. Because it is costly to shift to a DQP profile, this outcome (W) is only third best. If FL does not train in general and firm-specific skills and no other large firm trains, then it can hire graduates of the general education system and use the subsidies provided through the CQ to pay for training them in firm-specific skills. Firm FL prefers this outcome (Y) both to W and to Z. If FL does not train and others do train, then firm FL can poach trainees from other firms. This outcome (X) is only slightly preferable to Y, however, because firm FL will still not invest in changing its production profile to DQP to maximize the contribution of the poached trainees.

The preference ordering of firm FL is thus X > Y > W > Z. This ordering means that *for French large firms, there are no gains to be made from cooperation with each other.* They do not much care what other firms are doing because their optimal strategy is little affected by what other firms do. The French government urgently wanted to attract large firms to participate in the new training measures combining general and specific skills. But the certification options available to French large companies, combined with their existing product market strategies, left them with no incentive to change their training behavior. They could use the CQ to fill firm-specific gaps in their training while drawing on the school-based educational system for workers with general skills.

As a result of these economic interests, French large companies had different interests than did large firms in Germany in the development of associational capacity and in the politics of training policy. They had no need to use the employers' association as a mechanism of information circulation because they did not have any problems of coordination to solve, at least in the area of vocational training. They wanted the association to be able to provide firm-specific training, and they supported government measures that could be used to underwrite this training (cf. Hancké 2001). Yet, because they did not need to pursue a DQP product market strategy, they did not care whether the government convinced large numbers of SMEs to invest in general skills training through youth training contracts.[3] We expect French large firms to have been largely indifferent to the success or failure of the government's training reforms.

Eastern German and French Small and Medium-Size Firms
The basic preference orderings of SMEs in both countries were similar, although they had different contextual situations. Potential trainees considered industrial-sector SMEs in both France and in eastern Germany to be less desirable places to be trained and to work than the large firms. The reputations of large firms were more widely established, and they

---

[3] They had no reason to be hostile to such a measure, either, unless it limited their ability to use training contracts for firm-specific training.

appeared less likely to fail.[4] What differentiated the eastern German SMEs from the large firms was the importance of the broad general skills taught in the first year of German apprenticeship. Eastern German large firms, which operated at the most advanced end of the skill requirements for firms conducting a DQP strategy, needed the breadth of general skills that are taught in the first year of German apprenticeship. For German SMEs, however, these skills were needlessly broad. They too operated a DQP strategy, but they demanded a narrower range of skills from their employees than did the technologically advanced large firms. The fact that they had not invested so much in the capital facilities required for DQP means that it was relatively less costly for them to switch to a cost-competition strategy. However, given the regulatory and wage-setting environment in which they found themselves, they too preferred to operate a DQP product market strategy. What are the implications of this difference for their preferences in the area of human capital investment?

The hypothetical eastern German small firm (firm EGSME) is likely to prefer outcome X (EGSME does not train, but other firms do) to outcome W (EGSME trains, and other firms train). Whereas firm EGL needs the first year's training in general skills, EGSME is primarily interested in using the apprenticeship system to provide a more narrow range of general skills and firm-specific skills. This is clearly manifest in the evidence that large firms in western Germany invest substantially more per apprentice than do small firms (von Bardeleben 1995; Wagner 1999). Firm EGSME is simply constrained to use apprenticeship to attract workers of the appropriate level of general skill because there is no viable alternative system of skill certification for getting this mix of skills within the regulatory environment adopted through the eastern German reforms. (Firm EGSME would therefore be content to poach trained workers from other SMEs.) Like firm EGL, EGSME prefers not to train if no one else trains (Y > Z), but X and W are both preferable to either Y or Z. Thus, the preference ordering for firm EGSME is that of a typical *n*-person prisoners' dilemma: X > W > Y > Z. If the eastern German SMEs are not able to coordinate their training behavior around a training and no-poaching equilibrium, they all wind up with outcome Y, even though they all prefer outcome W to outcome Y.

The French SMEs did not differ from their large compatriots in their preferred strategy; they too were uninterested in paying for investment

---

[4] In western Germany, large firms also tend to have better training workshops and to invest more in the costs of training their young workers (Wagner 1999). I discuss the problems of poaching and coordination as largely internal to each set of employers (eastern German large, French large, and SMEs) because their potential labor pools tended to be different, although not totally independent of one another.

in general skills. However, unlike the French large firms, they were not powerful enough to force the employers' association to design firm-specific CQs to their exact requirements. If they wanted to use the CQ to develop specific skills, they had to agree to train in general skills as well as in skills specific to a given firm. If they had to provide general skills in order to attract workers (who found the large firms more attractive), it made sense for small firms to invest in the provision of machinery necessary to exploit the general skills of their workers. Thus, in order to attract trainable workers at all, French SMEs might have been willing to invest in developing a product market strategy that exploited the general skills of their workers. By virtue of their inability to compel the employers' association to tailor the CQ to their specific needs, they might have been willing to adjust their productive strategy to make the best use of the general certification they needed to attract workers and train them in firm-specific skills.

What, then, are the preferences of the hypothetical French SME (firm FSME)? Neither outcome Z (FSME trains, but others do not) nor outcome Y (FSME does not train, others do not train) provides a way for small firms to attract the workers they need for production. Their need for workers on whom they can confer their own firm-specific training leads them to prefer both X and W to Y or Z. Firm FSME clearly prefers to poach workers trained in general skills elsewhere (X) rather than to train in general skills itself (W). Thus, just like the typical eastern German SME, firm FSME has the preference ordering X > W > Y > Z. The French SME is caught between its needs to attract workers (by training in some general skills) and its temptation to let other SMEs bear that cost and poach their workers after they have been trained by offering higher wages. In a stylized world with only one round of play, the nature of the strategic situation facing individual SMEs in France and in eastern Germany leads them to defect rather than to cooperate with one another.

However, this was in reality an iterated game for the companies; depending on their discount rates, there was a potential equilibrium of high investment in training without poaching. Policy-makers in both countries tried to convince them to choose this cooperative outcome, even though this choice did not maximize their return in any single round of play.

STRATEGIC INTERACTION, COOPERATIVE THRESHOLDS, AND INTRAGROUP HETEROGENEITY

In delineating this basic set of employer preferences, I have made two important simplifications that need to be discarded in order to identify problems relevant to securing decentralized cooperation. First, the preference orderings assume that there are two states of the world confronted by individual firms: one in which every other firm trains apprentices and one in which no other firms train apprentices. Second, the previous discussion implies that the interests of firms within any given size category are essentially identical. Both these assumptions are false.

In almost any imaginable scenario, some firms will invest in apprenticeship training and others will not. The payoff for an investment in general skills training then depends on how many other firms are in fact training. Companies therefore encounter a threshold problem analogous to that faced by actors engaging in collective action, such as political protest. The intuition behind the threshold is that whether I engage in a costly action such as a protest for the collective good depends on how many other people I think will engage in that same action; my threshold is the number of other people I must believe will protest before I will join the protest (Granovetter 1978; Lohmann 1994; Chwe 1999). We can conceive of the individual firm's calculus using a cooperative threshold, where the threshold is defined as the number of other companies that must be investing in apprenticeship training in order to convince the firm that an investment in training will produce a payoff better than that of not training. Employing the notation of the previous section, the threshold is the number of other companies that must be training in order for a given small firm to conclude that payoffs W and X are both preferable to payoffs Y and Z.

My argument starts from the assumption that cooperative thresholds are heterogeneously distributed among firms in any given size category. This means that two firms that each have 150 employees are likely to have different thresholds at which they will find it rational to invest in general skills training through apprenticeship. The manager of one firm may be convinced to make the training investment if there are twenty-five firms of similar size that are training apprentices, whereas the manager at the other firm may require that seventy-five firms of similar size be training before the training investment appears rational. Let us now consider the effect of this heterogeneous distribution of cooperative thresholds for each category of firm.

The French large firms constitute the easiest analytical case, but the most intractable group from the perspective of the French government. It is easy analytically because French large companies stood to gain nothing from changing their training practices, given the contemporary institutional and regulatory environment. Introducing the assumption of heterogeneous cooperative thresholds does not change this picture. Individual employers in France were too strong, in comparison with the unions, to be compelled to invest in general skills when they could make the state and individuals pay for those skills through the general education system. Because large firms were often the most technologically advanced companies in a given sector, the French state intently tried to woo them to invest heavily in youth training contracts to provide general skills. If my stylized interest analysis is correct, this is a lost cause. French large firms have no interest in investing in such a system, and there is almost no way—given the current regulatory, institutional, and product market environment—that the government would be able to persuade them to use these instruments to develop the general skills of the workforce.

The interests of the eastern German large firms merely required them to have an adequate mechanism for the credible circulation of information in order to coordinate on a high-skill equilibrium, in which almost all firms invested in general skills training. The employers' association, which was the mechanism of interfirm discussion and information circulation in western Germany, would be the most likely means of credible communication in eastern Germany. Only if they failed in establishing the coordinating capacity of the eastern German associations would it be difficult to convince the large firms to invest in training. The heterogeneity of cooperative thresholds for large German firms is therefore relatively unimportant. If they have access to credible information about what other firms will do, then even those with high cooperative thresholds—that is, those that will train only if a large proportion of other firms in their size category will train—will be willing to invest in general skills.

The SMEs in both countries constitute the most interesting case, both analytically and politically. SMEs made up the bulk of the firm population and accounted for the majority of employment in France and in eastern Germany. In order for the reforms to succeed in either country, a substantial number of these firms would have to be convinced to begin investing in the training of apprentices. Yet the interest analysis in the previous section suggests that SMEs are involved in a strategic situation in which there are constant temptations to free ride on the training investment of other companies by poaching.

Introducing the heterogeneity of cooperative thresholds among the SMEs underlines an obvious feature of the real world: some of these firms are much more likely than others to be persuaded of the value of training. In a situation in which there are only a few existing cooperators—that is, firms investing in general skills training—those small firms with high cooperative thresholds are very unlikely to be convinced of the value of investing in training. They will only be convinced if they observe many other companies also investing in general skills training. Those with low cooperative thresholds, on the other hand, do not require that virtually the entire population of SMEs be training in order to be persuaded of the value of investment in general skills training. I call actors with low thresholds waverers to highlight the uncertainty of the choice facing them, which leaves them wavering between coopera- tion and defection. In other words, if we arbitrarily set the current level of cooperative behavior in the population at twenty-five, the waverers are those actors with a threshold of between twenty-four and twenty-six.[5]

The Dynamics of Policy Change

In light of this understanding of the heterogeneity of thresholds, we can now return to the tipping character of rationalist institutional change (discussed in chap. 1). The challenge facing both the French and eastern German governments—convincing private actors to coordinate their behavior around an equilibrium that yields high individual and social returns—is not likely to be characterized by a linear dynamic. Training reforms look different to large firms in the two political economies than to SMEs, but we are now considering the problem of reform from the perspective of the state, which is interested in the actions of the entire population of firms. We have already mentioned that, at the outset of the reform project, the one-shot strategic situation of SMEs resembles a prisoner's dilemma. When the game is iterated, there are multiple potential equilibria, depending on individual dis- counting rates. Yet the introduction of threshold considerations means that the situation of reform has a potentially accelerative dynamic, in which additional individual choices to cooperate have increasing returns on the probability that others will cooperate (cf. Marwell and Oliver 1993). Two features of the situation of SMEs suggest that this will be so. First, given the heterogeneity of cooperative thresholds, each round of play in which one set of firms is convinced to begin investing in train- ing will trigger the (slightly higher) thresholds of other firms that observe the first group investing in training. At some point, the decision of each individual company to cooperate catalyzes another company to cooperate, and so on. Eventually the probability of triggering one addi- tional cooperating firm will decline as it becomes difficult to cross the high threshold of the committed defectors.

---

[5] Recall from the earlier discussion of thresholds in Granovetter (1978) that these numbers represent the number of other actors who must be engaged in the new cooper- ative activity before a given individual judges participation to be worthwhile, given com- plete information. However, as discussed in chapter 1, some companies have substantial analytic uncertainty. If there are twenty-five other companies engaged in high-skill train- ing and a firm with a threshold of twenty-four is uncertain about the benefits of training, that firm may not begin training even though its threshold has been crossed. Uncertainty lowers the perceived benefit from cooperation and heightens the perceived risk of defection.

Second, as more firms begin to invest in training through apprenticeship, this changes the nature of the available labor pool from which companies can recruit. If many companies train and retain their own apprentices, then the apprentices available on the market are likely not to have been retained because of some unobserved individual defect (i.e., they are lemons). In such a situation, it will make more sense for a company to invest heavily in training its own apprentices because the few hires available on the market are likely to be lemons (Soskice 1994). By contrast, if few companies are retaining their apprentices, the lemon problem does not come into play for SMEs because most post-training apprentices are on the market (not just the lemons). But if the number of firms training and retaining does rise, then at some point the increasing level of retention will increase the costs of hiring directly from the labor market because the probability of hiring a lemon increases. This will make companies that were previously hesitant to train more likely to do so. It is at this point that the accelerative dynamic can kick in, causing the number of companies training apprentices to increase dramatically.

Over time, then, the interest of actors in decentralized cooperation has the character of an S-shaped curve (see figure 2.1). At the

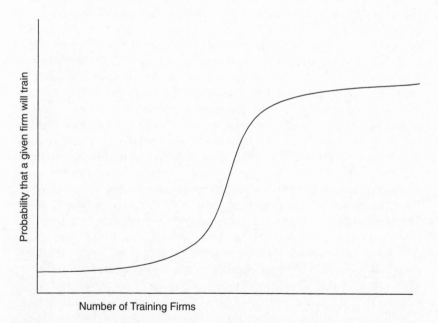

Figure 2.1 The Dynamics of Decentralized Cooperation

beginning of the reform project, the participation of a few companies does not much affect the payoffs of other companies considering cooperation. This is indicated by the flatness of the curve in the early stages. However, as the number of participating companies increases, there is a point at which the growing number of participating firms yields additional returns to cooperation. At this point, the slope of the curve steepens, meaning that the additional participation of each additional firm has a marginally larger impact on the probability that others will begin to invest heavily in apprenticeship training. If the state can succeed in generating enough cooperating firms to get to the steeper part of the curve, it increases the likelihood of succeeding in its goals of changing societal patterns of coordination.

At the early stages of the reforms, however, the accelerative part of the curve is still a far-off objective. The governments in France and eastern Germany in the 1990s found themselves at the early, flat part of the curve. As in collective action, the problem of governments was how to pay some of the start-up costs of cooperation in order to increase the net number of participants, and so move toward the accelerative part of the curve (Marwell and Oliver 1993; Heckathorn, 1996). In looking at this curve, we can see an advantage of the eastern German situation compared to the French situation. A portion of the left-hand, flat part of the curve is likely to be occupied in eastern Germany by the large firms, provided they can devise a means of communication in order to coordinate on their preferred outcome (in which all large firms train). The large firms in France, by contrast, are located on the right-hand, flat part of the end of the curve: no matter what happens among the SMEs, the large firms are very unlikely to be persuaded of the value of investing in general skills through in-firm training. The problem facing eastern Germany is easier, then, even though the large firms are not sufficient in number to move to the accelerative part of the curve on their own. In both countries, however, the principal challenge facing states is to convince wavering SMEs to begin engaging in high-skill training practices.

ANALYTIC UNCERTAINTY AND GROUP POLARIZATION

How can wavering companies be convinced of the value of cooperation? The question underscores the importance of uncertainty in subverting reforms premised on decentralized cooperation. Up to this point, our discussion has proceeded on the assumption that actors understand the payoffs involved in choosing whether to invest in general skills training. The logic has been strategic—companies consider how their choices will interact with the choices of other firms. Recall from chapter 1, however, that the uncertainty created by these reforms is not merely strategic, or related to the actions of other companies. This uncertainty is also cognitive: What would the payoffs to cooperation be if the other players cooperated? This is analytic uncertainty, and overcoming it is a critical element in resolving problems of decentralized cooperation.

The description of the strategic situation for SMEs assumes that they correctly understand the payoffs for a given course of action (the value of training vs. the value of poaching). But are the premises of public policy-makers correct? Does the investment in the firm-level provision of general skills indeed provide the higher joint payoff promised by the government? This is uncertain to the managers and personnel directors of French and German SMEs, and it is here, I argue, that public policy may be effective in convincing actors of the value of coordinating around a high-skill training equilibrium over the long term.[6]

Overcoming analytic uncertainty requires that actors be convinced that the payoffs attributed to cooperation are indeed accurate. This is fundamentally a cognitive problem: in situations of analytic uncertainty, either the complexity of an issue is high or the cognitive familiarity with the mechanisms of a system for adding value is low. Either way, there are only two ways to get actors to change their preferences: it can be demonstrated to them, empirically, that there are higher payoffs associated with cooperation or they can be convinced, logically, that there are higher payoffs to cooperation. A combination of demonstration and persuasion is likely to be especially effective in convincing waverers of the nature of the payoff structure of the new game of cooperation introduced by the government.[7]

---

[6] Analytic uncertainty is only important for the SMEs in the case of training reform in France and eastern Germany. Managers in French large firms were certain there is no value in cooperating. Eastern German large firm managers had their uncertainty ameliorated by the fact that their principal owners were western German conglomerates. These conglomerates had an experienced corps of western German human resource personnel who could give eastern German managers good information about the likely payoffs of a training investment. This informational advantage means that analytic uncertainty would be greatly reduced, if not eliminated, as an obstacle to training for most large firms in eastern Germany.

[7] For ease of exposition, I assume that changes in organizational (firm) knowledge operate through the updating of expectations by relevant individual decision-makers within the organization (personnel managers). This is consistent with the approach adopted by most of the literature on organizational learning (cf. Argyris and Schon 1978; Crossan et al. 1999). In the case of either individuals or of organizations, the analytical question is how to effect changes in the underlying cognitive structure that informs decision-making (Klimecki and Lassleben 1998). A fully developed theory of learning must address the issue of how individual learning is related to organizational learning, but as there is still great debate in the organizational behavior literature on how exactly this updating takes place, I merely join that literature in signaling the need for further empirical research on the question (cf. Levy 1994).

As do social scientists, individual actors use empirical experiences to update their theoretical apparatuses. If actor EGSME1 invests in general skills training at time t, then seeing a return on that investment will make it more likely to invest at time $t + 1$ because it sees that the investment does indeed produce the goods. Similarly, if it has access to information about actor EGSME2's investment and sees that actor EGSME2 is acting cooperatively and getting the return on its investment, then the same logic applies: the actor sees that the system works, cooperation yields a higher payoff than defection or nonparticipation, and this is factored into EGSME1's decisional calculus for the next round of play. The fundamental problem in this game is overcoming the uncertainty of the individual actor about its own payoffs through empirical demonstration of the benefits of cooperation.[8] The first element of convincing SMEs of the payoffs of training is therefore finding a way to have them experiment with training techniques.

Such an empirical method is likely to be reinforced if it is accompanied by a persuasive case for the benefits of cooperation. If there is a status quo bias that inhibits actors from changing their cooperative behavior for fear of loss, then it seems that a logical story confirming the prospect of gain will be useful in overcoming that bias. This is fighting fire with cognitive fire. For the sources of such a cognitively persuasive case, we need to make a brief detour through the literature on social psychology.

Group Polarization

Individuals tend to weigh the possibility of loss more heavily than the possibility of an equally probable gain from changing their patterns of interaction, which underlines the cognitive distortion that stands in the way of improving the prospects of social cooperation (Fernandez and Rodrik 1991).[9] Actors are not only biased against future loss, but are

[8] Macy (1991) has used computer simulations in an attempt to demonstrate the effects of this sort of adaptive expectation mechanism, in which actors randomly engage in cooperation and reap the mutually beneficial returns on cooperation without the benefit of foresight; that is, their cooperation is based on cooperation into which they stumble and which they then continue because it demonstrably yields high returns for them.

[9] These cognitive considerations are logically prior to the ones considered under prospect theory, in which people tend to overweigh losses with respect to gains and to have different risk propensities for the prospects of gain than the prospects of loss (Kahneman and Tversky 1979; Levy 1992). Prospect theory is fundamentally a theory of choice under risk, where the probabilities of a given outcome are known. The analytic uncertainty with which I am concerned takes place in the cognitive phase of framing, which is omitted in work on prospect theory. One proponent of this theory has noted that the "absence of a theory of framing is the single most serious limitation of prospect theory and the most important task for future research" (Levy 1996, 186).

also boundedly rational when it comes to evaluating the gains to be had from cooperation. In other words, people are afraid of trying a cooperative arrangement because they have difficulty estimating its benefits accurately. Being risk-averse, they prefer to remain in a situation where they can benefit a little less, but where they know exactly what to expect. Better the devil you know than the one you do not.

One way to overcome such uncertainty is to exploit a phenomenon known as group polarization. Repeated experiments have shown that group interaction has the effect of amplifying the summation of individual opinions of members of the group. The original experiment that led to this finding, since confirmed by follow-up studies in many diverse settings, is usefully illustrative. Stoner (1961) posed to his individual subjects a number of hypothetical dilemmas such as this one: "An electrical engineer may stick with his present job at modest but adequate salary, or may take a new job offering considerably more money but no long-term security." The results, as summarized in Brown (1988), were startling:

> The subjects were asked to judge the lowest acceptable level of risk for
> them to advise the main character in the scenario to give the riskier
> alternative a try. . . . The subjects were then randomly formed into
> groups and asked to reach a unanimous decision on each of the
> dilemmas they had considered individually. Stoner found to his surprise
> that these group decisions were nearly always riskier than the average of
> the individual group member pre-discussion decisions. These results
> were quickly replicated by Wallach et al. (1962), who also established
> that these shifts in group opinion became internalized because they
> reappeared when the subjects were asked once more for their individual
> opinions *after* the group discussion. (143)

This finding—that group opinions magnify the leanings of the individual group members—has been confirmed through studies in a variety of fields, from how juries decide to how individuals judge physical attractiveness (Lamm and Myers 1978; Brown 1988; Sunstein, Kahneman, and Schkade 1998).

Thus, in a population with heterogeneously distributed cooperative thresholds, one way to persuade the waverers of the value of cooperation is to promote intensive information exchange between them and some existing cooperators. The premise behind group polarization is that the individual leanings of a group are magnified through group discussion, so groups whose average opinion is risk-seeking will make their members even more risk-seeking, and risk-averse groups will tend to heighten their members' risk aversion. The key to polarizing actors in the right direction is to construct and promote discussion among smaller subgroups, whose members on average are likely to lean toward cooperation. That is, eliminate the confirmed defectors from the mix while concentrating the waverers together with existing cooperators. This strategy, following group polarization logic, is likely to promote a shift toward cooperation and away from defection, among the group of waverers. In other words, a cooperative attitudinal shift (polarization) should take place.

Why is that? Although this is a subject of dispute among social psychologists, the prevailing view is that the exchange of information and argument within the group is a driving force in producing this polarization of opinion (Isenberg 1986). Each member of the group has an argument or set of arguments for why he or she leans toward choosing cooperation. But these arguments are not all the same. As these participants exchange information and argument, those who are leaning toward cooperation discover (through this interaction) different arguments that confirm their preexisting belief that cooperation is a strategy with long-term benefits (Burnstein and Vinokur 1977; Brown 1988). Because this is a group that, by design, tends to lean toward cooperation, the balance of arguments circulating through the group will favor cooperation, and thus these opinions will be reinforced.[10]

In order to take advantage of the phenomenon of group polarization, reforming states need to know who the waverers in the population are, and they need to know how to convince them to engage in intensive information exchange with existing cooperators. If a government can do these things, its probability in succeeding in a reform based on securing decentralized cooperation is considerably improved.

RELATIONAL INFORMATION AND EMBEDDED POLICY-MAKING

The foregoing assumptions about the structure of firm interests, the way in which thresholds influence their engagement in strategic interaction, and the ways in which cognitive uncertainty can be resolved constitute the bedrock on which I build an explanatory framework for explaining the success and failure of certain types of institutional change. This is a rationalist framework, albeit one that concedes that there are cognitive distortions that interfere with the individual process of estimating expected utility. By introducing the idea of the cooperative threshold

---

[10] The principal alternative explanation of the process of group polarization is that social comparison takes place: individuals observe within the group a preponderance of individuals sharing similar opinions and are thereby reinforced in the belief that their views are correct (polarizing them). Most versions of this explanation contend that social comparison acts in concert with the persuasion-information effect and that the persuasion effect seems to be stronger (Isenberg 1986). See Brown (1988) for a further discussion.

and the limits of cognitive uncertainty, the framework makes predictions about the conditions under which actors can succeed in coordinating around a new societal equilibrium. The influential approach based on varieties of capitalism, by contrast, predicts failure for policies that seek to establish nonmarket coordination where it has not previously existed (Hall and Soskice 2001, 63). In the absence of institutions that can credibly monitor and sanction defection, the rationalist approach of Hall and Soskice possesses no mechanisms to create reliable expectations about how other actors will behave in the face of political reforms. The importance of credible monitoring and sanctioning—which are indeed extremely difficult to establish for states trying to secure decentralized cooperation—is common in rationalist theories that address the issue of societal cooperation (cf. Ostrom 1990, 1998; Putnam 1993).

Yet credible sanctions, for all their potential force, may be overrated. The problem of transition between equilibria for many rationalist theorists is one of creating common knowledge among participants about the way in which other actors will play the societal game. If we believe that cooperative thresholds are heterogeneously distributed, as I have argued, then common knowledge among actors is not required. Some actors, for their own idiosyncratic reasons, need only observe that a relatively small number of other actors are willing to adopt a new cooperative stance in order to change their behavior. They do not need to believe that everyone else in the population is likely to engage in cooperative behavior and know that everyone else believes this, but only that some proportion of the population will cooperate. This proportion is their individual threshold. And sometimes it is not the strategic worry of defection by other players that limits their willingness to engage in cooperation. Instead, it is their own cognitive limitations in estimating the payoffs of adopting a new pattern of behavior. If their hesitation originates in cognitive, rather than strategic, considerations, then sanctions are not the only way to create cooperation de novo.

Does this mean that interests are infinitely plastic and that cooperation is always possible, given the right deliberative institutions? No. Certain classes of actors have preferences that are objectively given, and no amount of deliberation will persuade them to revise those expectations in recognition of their common interests with other actors. As discussed in chapter 1, the deliberative associational approach is more successful than most rationalist approaches in acknowledging the multiple sorts of uncertainty that can undermine cooperation, but these uncertainties are not so sweeping that they completely obscure objective preferences, making all potential alliances possible. French large firms provide a concrete example of this phenomenon. Constructivists see worlds of possibility in which participation in deliberative institutions might convince even large French firms of their wider interests in investing in general skills training. The approach taken here sees the large French firms, unimaginatively, as confirmed defectors who have no incentive to cooperate.

Is there a theoretically viable course between the overdeterminacy of the equilibrium analysis of rational choice and the indeterminacy of comparative constructivists? I argue that such a course does exist, borrowing insights from both traditions to assemble a coherent set of rationalist propositions about the likely conditions of success or failure in the politics of decentralized cooperation. States require a certain type of private information—which I call relational information—to identify the waverers in the population and to develop policies that can succeed in overcoming their uncertainty. States are generally bad at getting such information, for reasons I explain later. I therefore build on the claim of Evans (1995) and Stark and Bruszt (1998) that states must be embedded in society in order to gain access to such information. This is a general theoretical claim, but its specific manifestation in our cases of reform—human capital investment in France and eastern Germany—deals with how policy-makers build links to employers' associations.

Firms are the actors that must be convinced to engage in cooperation, and there are good reasons to think their associations will be the most reliable societal interlocutors for the state. Yet not all associations are capable of playing this role, and there are good (rationalist) reasons why that is true. Only those associations that can exhibit what I call dialogic capacity—a capacity to use internal information to develop problem-solving strategies—are useful interlocutors for state policy-makers. Associations will only develop this capacity if they have to do so in order to attract and retain their members. The discussions that take place in these self-interested organizations constitute the most likely mechanism through which states can develop strategies to succeed in their goal of securing decentralized cooperation (cf. Fearon 1998).

States and Relational Information

The difference between success and failure in securing decentralized cooperation depends on how the state absorbs the costs involved in convincing wavering firms of the benefits of changing their training practices. The state will be most effective in so doing when it can minimize the allocation of those resources to actors who are unlikely to continue to cooperate in the future without receiving side payments. But policy-makers who want to intervene to aid waverers have an asymmetric information problem; the state does not have the information necessary to distinguish an actor with a cooperative threshold of twenty-six from an actor with a threshold of one hundred. The latter has a threshold for cooperative behavior so high that it is unlikely to be reached in the current situation; it has an incentive to act as if it had a threshold of twenty-six, if doing so will allow it to gain access to the resources offered by the state. I call these actors with high cooperative thresholds confirmed defectors; they are not likely to be persuaded of the benefits of cooperation during a policy transition.

It is important for the government to entice only waverers because this aid is supposed to be transitional—to get on board those who will participate and continue to participate (without aid) in the future. Marginal shifts in the cooperative thresholds of confirmed defectors will not change them from defectors to cooperators in a situation of transition.

Moreover, companies involved in training apprentices may work with one another through a cooperative arrangement over the lifetime of the training contracts of their young workers. If the managers of these companies have an opportunity to exchange information, how does this interaction change the expectations of participants about the payoffs of the training investment? The answer to that question depends on whether the group polarization dynamic can be exploited. Policy-makers have an incentive to ensure that the average opinion of the group of firms training through a cooperative arrangement is more convinced of the payoffs of apprenticeship training than are firms in the general population. In particular, it wants to avoid involving confirmed defectors, who see no value in training and will merely exploit the subsidy as a rent. Thus policy-makers face two questions: What sort of policies will be most successful in attracting the participation of waverers rather than confirmed defectors, and how can these policies be structured to best convince the waverers of the benefits of cooperation?

The difficulty facing public policy-makers lies in the fact that they do not have access to information about waverers. Who are they? How do they perceive the obstacles to cooperation? What policies would persuade them to gamble on an uncovered investment in apprenticeship training for one or more rounds of play, so that they could better estimate the returns to cooperation? Because the bureaucracies through which states typically gather and process information have difficulty identifying these actors, public policy-makers need to rely on alternative sources of information to design policies that are especially targeted to appeal to waverers.

What sorts of information are states well equipped to find out? States have access to expertise, through the bureaucracy or through research institutions set up to study a particular policy area. Yet the information the state can acquire by using its own research potential is limited by the difficulty a corps of state experts has in getting access to private information about the propensity of one actor, relative to others, to engage in cooperation. Like the drunk in the dark who looks for his keys under the lamppost—because that is where he can see them—the sort of information available to bureaucrats and experts is premised on what their tools enable them to observe. What they are very good at observing is aggregate outcomes. As James Scott points out, states need aggregate measurements in order to grasp the large complex reality that they are supposed to govern: "[I]n order for officials to be able to comprehend aspects of the ensemble, that complex reality must be reduced to schematic categories. The only way to accomplish this is to reduce an infinite array of detail to a set of categories that will facilitate summary descriptions, comparison, and aggregation" (1998, 77).[11] But in so doing, state officials necessarily lose contextual aspects of information about their societies.

It is this sort of contextual information that states require in order to discriminate between waverers and confirmed defectors. The state wants to know which firms have low cooperative thresholds, but this is a relative, that is, relational, piece of information. It concerns how the cooperative threshold of a given firm relates to the thresholds of other firms in the population. The advantage of the state in transitional situations remains its ability to provide subsidies to promote the sorts of behavior it wants to encourage. Yet a company's cooperative threshold constitutes privately held information, and actors will not reveal their true thresholds to just anybody. Bureaucracies can conduct sophisticated surveys that include on-site visits in an attempt to get access to such information. But private actors in the political economy—such as business firms—will not readily share inside information with the state. As noted by David Finegold and Soskice (1988), in normal times companies distrust the state and are leery of sharing information with it. In times of transition, their distrust is only magnified by their uncertainty about the motives of the state in trying to convince them to train (cf. Wood 1997). Companies not only distrust the state, they also have an incentive to misrepresent their true preferences to the state in order to gain access to subsidy money. Their motives can be seen as strategic (because they want the government to bear as much of the cost of a public good as possible) or ideological (because they believe this is none of the government's business), but companies will not readily volunteer this sort of sensitive information to the state.

---

[11] To illustrate such state simplifications, Scott cites the example of employment as a category: "The working lives of many people are exceptionally complex and may change from day to day. For the purposes of official statistics, however, being 'gainfully employed' is a stylized fact; one is or is not gainfully employed. Also, available characterizations of many rather exotic working lives are sharply restricted by the categories used in the aggregate statistics" (1998, 81).

The Role of Private Associations

The problem of seeking private information is not an uncommon one for modern states in both advanced and developing countries. Peter Evans (1995) has argued persuasively that the capacity of states in the developing world to promote industrial transformation requires an autonomous state bureaucracy, meritocratically selected and following a Weberian rationalization of tasks. But, Evans crucially adds, autonomy is not enough to promote effective economic adjustment: "a state that was only autonomous would lack both sources of intelligence and the ability to rely on decentralized private implementation" (1995, 12). State bureaucracies need information that is located within society, and cloistered bureaucrats have great difficulty acquiring such information. How can they get it? Stark and Bruszt (1998), examining strategies of privatization in postsocialist eastern Europe, suggest that industrialized societies often possess organized networks of companies that are well suited to play this role. Yet when a state has to rely on private organizations for information, it faces a dilemma: "strong networks are a resource, but they are not unproblematically so. They have the capacity to be agencies of development—or to be rent seekers depleting the public treasury and inhibiting economic growth" (Stark and Bruszt 1998, 129).

To get the relational information that they need to secure decentralized cooperation, public policy-makers must build links with private networks. The state needs to rely on an organization that actors in the political economy trust sufficiently to reveal potentially sensitive information about their propensity to cooperate. In other words, the state needs to work with organizations it cannot control in order to have an interlocutor that is a credible, trusted intermediary and that has access to private information about the identity of waverers and the problems that make them uncertain about the returns to cooperation. Existing private-sector associations can sometimes perform these functions. If not, the state will have to create some sort of forum for information circulation and collective discussion, that it is not able to control.

In the case of vocational education reform, the primary problem of coordination is among employers, so employers' associations are those especially likely to be called on by the state. But how can we assume that employers' associations will be willing to share this information with the state? And how can the state be sure that it is not merely being taken for a ride by a rent-seeking association that exploits its informational advantage to procure subsidies for its members?

Employers' associations, like other voluntary associations, seek to establish a secure base of members and to acquire organizational resources. Although associations claim to further the interests of a given category of individuals (such as employers), their principal means of attracting members is the provision of selective incentives: goods that are available to members and not available to nonmembers (Olson 1965, 51). Recall from an earlier section of this chapter that the interests of large companies appear substantially different from those of small companies both in France and eastern Germany. However, for three of the four groups analyzed—large firms and SMEs in eastern Germany and SMEs in France—the structure of company interests was such that there were potential gains for companies to invest in general skills through the training contracts, if they all agreed to invest. It is not surprising, therefore, that the associations in both countries were strong proponents of the training reforms.[12] Yet the associations can only usefully assist the state if they possess the capacities to promote information circulation and collective discussion. Whether associations develop these capacities is a function of the selective incentives they provide their members, which vary both within and across the national samples. Thus, in both countries the national associations favored the training reforms, but their capacity to serve as relays of relational information varied markedly (see chaps. 4–5).

Associations can gain access to relational information if such information allows the associations to fulfill collective functions that individual member companies appreciate (the selective incentives). Associations, supported by companies, are rightly perceived to be trustworthy by the individual companies whose dues support the associations. This is not so much an issue of control (i.e., that companies trust the association because they control it) because only the largest companies can feel that this is even partially true. Rather, it hinges mainly on reputation: the association cannot do its job of technical support without having a reputation for being a reliable guardian of information because the other companies belonging to the association are also competitors. Each individual company knows that the association will cease to be effective once its reputation for confidentiality has been breached, and thus it is confident that sensitive information will not be circulated. The association is the only intermediary to which companies will be willing to grant access to their private information. An association can be credible in two directions. First, to the state, if its membership base is encompassing, it can credibly claim to have a broad perspective on the needs of firms that the state lacks. Second, to firms, the association can carry

---

[12] The French large firms had no interest in investing in general skills, but they too were in favor of the reforms of the system because their power within the association allowed them to develop subsidized contracts in which they provided only firm-specific skills. Thus, there was no important group in the French associations opposed to the training reforms, in principle.

information about the proposed subsidies of the state and (more important) about how other firms are reacting to them. And members of
employers' associations are not nearly as likely to misrepresent their
views to the association as they are to a state carrying a big wallet: associations take money from member firms rather than potentially giving
it to them. Just as clients have every incentive to give their lawyers the
most accurate information in order to represent them, a company has
a similar incentive to give complete information to its association so that
the association can help fashion a collective response to the problems
of companies. Thus, the capacity to be the trusted intermediary is one
that associations are uniquely well suited to play in reforms premised on
securing decentralized cooperation.

Moreover, private associations have other capacities that the state can
imitate only ineffectively. An association may be able not only to circulate information, but also to serve as a forum for extended discussion
and as a powerful persuader. The association can be a center for coordination and strategy development among boundedly rational actors
(firms), which not only have to bargain over their divergent interests
but also need a strategic capacity to help them develop responses to a
constantly changing environment. Associations can also deploy exhortation and the use of persuasion to convince companies to engage in
cooperation. Although individual companies may have no reason to
contribute to the provision of a collective good, an association does; its
entire reason for being is to pursue interests declared to be collectively
good for the membership. And, just as its information is good, it is able
to use its legitimacy as the agreed-on locus for bargaining and discussion among firms. Thus, agreements to which firms have acceded
through associational bargaining become acknowledged and accepted
focal points for coordinating company behavior (cf. Schelling 1960;
Hall and Soskice 2001, 11). Although the association in most instances
lacks the ability to threaten credibly, it can certainly cajole members
and remind them of their collective responsibilities. The fact that it is
the representative of company interests grants these claims a good
deal more legitimacy than similar claims from the state or from other
organizations in the economy.

Encompassing private associations are thus much better positioned
than the state to craft subsidies that appeal specifically to companies
wavering on the border between cooperation and defection. The
waverer is uncertain about deriving the benefits from a coordinated
investment in general skills because it is not sure that the payoff structure is one in which the highest payoff in an iterated game accrues to
an outcome of mutual cooperation. The state is in a position to provide
the waverer with side payments (subsidies) to compensate it for the

potential downsides of choosing cooperation, that is, for the possibility that the payoffs to cooperation are indeed low. The waverer who accepts this side payment agrees to cooperate initially only because its expected value increases by the value of the side payment, not necessarily because it believes that cooperation will yield its own rewards without the side payment. In other words, the waverer's payoff has been changed, not its underlying understanding of the expected value of cooperation in the absence of these payoffs.

The problem of transition to a different coordinated equilibrium requires that being engaged in (at least) one round of cooperation increases the expected value of cooperation in a future round. Otherwise, the transition to the new equilibrium can never be achieved because the system will always depend on the presence of side payments from the state. Thus, the state first uses a subsidy to reduce the perceived risk of cooperation on the part of the waverer, in order to get it to suspend disbelief about the payoffs to cooperation. How then can the subsidized act of cooperation change the waverer's expected value of cooperation in future rounds of play, so that its cooperation no longer needs to be subsidized? The waverer is uncertain about deriving the benefits from cooperation, either because it is not sure what the payoffs of mutual cooperation are or because it is afraid that not enough other actors will participate to make it worthwhile. Actors revise their expectations in light of experiences that increase their confidence in the payoffs of cooperation and the functioning of the institutions that support it. If they can be concentrated together with other wavering actors and confirmed cooperators, the exchange of information among them will reinforce through group polarization their tenuous belief that the system will deliver the long-term payoffs promised by policy-makers. Turning the subsidized cooperation of waverers into stable equilibrium behavior requires that the period of subsidized cooperation facilitate an improved estimate of the benefits of cooperation relative to its costs. Otherwise, the subsidy is wasted.

Private associations, by virtue of their access to relational information, have the potential to improve the effectiveness of state policy-making. And in the cases studied here, they had incentive to do so. Why might states not work together with private associations to develop effective policies to secure decentralized cooperation? We can imagine that this might happen if policy-makers suspected that the losses due to rent-seeking would exceed the gains from securing decentralized cooperation, if policy-makers doubted the capacity of private associations to provide them with the relational information necessary to develop targeted subsidy programs, or if policy-makers doubted that the interests of the private associations were sufficiently similar to those of the state to risk the delegation of a stronger voice in policy implementation to the associations.

For purposes of the explanatory framework here, the reason policy-makers fail to develop embedded links to associations is irrelevant. In all cases, we expect a similar empirical outcome. In the absence of reliable relational information, public policy will fall back on what states do best: collecting standardized information about the economy. The bureaucratic tools of information gathering are very adept at summarizing aggregate features of the labor market. How many total apprenticeship contracts were signed in a given area? What occupations are particularly sharply characterized by a shortage of apprenticeship places? What demographic groups have the most difficulty finding apprenticeships? One of the core predictions that emerges from this explanatory framework is that, faced with problems of decentralized cooperation, states make policy based on the information to which they have access. Regardless of the partisan orientation of governments, we can expect that states without access to relational information will make policies exclusively targeted at these observable aggregates. And, given the inability of these policies to target and persuade waverers, such policies are likely to fail in securing decentralized cooperation.

The view of the state in this process is one of facilitating coordinated change in economic behavior rather than controlling it through regulatory enforcement. The Weberian state, with its monopoly on force and its rationalized bureaucracy, has the means to set standards through a state corps of experts, to monitor compliance through a corps of state inspectors, and to sanction those not in compliance through an established legal system. In policy areas such as vocational training, in which reforms depend on creating private cooperation, none of the principal strengths of the Weberian state is particularly useful. For example, a classically state-managed solution to the problem of creating more investment in general training is to impose a training tax, which the French government tried. The state sets a level of money that must be apportioned to training, monitors that such money is indeed applied to training, and then requires firms not in compliance to pay the state to compensate for not training. But in practice, companies can use creative accounting and legally approved alternatives to evade the goal of spending the training money on general skills, often concentrating it on already highly skilled employees (Boyer 1995; Lynch 1994). When firms do not invest in training and cannot conceal that fact from the state, they simply pay the tax and do not train, which leaves the state no closer to its goal of increasing investment in general skills training.

The goal of securing decentralized cooperation requires the state to move from a model of autonomous policy-making to one of embedded policy-making. The goal of state policy-makers in such a reform is to change societal patterns of coordination. It therefore needs to address the interdependence of individual decision-making. The sort of information it requires is relational: How does a firm's decisional calculus invoke the anticipated decisions of other firms? How, in other words, can the state find the firms with low cooperative thresholds in order to target them with its subsidies? To do so, the state needs to build bridges to private interest groups with strong coordinating capacities, even as it tries to establish alternative venues in which actors can talk with one another and form expectations about how others are likely to act. Given the prevalence of analytic uncertainty, the old reliable strategy of state policy-makers and of the game theorists who study them—sanctioning capacity—is not likely to be a particularly effective lever to achieve its outcomes. The state policies that will be most successful in triggering Pareto-improving social coordination are those developed in concert with private associations.

CHAPTER THREE

Employers, Public Policy, and the High-Skill Equilibrium in Eastern Germany and France

How did politicians in eastern Germany and France try to persuade employers to move to a high-skill equilibrium? And, once their proposals became law, how did companies respond to them? This chapter investigates whether firm practices in the two economies confirm the stylized depiction of interests presented in Chapter 2, and it identifies variation that is not clearly explained by the interests shared by all firms of a given size category, particularly among the SMEs, in which managers face both analytic and strategic uncertainty. Explaining this variation is the task of Chapters 4 and 5.

In order to evaluate the response of companies to the reforms, I draw on three sorts of information. Agencies in both countries collect indicators of how many youth training contracts have been signed, in what sectors those are located, and (sometimes) the extent to which they are subsidized. Survey research yields supplementary information on why companies say they are training, the obstacles they say they face, and the number of trainees hired or fired after their traineeship. These tools measure important summary statistics, but they have great difficulty connecting detailed analyses of firm-level decision-making about training investments with the extent to which a given firm actually invests in the general skills of its workers. In order to acquire such information, I have constructed a sample of companies from France and eastern Germany, and the evidence from this sample provides the basis for most of the empirical inferences made in this chapter.

The chapter starts with brief sketch of the human capital reforms adopted in eastern Germany and France. I then discuss the aggregate results of training reforms, as depicted in government statistics and studies of patterns of training and retention, and present the characteristics of my firm sample and the overall findings from it. In the subsequent sections, I break down the training behavior of companies according to their size, discussing uncertainty and the use of subsidies. The way in which subsidies are used by firms in the two employment

zones in the eastern German state of Saxony and in the French Valley
of the Arve underlies the greater success of firms in these areas
in coordinating their training practices around a new high-skill
equilibrium.

THE REFORMS

Eastern Germany

To transfer the western German dual system to eastern Germany after
1990, the German government had to convince companies to invest in
the development of human capital through apprenticeship. The legal
architecture of such a project was easily established through the adoption, in August 1990, of the West German framework law for vocational
training (Berufsbildungsgesetz, BBiG) by the moribund parliament of
the German Democratic Republic (GDR). This reform gave the five new
federal states of eastern Germany, which had just been created, responsibility for the in-school component of apprenticeship training (Goetz
1993).[1] Similarly, this law established the supervisory responsibility of
the chambers for training, and it allowed employers' associations and
unions to staff the corporatist institutions that supervised training at
the national, state, and local levels (Johnson 1995). These steps were
intended to establish the governance structure that would persuade
firms to hire apprentices. Prior to 1990, companies in eastern Germany
had trained apprentices in a system that looked like the western German
system; the key difference was that managers exercised very little autonomy in choosing how many apprentices to train. For this investment
decision, they had in the past deferred to state economic plans, which
stipulated how many apprentices they would hire. Decisions about
apprenticeship were among the multiple new investment decisions that
were abruptly thrust on firm managers after the sudden introduction of
the market economy in 1990. Convincing them to make this costly long-
term investment was the challenge behind transforming the system of
human capital formation in eastern Germany.

The transformation of the eastern German training system put the
onus of investing in youth training on individual companies just as those
companies were undergoing the shock imposed by the revaluation of
their currency. The monetary union of July 1990, by means of the high
real wages it established for eastern German firms, rendered many of
them completely uncompetitive with the western German companies

---

[1] The dual system of apprenticeship is characterized by dual locations of learning: one
or two days per week in a public vocational school learning general skills related to the
profession studied, with the remainder spent directly in the training firm learning
practical applications of these skills.

that were now their market rivals. Eastern German markets were suddenly flooded with high-quality western goods; the adoption of the currency conversion policy based on parity of the lowly Ostmark with the mighty Deutschmark combined with the low productivity of eastern German workers to make most of their goods hopelessly overpriced (Baylis 1993). The results were predictably drastic: by 1991, eastern German manufacturing had collapsed, falling to one-third of its 1989 levels (Collier 1993). The effect on the competitiveness of firms in eastern Germany was exacerbated by the wage deals struck by western German unions and employers, in which the principle of reaching early parity with western German wages—while lacking western German productivity—was enshrined and ratified by collective agreement (Ettl 1995; Silvia 1997).[2] The original terms of monetary union, followed by these agreements, contributed to high eastern German unemployment, which persists into 2002. Including those workers removed from employment along with those in hidden unemployment (i.e., masked by work-creation schemes), one-third of the eastern German labor force was unemployed within a year of the formal unification of the two Germanies (Lange and Pugh 1998).

The high unemployment that followed unification exacerbated the challenge of convincing eastern German employers to adopt the cooperative training practices characteristic of the western German dual system. The sudden immersion in a market economy hit the inefficient industrial sector in eastern Germany especially hard, putting many skilled industrial workers out of work and on the labor market. Eastern German companies that hired these unemployed workers could receive government financing to support their further training in firm-specific skills. Moreover, the limited work available increased the likelihood that existing employees would resist management's attempts to hire apprentices, who were seen as rivals to current workers (Wagner 1999). If eastern German works councils, which in western Germany generally encouraged the hiring of apprentices (Soskice 1994), became driven principally by the goal of preserving existing employment, this would be a further obstacle to using apprenticeship as a mechanism for providing for future skilled labor. Finally, the effect of the severe contraction of industrial employment was to push young eastern Germans to desert the industrial professions, so that (despite the high unemployment) industrial companies in the east with advanced skill demands soon had

---

[2] The 1991 agreement by employers' associations throughout eastern Germany set up a stepwise march to parity, in which wages would be equalized in the two parts of Germany by 1994. By end of the year 2001, parity with negotiated wages in the west still had not been reached in most sectors in eastern Germany.

difficulty finding qualified applicants (Locke and Jacoby 1997).[3] In the industrial professions, policy-makers in eastern Germany in the aftermath of unification faced numerous obstacles to convincing firms of the importance of investing in apprenticeship: industrial apprenticeship was in disrepute, high youth unemployment gave employers other options for developing human capital than apprenticeship investment, and the productive system was one in which many existing plants were organized for low-skill Fordist production rather than the profile of incremental innovation typical of western Germany. Coordinating on a high-skill equilibrium was not an obvious course of action to the beleaguered managers of eastern German companies.

France

Whereas training reform was part of the single tidal wave of institutional transfers that swept over eastern Germany after 1990, the reform process in France more closely resembled an encroaching tide, in which successive waves of legislation steadily expanded the regulatory framework designed to convince companies to make high investments in youth training.[4] A 1984 law established new firm-based youth work contracts, of which the most important (the CQ) eventually rivaled apprenticeship. The apprenticeship contracts and CQs were the two certifications on which the French attempts to elicit increased in-firm training were constructed, but they differed in an important way. Unlike in Germany, where the content of vocational qualifications was the subject of negotiation between employers and unions, apprenticeship qualifications in France were controlled by the Ministry of Education (D'Iribarne and Lemaître 1987). By contrast, the CQ effectively mim-

---

[3] This effect was not felt identically across all occupations: service sector professions, in particular, were steadily oversubscribed because they held the prospect of greater security of employment than those in industry.

[4] At the same time, other changes in the school-based education system were responses to demands of the private economy for the skills needed for production (such as the bac professionnel, bac technique, and the development of the bac + 2 degrees) (cf. Bouyx 1997). I do not deal with these here except when they intersect the problems of firm-based training, but any exhaustive treatment of the French system of skill provision must also treat the school-based reforms in detail. Here I focus specifically on the in-firm reforms because they attempted to develop a qualitatively different approach to education, one that epitomizes the politics of decentralized cooperation.

The baccalauréat is the post-high school examination in France. Post–secondary schooling is typically referred to by the number of years following high school (the bac); e.g., bac + 2 refers to two years of post–secondary schooling. The CAP (Certificat d'aptitude professionnelle) is the lowest level occupational qualification in the French system, given after ten years of general schooling and the completion of a two-year apprenticeship.

icked German apprenticeship, in that trainees combined work in a company with time devoted to theoretical general training taught through a training center. The content of the qualifications was negotiated between employers and unions alone.[5] A 1987 law gave employers the opportunity to use apprenticeship for young people with up to two years of post–high school education (Comité de Coordination 1996b).[6] French employers, who had perennially complained about the theoretical nature of the curriculum in the educational system and the low qualifications of recruits attracted to vocational training, gained in these two measures powerful new tools for investing in skilled labor through youth training contracts.

In 1993, the Balladur government passed a law that aimed to unify these past measures and tried to convince companies to move the principle of *alternance*—training alternating between school and the workplace, on the model of western German apprenticeship—to the center of their skill-provision strategies. The Five-Year Law on Work, Employment, and Professional Training (hereafter, the Five-Year Law) established new institutions that provided a forum for interemployer and employer-union coordination at the level of the regions; and the regional councils were given the primary responsibility for the development of training policy by the Five-Year Law. By creating these new institutions of governance, the national government hoped to clarify responsibility for training policy so as to convince firms to use the principal *alternance* training contracts—the apprenticeship contracts and CQs—as an important means of securing their future skilled labor. The law also established clear, generous subsidies for these contracts as an additional inducement to firms that had hesitated to use them during the previous decade. The law delegated many of the issues of implementation to employers and unions on the presumption that they should be the ones to negotiate the details, given their close involvement in the governance of further training in France. By establishing this comprehensive framework supervised by private-interest organizations, the government hoped to entice employers into youth training at the level of their neighbors across the Rhine.

Like their counterparts in eastern Germany, the regional governments in France faced a daunting task—the woeful state of in-firm voca-

---

[5] The duration of the CQ varied between six months and two years, and it was available to youth between the ages of 16 and 25, who had to spend at least one-quarter of their time receiving instruction in a training center external to the firm where they have the contract.

[6] In 1990 the government expanded this project further, passing a law making apprenticeship possible at the university engineering level (five years after the baccalauréat, or bac + 5).

tional training had previously led French firms to pursue alternative means of recruiting skilled labor. With no mass educational system capable of providing workers with general intermediate-level skills, French companies had relied less on shop-floor workers and more on supervisors to maintain strict control over the production process, using the continuing training system to develop the firm-specific skills of graduates of the general education system (Maurice, Sellier, and Silvestre 1986; Gehin and Méhaut 1993; Yakubovich 1998). These employers had responded to the structure of the existing skill-provision system by taking advantage of what it did best (managerial and general technical training) while complaining politically about what it did worst (provision of broadly skilled production workers). The expansion in the 1980s of youth receiving general education up to two years after the baccalauréat (bac) via BTS and DUT degrees, and the creation of the bac professionnel in 1985, multiplied the potential alternative sources of workers with general skills, and the majority of youth in the vocational training system in France still passed through the school-based general education system (Bouyx 1997). Although employers continued to disparage the quality of general education, their hiring habits were well established by the 1990s. In order to increase the participation of companies in the youth training contracts, the government had to convince them that the potential payoff for doing so was more lucrative than the option of hiring workers with a general degree and giving them purely firm-specific training. For French firms, as for those in eastern Germany, the high-skill equilibrium preferred by the government was not an obvious choice on which to coordinate.

AGGREGATE RESULTS

Convincing companies across eastern Germany and France to coordinate on a high-skill equilibrium was in fact extremely difficult. Successful reform required firms to make substantial uncovered investments in general skills when they were uncertain what other firms would do. Yet in both eastern Germany and France, the politics of youth training was highly charged because both political economies suffered throughout the 1990s from the problem of high youth unemployment. Politicians like the dual system of western Germany because, among other reasons, it eases the transition from school to work, thus reducing youth unemployment (Wagner 1999, 58). The short-term imperatives of politicians to adopt policies that kept young people off the unemployment rolls were in constant tension with the goal of establishing a system in which firms invested heavily in high-skill training. And this tension marked the development of training policies in both countries, particularly through the question of how best to subsidize youth training.

Table 3.1 Apprenticeship Market in Eastern Germany, 1991–1994[a]

	1991	1992	1993	1994
Youths seeking apprenticeships[b]	145,693	138,342	145,580	171,103
In-firm posts available[c]	62,659	75,084	83,959	87,529
Youths/Available posts	2.3	1.8	1.7	2.0

[a] Source: BMBW (1995, 24).

[b] Includes all youths who registered as apprenticeship seekers at the local employment offices.

[c] Includes subsidized in-firm places, but excludes the out-of-firm places subsidized by the federal government.

In eastern Germany, the federal and state governments had to persuade firms in the midst of a restructuring economy to bear the costs of training apprentices; and the firms had to offer sufficient places to cover the demand of young people desiring an apprenticeship. This was a tall order. As shown in table 3.1, in the first four years of the united German labor market, there were nearly twice as many eastern German youths registered for apprenticeships as there were available in-firm places in the new federal states. Soaring eastern German unemployment and the contraction in the number and size of firms that followed reunification meant that the firms that did survive were likely to be on the edge of bankruptcy, having no money to spare for the luxury of ensuring future skilled labor. And in any case, the market was flooded with skilled laborers whose firms had either gone bankrupt or had curtailed employment severely, so that firms in every eastern labor market had easy access to skilled labor to meet their needs for the future (Schober 1994, 8–9).

The lack of in-firm apprenticeship places, relative to the number of young people seeking places, was the foremost training-related problem facing the governments and social partners in eastern Germany.[7] And

---

[7] The lack of sufficient apprenticeship places is a staple of public debate between German unions and employers' representatives, with each side employing creative accounting to create its desired picture. Unions point to a lack of places—or a lack of places in the most desirable careers—as evidence that the employers are failing to take on their responsibilities for training the young; the oft-stated conclusion is that the state should take a more active role in the functioning of the dual system, forcing recalcitrant firms to contribute to training costs. Employers' representatives, for whom any intrusion of the state into their training prerogatives is anathema, tend to see the glass as half-full. They point to the inability of many firms, especially in industry, to fill the places they offer. The important point for the new states of eastern Germany, on which all parties agreed, was that there were not enough apprenticeship places for the young people desiring apprenticeships.

their response was to use state money to create apprenticeship places. Thus, three-fourths of the new apprenticeship contracts signed in 1998 were in fact subsidized by state or federal authorities. By contrast, in the western German system, which the government was trying to establish in eastern Germany, fewer than 3 percent of apprenticeship places were subsidized (Bundesministerium für Bildung, Wissenschaft, Forschung und Technologie [BMBW] 1999: 41). More than 10 percent of the eastern German places were created by governments, and these places were not (as was the practice in western Germany) based on a work contract between an apprentice and a firm. They normally took place in a school or a training center, and the apprentices who filled these places lacked the same exposure to productive work as their in-firm counterparts.[8] In-firm apprenticeship places subsidized by the state governments constituted the bulk of the places in eastern Germany, as they have every year since unification. These places were governed by a work contract and apprentices were integrated into the production process of the company, but the employer received a subsidy to help cover the costs of training; thus, the net employer investment in the costs of training was reduced.

In other words, eastern German employers overwhelmingly depended on government money to train apprentices. Unlike employers in western Germany, they were not willing to invest substantial amounts of their own money in apprenticeship training.[9] What these aggregate data do not tell us is whether or not this subsidized training enabled companies to make the transition to western German patterns of investment in skill provision or whether, instead, a new form of subsidy dependence became durably embedded in the eastern German apprenticeship system. The outcome depended on the ability of the government to use these subsidies to convince companies to coordinate around a training and nonpoaching equilibrium.

In France, the attempt to implement a high-skill equilibrium moved no further, and the development of training depended on the sorts of subsidies offered by the state. Laws enacted in 1982 and 1983 had decentralized the power over youth vocational training to the French regional

[8] The postapprenticeship employment rates of these youth tended to be much lower than those of apprentices with firm-based training contracts, because there was no company that had had three years to evaluate their possibilities and groom them as future employees (Ulrich 1995; BMBW 1999).

[9] Eastern German firms with more than fifty employees—firms of the size that make the large investments in apprenticeship training in western Germany—also retained their apprentices at a much lower rate than western German firms of comparable size, which implies that they were not yet sinking substantial resources of their own into youth training, on average (BMBW 1999).

Table 3.2 New *Alternance* Contracts in France, 1987–1992[a]

	Apprenticeships	CQs	Total
1987	130,576	38,566	169,142
1992	126,165	103,326	229,491
Change 1987–92	–3%	168%	36%

[a] Source: Reported in Möbus (1996, 20); author's calculations.

governments, but the creation in 1984 of CQs, which were not under regional control, almost immediately undercut the capacity of the regions to coordinate policies on youth vocational training because employers started to use CQs. As shown in table 3.2, the use of apprenticeship contracts slumped between 1987 and 1992, whereas CQs soared in popularity with employers.

By itself, the rapid growth of CQs might appear to be a sign of governmental success in encouraging employers to use in-firm training contracts to hire youth. In fact, French firms appeared to use CQs more as a means of hiring workers cheaply rather than as a tool for investing in general skill development. A study by the French Centre d'Études et de Recherche sur l'Emploi et les Qualifications (CEREQ) found that the majority of employers who used CQs reported that they were exploiting the financial advantages of the qualification for hires that they would have made anyway; a majority of these firms also reported that the youth they had trained had not attained a higher level of educational qualification as a result of their training (Lhotel and Monaco 1993, 41). Meanwhile, the apprenticeship law of 1987 had completely failed to convince large companies to begin investing in highly educated apprentices; the overwhelming majority of firms using apprenticeship during the early 1990s were still very small companies that hired apprentices at the lowest educational levels.[10] A critical parliamentary report voiced the widespread view that the similarity of the CQ with apprenticeship had engendered a competitive dynamic between the two certifications, whereby firms hunted for the most financially advantageous measure rather than using them to invest in the development of their own skilled workers (Goasguen 1994, 45).

[10] Eighty percent of the apprentices hired in 1992 went to firms employing fewer than eleven employees; 62 percent of the 1992 apprentices possessed no school diploma, and another 34 percent had only the lowest level diplomas (CAP; or Brevet d'études professionnelles, BEP) (Grezard 1993).

Table 3.3 New *Alternance* Contracts in France, 1993–1997[a]

	Apprenticeships	CQs	Total
1993	127,887	95,008	222,895
1997	211,458	101,163	312,621
Change 1993–97	65%	6%	40%

[a] Source: Reported in Möbus (1996); Sanchez (1998, 44–49).

In the 1990s, employers reversed their apparent preference for CQs, as the number of apprenticeship contracts increased sharply (see table 3.3). The reason is simple: prior to passing the Five-Year Law, the government had introduced a new subsidy to make apprenticeship much more financially lucrative to employers. Employers received 7,000 FFr on signing an apprenticeship contract and also received a tax credit of either 5,000 or 7,000 FFr per apprentice (Comité de Coordination 1996a, 12).[11] The presence of these subsidies again raises the problem of subsidy dependence, suggesting that employers in France were using the measures merely to procure cheap labor. If French firms had been investing heavily in their trainees, they would not want to lose them after their training. Yet only 10 percent of apprentices and 29 percent of youths in CQs were hired into regular work contracts after their training by the firm that had trained them (Charpail and Zilberman 1998, 50; Vialla 1997, 189).[12] In aggregate, then, French firms were clearly using the subsidies associated with the training reforms to lower their labor costs rather than to invest in developing the skills of their future workers.

A SECTORAL VIEW OF THE TRAINING REFORMS

Have these subsidies persuaded at least some firms to coordinate around a general skills training and nonpoaching equilibrium? To answer this question required developing a comprehensive picture of the determinants of firm-level decision-making about vocational training, which requires on-site visits and extensive interviews of managers. This placed logistical limitations on the number of firms that I could include in this study. The total sample of the industrial metalworking firms used in this study comprised fifty-nine firms, of which fifty-two were located in France and eastern Germany and seven were in the comparison group located in western Germany. I concentrated on the firms that have been most

[11] At 2002 exchange rates, 7,000 FFr equals approximately $1,000.

[12] The figures on apprenticeship come from a survey of 2,006 youths and those on CQs from a panel of 6,800 youths, both conducted at the end of 1996.

central to the debates about the competitiveness of firms in international markets—those in the metal and electronics sector. When observers talk about the advantages of the western German training system, they almost always mean German industrial prowess in the export sector, with machine tools and automobiles being the most frequently cited examples (Streeck 1992; Culpepper and Finegold 1999). Indeed, German training became such a darling of industrial country policy-makers because of the revolution in the organization of production that increased the importance of skilled labor for manufacturing companies, which could use their comparative advantage in human capital to maintain a niche in competitive international markets (Streeck 1992; Finegold and Wagner 1999). Moreover, this sector is central to the German dual system: in 1995, the metalworking and precision-engineering sectors had the highest proportion of plants training apprentices of any sector in western Germany (Wagner 1999).[13] This sector thus seems the best suited for evaluating which firms in eastern Germany and in France were training apprentices in a manner consistent with the patterns characteristic of the western German high-skill equilibrium.

My eastern German firm sample contains twenty-three companies in the metal and electronics industries, all of which were members of the chambers of industry and commerce.[14] The information was collected through interviews conducted on plant premises; supplementary information was frequently gathered through follow-up phone calls or documentation supplied by the company. The companies were drawn from four employment zones: Plauen and Leipzig in Saxony and Halle and Sangerhausen in Saxony-Anhalt.[15] They include firms from different parts of the metal sector, including mechanical engineering, steelmaking, and electronics, and firms ranged in size from 9 to more than 4,500 employees.

[13] Just over one-third of the plants in these sectors trained at least one apprentice in 1995, compared with 24 percent of the plants overall in the German economy (Wagner 1999).

[14] For both countries, the sample comprises almost entirely single-plant companies. Four of the largest companies (two in eastern Germany, two in France) had multiple plants for which personnel and training decisions were handled by a single office, and for these cases the data refer to total company employment managed through the single office. Legally separate subsidiaries are not included in the data.

[15] The employment zones sampled were chosen to create variation on two of the independent variables tested in this research: social capital and the design of state policy. This method of selection creates no problems of bias (King, Keohane, and Verba 1994).

Unlike the French company sample, which was constructed with the help of employers' associations in France, the German sample was constructed entirely from published lists of German private employers (Hoppenstedt 1993, 1994). The sample frame included 112 eastern German firms in these four employment office districts, to which I sent letters

My French sample contains twenty-nine industrial firms in the metal sector; the interviews were similar in structure and duration to those conducted with the eastern German companies.[16] As in Germany, the companies produced for different subsectors of the metalworking industry, including complex mechanical industries (including several firms in the bar-turning sector), electronics, and machining and toolmaking, and the firms ranged in size from 15 to 2,400 employees. The companies were located in the employment zones of Lyon and the Valley of the Arve in the region of Rhône-Alpes; Amiens and the Vimeu in Picardy; and Greater Strasbourg in Alsace.[17] In each of the French

inviting their participation, followed by at least one telephone call (and usually many more). This method of sample construction was quite time-consuming, which is why I enlisted the aid of the employers' associations in constructing the French sample. The eastern German sample should be free of obvious sorts of bias, except for two. First, as always with voluntary research, participants who agreed to take part were self-selected. It is probable that the firm representatives who agreed to participate were interested in issues of vocational training. However, I stressed in both the letters and phone calls the importance of including the perspectives of firms that did not have trainees, and the sample for every employment zone included at least one company that had no trainees. Second, those firms whose representatives chose to participate were larger than the sample frame average, which is consistent with the experience of researchers in the United States who have tried to investigate employer participation in youth training programs (Cappelli, Shapiro, and Shumanis 1998). The lower participation of small companies is understandable: in companies with fewer than one hundred employees, I generally spoke to the company manager, whereas in larger companies I spoke to the personnel manager or the director of training. Thus, in larger firms, I was more likely to talk with someone whose job dealt largely or exclusively with issues of apprenticeship training, and it is probably fair to say that these people were more likely than company managers to take an interest in my project. Neither source of bias is likely to have a substantively significant effect on the results I find for firms that do train.

[16] The questionnaire used in the French companies was modeled on the questionnaire used in the German companies, but it also included different country-specific questions (e.g., on the relevance of the training taxes to decision-making in French firms). As in the eastern German sample, almost all the companies in the sample had a single plant or were legally independent (single-establishment) companies belonging to a larger industrial group. Two French companies in the sample had multiple plants for which personnel and training decisions were handled by a single office, and for these cases the data refer to total company employment managed through the single office. One of the firms in the sample comprises two separately incorporated companies, each serving a discrete product market and having a different training policy, although they shared a chief executive. This case is treated as two different establishments in the sample.

[17] As in eastern Germany, the zones were chosen to create variation on the independent variables of social capital and regional policy. A sample from an area in Alsace was included to test the effect of the distinctive regional regulations in training that the region retains from its time under German rule between 1871 and 1918. As shown in chapter 5, the legal and cultural inheritance of Alsace had no effect on the training patterns of French companies located there.

employment zones, the relevant employers' associations assisted in the construction of a list of firms to be contacted.[18]

As a condition of participation in the study, all firms were guaranteed strict confidentiality, and the presentation and discussion of the data are couched in categories sufficiently broad to shield their identities. Each company was assigned an anonymous reference name based on its size; for example, EGSME7 is one of the eighteen eastern German companies in the sample with fewer than five hundred employees. I use these anonymous reference labels when discussing the training practices of individual firms. Appendix B provides a complete list of firms by reference label and their basic training characteristics.

In this chapter, I present the outcomes from the samples of firms according to the three categories established in chapter 2: large firms in eastern Germany, large firms in France, and SMEs in eastern Germany and France. To assess firm-level investment in general skills, I have relied on the training ratio (the number of apprentices as a proportion of the total workforce) and on the retention rate (the proportion of trainees hired after their apprenticeship). I use one or both of these measures because they represent the best available indicators of a firm's investment in youth training (von Bardeleben, Beicht, and Fehér 1995; Wagner 1999, 63–64). I use ranges of training derived from western German training practices, as well as the declared goals of political actors in eastern Germany and France, to establish a target range for the training ratio that is characteristic of investment in general skills commensurate with the high-skill equilibrium: 4–8 percent in eastern Germany and 2.5–6.5 percent in France. The higher the retention rate, the more likely that firms have invested heavily in the general skills of apprentices (whom they do not want to lose by not hiring the apprentices). I discuss the derivation and justification of these measures at length in appendix A.

Results from the Firm Sample
Table 3.4 lists the results from the firm sample, distinguishing between large firms (those having at least five hundred employees) and SMEs

---

[18] When contacting the companies to ask for their participation, I made clear that I had no connection to the employers' association and that results specific to the company would be held in confidence and would not be passed on to the association. Of the thirty-three firms I contacted, twenty-nine agreed to participate. There are two sources of potential bias introduced by this method of developing a sample of companies in France. First, there is a likelihood to overstate the effectiveness of the association (because the association would not be likely to send me to its most discontented members). Second, companies in this sample are probably more likely to have invested in training at higher levels than a representative sample of the entire French metal industry. In other words, to the extent that my results are biased, the fate of the French reform may be even bleaker than I claim.

Table 3.4 High-Skill Training Index by Size of Firm[a]

	High-Skill Training Index (%)[b]	N
Eastern German large firms	80	5
French large firms	0	9
Eastern German SMEs	22	18
French SMEs	25	20

[a] Source: Interviews conducted in 1995 and 1996 in France and Germany. Large firms are those with 500 or greater employees, SMEs (small and medium-size enterprises) are firms having fewer than 500 employees. The results for eastern German SMEs are based on the projected rate, as shown in Table 3.5.

[b] Proportion of companies judged to be training according to western German standards, as determined by the training ratio and the retention rate. (See appendix A.)

(those having fewer than five hundred employees). These data confirm that the training behavior of large firms in eastern Germany and in France conforms to the analysis in chapter 2 of their strategic situations. That analysis predicted that privatized large eastern German companies were those most likely to have invested in the provision of general skills at levels consistent with the high-skill equilibrium. Their best outcome was to invest in training and to have other large firms train; they depended only on the presence of a credible mechanism of information circulation so that their intention to train became common knowledge. And, with the successful establishment of eastern German employers' associations, that was exactly what they did. Four of the five large eastern German firms in the sample invested heavily in apprenticeship training. The only one that did not invest heavily in general skills was not privatized at the time of my interviews. These data are consistent with large-*n* surveys of the behavior of large firms in eastern Germany; this panel evidence indicates that large firms in eastern Germany were in 1996 the group most likely to increase their training and in 1997 the group most likely to continue their level of training over the next two years.[19] In other words, large firms were early to adopt the training habit and appear to be the most steadfast upholders of those habits.

For large firms in France, the discussion of interests in chapter 2 suggested that investing in youth training contracts would have no appeal.

[19] The panels, conducted by the statistical office of the German employment agency consisted of over 4,000 firms from all sectors in eastern Germany. For details of the surveys, see BMBW (1998, 126–41; 1999, 130–49).

In practice, this is exactly what we observe. None of the large companies in France was training and retaining at levels suggestive of a heavy investment in general skills training. On average, the large French companies in my sample retained approximately one-third of their trainees after the completion of their training contracts, which is less than one-half the retention rate observed in western Germany.[20]

Although most of the large French companies have used the policy tools available for youth training in a deliberate strategy to maintain or upgrade the skill base of their workforce, the ways in which they have done so bear little resemblance to the practices of the dual system in western Germany. The existence in the French system of CQs, which allow large companies in pressing need to pursue firm-specific skill upgrading, provides an exit option should the apprenticeship system, dominated by the national education ministry, prove insufficiently pliable to the demands of employers for new skills (Culpepper 1999). In addition, CQs provide firms of all sizes with a means to hire workers with a sound foundation of general skills at the bac + 2 level and to give them firm-specific training while paying a fairly low wage.[21] In some cases, the CQ serves as a two-year probationary period for workers who, once they are permanently employed, entail high wages and social charges on the company's payroll.

The interest analysis for SMEs in chapter 2 was more ambiguous, as are the overall results from my sample for these companies in eastern Germany and France. In order to attract motivated young workers to their companies, SMEs may be required to offer training in certifiable general skills. Yet any small company that invests heavily in general skills leaves itself open to the risk of poaching by other SMEs. If we assume only a single round of play, the rational expectation is that no firm will train in general skills. However, the real world is an iterated game, in which companies confront these choices—and observe the choices made by other companies—repeatedly over time. Thus, there is a potential for companies to coordinate on the high-skill equilibrium if their time horizons are sufficiently long.

The results from my sample show that, even with subsidies, only approximately one-quarter of the SMEs in each country were investing in general skills at levels consistent with the high-skill equilibrium in western Germany.[22] One-quarter of the SMEs is not enough to consti-

---

[20] This is consistent with the findings on the very low overall retention rates of trainees in the French economy (Charpail and Zilberman 1998; Vialla 1997, 3).

[21] The availability of the technical and professional bac and bac + 2 degrees in France expands the number of alternative training options available to French companies.

[22] The data on eastern German SMEs are based on projected training ratios, using information about first-year trainees.

tute a high-skill equilibrium, to be sure, but neither does it suggest that all firms chose not to participate in the training programs set up by the governmental reforms. Almost all of the firms of this size received public subsidies. Even so, only a few had developed training patterns that would be recognizable to their western German counterparts. It would appear that some subsidies were more effective than others in eliciting invest-ment in general skills (in the context of a reform aimed at adapting the benefits of a high-skill equilibrium). The high-skill training was not dis-tributed evenly among the regions studied. Firms in the two employ-ment zones in Saxony in eastern Germany, and in the Valley of the Arve in France, seemed particularly likely to engage in this sort of training behavior.

In all companies in the sample, the variable of ownership plays an important role.[23] This is most notable among eastern German firms, both large and small. None of the firms still owned by the Treuhand (i.e., those firms that had not yet been privatized) trained at levels consistent with the western German model. Apprenticeship is a long-term investment decision, and so it is not at all surprising that those firms with a short-time horizon were not participating in the training system at western German levels. A second ownership characteristic is almost equally salient for training outcomes: whether a company was independently owned or instead owned by another (usually western German) company or corpo-ration. Ownership by a western German company entailed certain attrib-utes that made these firms more likely than others to invest in general skills training. Carlin and Mayer (1995, 10–11) argue that the collateral and reputational effects that eastern German firms gained by having a western ownership structure could greatly ease their access to long-term finance. The importance of such access to finance would certainly be consistent with arguments about the importance of long-term finance in sustaining the high-skill equilibrium (Soskice 1990b; 1994, 33–34; Finegold and Soskice 1988, 36). Of equal significance may be the access of these companies to the rich internal networks of information exchange of the large western German conglomerates. These networks were a resource for eastern German managers, who might have been uncertain of the value of western German training practices. They could draw on these informational resources both to increase their knowledge of the system and to increase their confidence in its functioning, thus reducing their degree of analytic uncertainty.

In France, too, ownership is an important variable, but it has exactly the opposite effect observed in eastern Germany. Whereas the success-

---

[23] This finding is supported by the work of Katharina Bluhm (1999, 248) on interfirm cooperation in Saxony.

fully training companies in eastern Germany were all corporately owned, in France the successful companies were all independent (or family-owned) businesses. If we can assume that corporate ownership also gives French firms greater access to finance, then the finding that French corporate firms were unlikely to be high-skill trainers suggests that access to finance is not a decisive variable in the training decisions of SMEs in the transitional situations following significant political reforms. At the French firms that were corporately owned, those officials responsible for training policy did not refer to discussions within their conglomerates or with their parent company as an important source of information for making decisions about youth training. This is true even of the three French companies in my sample owned by western German corporations. It would appear that corporate ownership influences decision-making, but that individual companies respond mostly to the likely actions of other actors in the political economy in which they are located, not that in which their parent company is located. Western German ownership was no panacea for either the eastern German *Mittelstand* or for French companies.

The fate of the eastern German and French reforms ultimately rested on the training behavior of SMEs. These firms created, or did not, the bulk of the apprenticeship places following the training reforms. Large firms in western Germany account for only 20 percent of the training places in the dual system, and even fewer in eastern Germany. And large firms in eastern Germany knew this. As shown in chapter 2, their product market strategies depended on the sort of skills they could procure through the dual system of vocational training. A persistent failure by private companies to offer enough apprentice places would have provoked the government to assume a larger degree of control over the system of training, which large firms desperately wanted to avoid. They were therefore politically engaged in trying to convince smaller companies to develop their own apprenticeship programs. This political involvement of the corporate giants was an important resource for eastern German governments, but it was not a sufficient condition for success. Contrariwise, the low likelihood that large French firms would invest in the new measures for human capital investment did not condemn that reform effort to failure. But it did handicap the reform because large firms were not a political constituency committed to providing more investment in general skills through youth training contracts.

Large Firms in Eastern Germany
Large privatized firms in eastern Germany shared the government's objectives of transferring the dual system successfully to eastern

Germany. These companies had accepted the regulatory and wage-bargaining institutions of the coordinated market economy of western Germany, and they therefore depended for their competitive success on their ability to implement a product market strategy of DQP. This fact affected their strategies in three ways that are highly germane to the course of the human capital reforms. First, they were strong partisans of establishing the western German model of employers' associations in the east because they required the capacity of such associations to circulate information to be sure that other firms were likely to invest in general skills. Second, and following from the first, they invested heavily in their physical and human capital, and thus they invested in apprenticeship at levels consistent with the high-skill equilibrium. Third, they were active politically in trying to convince small firms to use the dual system to make large investments in apprenticeship training. Despite their disproportionate political power in the economy, large companies knew that the bulk of the training places in a functioning dual system must come from the SMEs. Thus, they were active in promoting the development of training at smaller companies. All three of these can be cloaked in the language of altruism, in the sense of the duty of large firms to the political economy. But it is clear that all three are completely consistent with the self-interest of large firms, which lay in establishing a dual system based on company responsibility for training in eastern Germany.

The eastern German employers' associations quickly established a strong capacity of information circulation after unification (Wiesenthal 1995; see chap. 4). As a representative of one large firm in my sample noted explicitly, the association was good for two things: "they look for extra apprenticeship places, and they allow issues to be coordinated among firms." The coordination of firm activities had two components: first, passing information among companies about other companies' training practices; and second, promoting ongoing discussion about which old qualifications needed updating, and which new ones needed to be created to respond to their needs for skills relevant to production. The presence of this capacity was the prerequisite for their engaging in heavy investment in the apprenticeship system. But the development of apprenticeship places was an equally important goal because political support for the dual system depends on the public perception that firms are delivering on their responsibility to invest in youth training (Wonneberger 1994). Large firms cared if other large firms were training because they did not want to have their apprentices poached. Small firms, which had less desirable internal labor markets than large firms, could not successfully poach from large firms. But the failure of small firms to train put pressure on the state to intervene more heavily in the system of training, which was governed by employers' associations and unions.

With the mechanism for coordination firmly in place, large firms with western German ownership were indeed disproportionately likely to invest in training at western German levels. The five large companies in my sample (those with more than five hundred employees) all maintained a ratio of apprentices to the total workforce well above the floor of the western German target range for sustainable training (4 percent of the workforce). Two of the companies, ever cognizant of the need to create more apprenticeship places to support the system politically, had hired extra apprentices at the behest of the Chamber of Industry and Commerce in the early years after unification. As a result, one of the companies actually trained above the western German target range, with a training ratio of 12 percent. This company was part of a well-known western German conglomerate that was one of the paragons of virtuous dual training in the west. Between 1992 and 1995, after calculating its own need for apprentices, the company hired one hundred extra apprentices (i.e., above the calculated need for replacing their skilled workers) per year in its eastern German plants because of the lack of in-firm training places available to eastern German youth.[24] Without these extra, politically motivated places, this firm would also have been training in the target range.

For these companies, apprenticeship training was an investment in future skilled workers, and only in exceptional cases were trainees who pass their final exams not retained. In cases in which the companies did train beyond their own projected skills needs, this was as a political action in response to weaknesses in the local labor market. Moreover, all of the companies had offered to train in partnership with smaller companies that lacked the machinery or personnel to train their own apprentices according to the broad requirements of the Industrie- und Handelskammer (IHK) training regulations. None of the private companies received subsidy support for its own training program, nor did any receive direct public support to participate in partnership training schemes (although they were reimbursed for administrative costs). These companies, owned by western German conglomerates, were

---

[24] Because it was one of the most prominent German corporations, it is safe to conclude that the company faced very intense political pressure to take extra apprentices in the anemic eastern German youth labor market. The company certainly derived a public relations windfall from the extra training, and it made this extra commitment very public in company literature about its training program.

model citizens of the new market world of eastern German training. They were also among the strongest believers in the value of the dual system.[25]

Large companies not only invested in their own human and physical capital, but also encouraged the development of training at other, smaller companies. The two motives jointly influenced their political strategy. In 1993, the peak association of metal employers, Gesamtmetall, convinced the federal government to spend close to 30 million DM to modernize certain large plants in eastern Germany. These *Leitbetriebe* (model plants) of the metal and electronics sector had been designated by the regional affiliates of Gesamtmetall, and they usually consisted of the largest member companies. This program had at least two advantages for the large companies: first, it subsidized the upgrading of machinery that was outdated, allowing them to become competitive under a DQP strategy; and second, it allowed these companies to develop the facilities to serve as partner firms for smaller companies lacking sufficient training machinery. Rather than pushing for flexibility in the system (i.e., relaxing the regulations), they lobbied for federal support to enable them to aid smaller companies in providing training places, in addition to lowering the cost of their own investment in training machinery. Among large private firms in eastern Germany, the high-skill equilibrium quickly became a reality. But these companies were well aware that this equilibrium was only partial. Without the sustained participation of many SMEs, the dual system was politically unsustainable in the long run.

Large Firms in France
The contrast between French and eastern German large firms could not be starker: none of the French companies exhibited training behavior

[25] The fifth firm in this group, which was the only one not owned by a western German parent corporation, had not yet been privatized in 1995. This company was in fact training far above its own future need for workers and was doing so only because its training was heavily subsidized by both the federal privatization agency and the state government of Saxony. This company hired none of its apprentices who finished their training in 1995 and had no plans to retain any of its younger apprentices when they finished their training. Anticipating further layoffs in order to make the company an attractive privatization candidate, the appearance of this company in the target range is a spurious reading on the high-investment metric. The firm was neither investing in the training of apprentices nor planning to use them as future workers.

The data on all these companies are given in appendix B. Of all the companies in the sample, only the large firm that had created extra apprenticeship places (EGL5) and the nonprivatized firm (EGL1) appear to be wrongly classified: EGL1 falls in the target range but did not invest heavily in training, whereas EGL5 falls above the target range (due to the extra places it created in response to political pressure) and did invest heavily in training. Fortunately, both EGL1 and EGL5 are located in the same employment zone, so their erroneous scores cancel one another out in the high-skill training index results.

consistent with a high net investment in general skills training. That they differed so dramatically is not surprising, in light of the interest analysis of chapter 2. French large companies did not demand the set of general skills required by the German large companies that operated a DQP strategy, and so they had no interest in investing in youth training contracts. The general-skill pool available to them from the French school-based system may need firm-specific training. Because the employers' associations dominated the development of the CQ, and because large employers typically dominated the employers' associations, large firms could use the subsidized CQs to train workers in skills that were almost completely firm-specific. Those large firms that did choose to use the training system either used this approach or instead trained because of so-called social obligations to disadvantaged young people. Training motivated by social obligations was generally characterized by a low level of firm investment and very low chances of workers getting post-training jobs in the training company. It is hard to imagine a less propitious terrain for the establishment of a high-skill equilibrium than among French large companies that had no incentive to invest in them.

At the most technologically advanced firms in the sample, the strategy of developing firm-specific skills is clearly apparent. Representatives of two of these companies reported developing specific strategies of youth training to cope with new product development and consequently increased skill demands or to replace the know-how of existing workers nearing retirement. One of these firms (FL2) was the only one among the French large firms to retain its trainees at levels consistent with high-level investment in their training. However, the training program developed at this company was targeted only at meeting a minimal level for the company's skill requirements over a short time period. The adoption of new production technology compelled the company to embark on the training program because the existing local labor market was not able to meet its needs for skilled labor. The firm had previously hired production workers with no qualifications and had not engaged in any programs for training young people. Yet the new technology and production methods it introduced required the company to impose a minimum CAP qualification for production workers, with a long-term goal of establishing the bac as the minimum level of hiring for workers in production. The decision to train was a stop-gap measure rather than a durable change in the way the company did business. Fewer than 1 percent of those employed by the company were involved in this sort of training, and the company had no plans to use the training contracts for further skill investments.

For the remaining large firms in the sample, the rates of retention are very low indeed. Four of the nine had retention rates of zero, meaning that *none* of their trainees had afterward been hired. This was especially common among the firms that avowed their training to be a social mission. Typical was the account of one firm's personnel director, which had begun a training program with an eye toward the retirement of some older workers.[26] The firm wanted to replace them with younger workers at a minimum level of CAP (the lowest level French vocational certificate). However, the personnel director made clear that the purpose of the program was not to retain trainees at a high rate: "we will not necessarily [hire them after apprenticeship], but at least they will have the diplomas, and would do better on the labor market [than without any training]." When asked if the firm would train in the absence of state subsidies for training, the personnel director answered, "no, because [youth training] costs money, and the firm cannot support that cost. We do not do it because of the money, but without public money we would not be able to do it."

Despite the claim of this firm's representative, it is not clear that the youth training conducted by large firms cost them much, if anything, given the governmental subsidies they received. Only one firm in my sample reported having conducted a systematic cost-benefit analysis of youth training. To the surprise of the personnel director of this firm, its calculations showed that the firm was making a slight profit from its training program. The very low or negative net investment of French large firms lay behind their very low retention rates. They did not invest in their trainees, so they lost little if anything if those trainees left after their apprenticeship. What is more, those trainees could be replaced by another group of trainees whose cost was, again, subsidized by the government.

These cases exemplify the behavior of French large companies, for which training was more often considered a cost than an investment. For those firms with higher skill demands (the minority in my sample), in-firm youth training contracts had on occasion been used to bridge current or predicted shortages of skilled labor. Yet these programs were generally temporary and did not fit into any larger pattern of general skill development in the companies. Moreover, the existence of the CQ allowed companies to tailor qualifications very specifically to their own needs, without requiring them to bear the costs of conferring portable

[26] Company FL7 constructed a special training school for apprentices, as a result of a deal with the unions, signed in 1995. The firm agreed to take on a group of apprentices from disadvantaged neighborhoods in exchange for an agreement that gave management flexibility as to when the apprentices attended training; demand in the industry was highly seasonal. Trainees did not train in the winter months of peak demand and spent more time in the training center during summer periods of slack demand.

skills on trainees. And, even when investing in youth training contracts such as these, French large firms trained a lower proportion of workers, invested a lower amount per youth trainee, and retained a lower proportion of young people trained in such programs than did their counterparts in Germany. Given their existing systems of production, they are unlikely to be persuaded of the benefits of investing in this sort of training. If a high-skill equilibrium is to be established in France, it will probably have to function without the active participation or support of large firms.

Small and Medium-Size Enterprises in Eastern Germany
The patterns of company training in eastern Germany diverge along two dimensions: ownership status and region. In this section I first discuss ownership status and then the regional variation within one particular ownership status, those firms owned by other companies.

Certain types of ownership status increase the uncertainty facing company decision-makers, which affects their calculus about investment in apprenticeship training, an investment that only yields returns over the medium to long run. Companies owned by the Treuhand, the German privatization agency, were unlikely to take on heavy training investments with an uncertain return. These companies were being made into attractive candidates to be sold, and the thinking that characterized all firm decision-making was accordingly short term, focused on this end. Those firms that had been privatized (or newly founded), which were owned as individual or family businesses, did not have the problem of uncertain ownership. These were mostly smaller companies, though, and so they suffered more severely than did corporately owned firms from less easy access to financial markets. For these companies, too, an investment in the uncertain return of apprenticeship training was hard to justify. In both independent and state-owned SMEs in eastern Germany, the only way they trained apprentices is when that training was wholly subsidized by the state.

Table 3.5 depicts the training of all eighteen SMEs in my eastern German sample, organized by ownership. Unsurprisingly, none of the state-owned firms showed a high investment in the general skills of their apprentices.[27] Among the five independently owned companies,

---

[27] Two of the state-owned firms maintained very high training ratios, whereas another two had very low ratios. The variable accounting for the huge disparity between firms EGSME8 and EGSME9 (both 14.0 percent) and firms EGSME6 (0 percent) and EGSME7 (2.3 percent) is entrepreneurship in finding subsidies. Representatives of all four companies admitted they were extremely uncertain about whether or not the apprentices they had would be hired at the end of the apprenticeship period. Rather than operating according to any investment logic with respect to their future human capital, these companies

Table 3.5 High-Skill Training Index by Ownership in Eastern German SMEs[a]

Ownership Status	High-Skill Training Index (%)	N
Independent	0	5
State-owned	0	4
Corporately owned (actual)[b]	11	9
Corporately owned (projected)[c]	44	9

[a] Independent companies include companies and cooperatives owned by families or individuals. State-owned companies were still owned by the successor to the Treuhand in 1995. Corporately owned firms have at least a majority stake held by another company or conglomerate.

[b] Training index of corporately owned companies based on their total ratio of apprentices to workforce in 1995.

[c] Projection of the training index of corporately owned companies based on the apprentices they hired in 1995.

three were not training any apprentices, and all three of these reported that there was no subsidy programs that could convince them to train, suggesting that they are very far from the tipping point at which they would believe high-level training had its own rewards. The other two companies with independent ownership had a very high proportion of trainees in the total workforce, with ratios far above the western German target range between 4 and 8 percent of the work-force.[28] These high ratios suggest that their actual investment per worker

---

hired apprentices according to a pure subsidy logic: the more aid they could get, the more apprentices they hired. Company EGSME8 received 25,000 DM per apprentice per year from the Treuhand for more than one-half the apprentices it hired in 1995, a subsidy guaranteed over the three-year life of the apprenticeship; this was, by far, the most generous subsidy program available to any firm in my sample. Company EGSME9 received 170,000 DM in subsidies from the state government of Saxony-Anhalt to renovate its training workshop, and the amount of this subsidy was directly tied to the number of apprentices trained. By contrast, the personnel chief at company EGSME7 was unaware of the existence of Treuhand aid and had hired only a single apprentice in 1995. This hiring was in response to direct pressure from the Treuhand to hire more women, not because the firm expected to need the sorts of skills in which they trained her. Because these Treuhand firms operated outside the logic of the market even as they prepared for privatization, training apprentices only in view of the money they could get to underwrite the training, it is hardly surprising that their training rates fall outside the range that would be consistent with western German skill development practices.

[28] One of the companies (EGSME2) is simply a bizarre outlier: its training ratio of 46.5 percent means that almost one of two employees of this company was an apprentice. This situation resulted from the break-up of a much larger former conglomerate of the GDR

was very low.[29] There are likely to be few waverers in a population of firms such as these because they had firmly decided that an investment in the general skills of apprentices did not have a high payoff.

In contrast to the companies just discussed, the nine SMEs owned by western German or by foreign companies faced neither uncertain ownership nor uncertain access to capital. But at the time of my interviews, companies such as these were still very uncertain of the payoffs on investments in apprenticeship training, and this uncertainty limited their willingness to invest. It is among this group of firms that we find the waverers, the group uncertain about the benefits of investing in apprenticeship training. Richard von Bardeleben of the German Federal Institute for Vocational Training conducted surveys in 1993 and 1994 in order to find out why some firms refused to hire apprentices. Von Bardeleben, who has worked extensively with western German firms on estimating the costs and benefits of apprenticeship training, was puzzled by a paradox in his findings: although few eastern German firms thought that apprenticeship training was too expensive, two-thirds of them gave "financial help" as the measure that would convince them to begin training apprentices or to train more (no other measure was selected by more than 20 percent of firms). Von Bardeleben interprets this result as a clear sign of the analytic uncertainty of eastern German firms that apprenticeship delivers the long-term benefits attributed to it by the government: "many firms in the new federal states, as a result of their lack of economic experience with in-firm training and the lack of a longer-term apprenticeship culture, do not at all see the middle- and long-term

---

(*Kombinat*) into several different companies. EGSME2 took on all the former apprentices still under contract at the old *Kombinat* and received direct EU and state government aid to support the cost of this training until these apprentices finished their training. The company had no plans to retain these apprentices.

[29] The other company in this category (EGSME1) retained none of its trainees in 1995. This firm, which in the GDR fell under the *Handwerk* property law, conformed more closely to the model of craft firms discussed in appendix A, in which firms train at a high proportion of workforce, retain a much lower proportion of their trainees, and have very low or zero net training costs. This sort of training—in which apprenticeship serves as a three-year period of cheap labor—was not particularly hard to implement, nor was it the goal of the German government in eastern Germany.

Some observers have pointed to craft training as the "knight in shining armor" of the eastern German training system because these firms provided an abundance of apprenticeship places, compared with larger industrial firms (Schober and Rauch 1995). Although training by such craft firms undoubtedly kept youth unemployment lower than it would have been in their absence, it does not represent the sort of general skills investment that made the dual system so prized by the government. To the contrary, it is the industrial firms that are the linchpin of the high-skill equilibrium because of their heavy investments in general skill provision through apprenticeship training.

advantages of apprenticeship training" (1995, 86). Results from a 1997 panel survey confirm this finding—among eastern German firms that meet the minimum requirements of the chambers for being able to train apprentices, the reason most often given for not training apprentices was uncertainty about whether they would be able to hire the worker after the training period (BMBW 1999, 133–36).[30] Uncertainty about the returns on investments in training was a central obstacle to training for these SMEs.

Wavering SMEs worried not just about the *strategic* uncertainty of potentially having apprentices poached, but also about the *analytic* uncertainty of whether the investment in high-skill training would be worth the cost. As one of the firms in the sample from Saxony told me, "We could [just poach trained workers from other firms], but the apprentices trained here are much better acquainted with the firm. They also have a sense of belongingness to the firm." One of the firms in Saxony-Anhalt noted, "the best workers have the possibility of going west (to western Germany); I have lost some for that reason. But poaching is not a big problem here." Not worried about poaching, a representative of one firm in Saxony-Anhalt that was not training apprentices couched his reluctance in the following language: "if we were going to train, we would want to be certain the apprentices were learning their craft, and not just being cheap labor. To do that, you need the right equipment and the right personnel. . . ." For firms such as these, with little or no experience of western German training practices, the investment in general skills did not have a self-evident payoff.

Given uncertain benefits and certain costs, it is not surprising that of the seven firms in this group that were training apprentices, five were receiving subsidies to train. This contrasts both with the behavior of large, private eastern German corporations and with the prevailing standard in western Germany, in which firm training is not subsidized by the government. Despite this heavy use of subsidies, the third row of table 3.5 demonstrates that only one of the nine corporately owned companies of this size was training in the western German target range in 1995. On the subject of subsidies, the personnel manager of one Saxon firm (EGSME13) elaborated a position that was typical of firms in this size category: "for us, it was a financial question. Training at SMEs is overwhelmingly subsidized. The *Verbund* policy [cooperative alliance policy of the Saxon state government] enables someone else to develop the training plan for the apprentices in their first year. It is too expensive

---

[30] This answer was far less likely to be given by western German firms in the panel, whose complaints were either tied to high costs or to other, unspecified problems.

for us to fulfill the requirements of the [training system]." With uncertain benefits and certain costs and risks, training is not the obvious choice of these companies.

The fact that most of these firms were subsidized raises the question of how well the subsidies were persuading companies to mimic training levels associated with the high-skill equilibrium of western Germany. To answer this question, I projected the training ratios of the companies based on their 1995 stock of first-year apprentices. The results of this projection are shown in the fourth row of table 3.5 (these are also the figures used in the tables on high-skill indices in this chapter and in chap. 1). I used this method because in the year I carried out my in-firm surveys, the Saxon state government had just adopted its *Verbund* subsidy policy, and three of the five Saxon companies in this group had taken advantage of this new subsidy program. Those firms in Saxony-Anhalt that were subsidized had made their decision irrespective of the available subsidies. And in the future, they planned further to reduce or phase out apprenticeship entirely. Among the five Saxon firms, however, the *Verbund* had not only made it feasible for them to invest in the general skills of apprentices, but had also increased their reported willingness to train at the same levels for the foreseeable future. The projected ratio thus estimates their training after three years of the *Verbund* program.[31] And in adopting this dynamic perspective, the levels at which these firms were training were suggestive of training investments associated with the high-skill equilibrium in western Germany.

Seen in this light, it is apparent that the Saxon aid program succeeded where the more traditional subsidies in Saxony-Anhalt failed: they elicited training behavior consistent with the high-skill equilibrium among the medium-size firms in Saxony, where firms are training apprentices at four times the projected rate of those in Saxony-Anhalt. The amount of money given by the Saxon subsidy does not explain the success of the *Verbund* program, although the fact that it is generous certainly attracts firm participation. Even without the phased *Verbund* aid, Saxony-Anhalt spends more per capita on subsidizing apprenticeship training and subsidizes more places per capita than does the Saxon government.

The *Verbund* policy differed from the standard policy mix of the eastern states in two important respects. This training alliance supported

[31] To check the validity of the results using the 1995 projected training ratio, the three firms subsidized by the *Verbund* were contacted again in 2000 (five years after the initial interviews) about the company's current training practices. All three were training within or slightly above the target range, as projected.

SMEs that could not otherwise train apprentices in the use of the training facilities of large companies that had excess training capacity. Its differences lay first in the recognition that training for the wavering firms was not only a problem of money, but also one of satisfying the broad requirements in the metal professions in the first year of the training period. Second, rather than paying employers a single lump sum, the aid was structured to be phased and was concentrated in the first year of apprenticeship—during this first year the requirements of apprenticeship are the most weighted toward general skills and the apprentice is least productive for the firm. Companies were thus helped when they needed the aid most (when the apprentice was least productive) and the aid was structured over the lifetime of the apprenticeship contract. With other aid programs, employers were free to spend the money as they saw fit, but the *Verbund* program earmarked it for the expensive costs associated with training according to the broad requirements of the metal industry.

In other words, the phased *Verbund* aid responded more closely to the obstacles preventing SMEs in eastern Germany from investing in general skills training than did other policies. These concerns were not only strategic (i.e., the risk of losing an apprentice to poaching), but also about the quality of training that could be provided. To make the investment in apprenticeship training, they wanted to be sure it would deliver a return. The *Verbund* responded to the legitimate concerns of companies that might otherwise train by pairing financial assistance with the cooperation of the new giants of eastern German industry, which were generally owned by western German conglomerates and whose capacity for providing high-level training was beyond doubt. As a representative from a wavering firm in Saxony told me, "the *Verbund* allows someone else to develop the plan for the apprentices the first year. [Now, for the training of apprentices in their first year,] Siemens is the company with which we cooperate, and they do excellent training." By contrast, a firm from Saxony-Anhalt complained that there was "too little support from the government. It would be good if there were some sort of training center where small firms could send their apprentices to get good training. Large firms are needed for this to be effective." The way the phased *Verbund* was designed—combining generous, phased financial aid with access to the training facilities and expertise of larger companies—was especially likely to attract waverers in the population. Policies such as those of Saxony-Anhalt that were aimed at encouraging companies simply to hire more apprentices, regardless of what they needed for their long-term skill profile, were naturally less likely to appeal to wavering companies. The waverers were not interested in more training, but in better training. The Saxon policies appear to have been markedly better at attracting companies to begin investing at levels associated with the high-skill equilibrium (see chap. 4).

Small and Medium-Size Enterprises in France

SMEs in France were in a strategic situation similar to the one facing their eastern German counterparts, but the differences between large firms in the two countries was not without consequence for the observed practices of SMEs. Simply put, corporate ownership in France made a company far less likely to invest heavily in training, whereas in Germany corporately owned companies were most likely to gravitate toward high-skill training practices. In eastern Germany, large corporations were the anchor of the would-be high-skill equilibrium. They invested aggressively in training their own skilled workers and provided facilities to aid the training of workers from local SMEs. Within the German *Mittelstand*, it is only among the corporately owned companies in eastern Germany that we observed training practices consistent with high-level investment in apprentices. In France, by contrast, large companies had no incentive to invest in youth training in general skills because they had alternatives available to them in the French educational system. This raises the intriguing question of how the structure of ownership affected SMEs in France.

The advantage of corporate ownership in the eastern German case was that it gave companies access to information through corporate networks about the value of apprenticeship training, as well as easier access to finance. In other words, corporate ownership in eastern Germany ameliorated some of the uncertainties that blocked the SMEs from training. But in France, it is not clear a priori whether corporate ownership makes firms more likely to train (by virtue of greater access to finance) or instead less likely to train because much of the information to which they have access from their corporate networks does not provide reassurance about the value of apprenticeship. Empirically, it appears that the latter effect predominates: none of the French companies owned by other companies invested in general skills at levels consistent with the high-skill equilibrium. Table 3.6 summarizes the proportion of SMEs training according to the criterion of a French high-skill equilibrium in three categories: corporately owned firms, independent firms outside the Valley of the Arve River, and independent firms located in the Valley of the Arve. The table uses the same criteria for high-skill training used in table 3.4 for French large firms. And because the reforms in France are of older vintage, we are able to use retention data as an additional indicator of firm investment in apprenticeship (see app. A). Other things equal, a higher retention rate is indicative of a higher investment in youth training.

Table 3.6 High-Skill Training by Ownership and Location among French SMEs[a]

Ownership Status	High-Skill Training Index (%)	Average Retention (%)	N
Corporately owned	0	35	5
Independent (outside the Valley of the Arve)[b]	30	78	10
Independent (Valley of the Arve)[c]	40	88	5

[a] Corporately owned firms have at least a majority stake held by another company or conglomerate. Independent companies include companies and cooperatives owned by families or individuals.

[b] Includes all independent French companies of this size in the employment zones of Lyon, Amiens, the Vimeu, and Greater Strasbourg.

[c] Includes only those independent companies located in the Valley of the Arve.

Among the corporately owned firms, the two larger companies behaved similarly to the very large French companies already discussed. They trained at the lowest education levels and retained few of their trainees: 86 percent of the trainees are in CQs, the majority at the lowest possible qualification level (CAP). The three smaller firms that are owned by other companies, all of which had between 200 and 250 employees, trained like firms in the German craft (not the industrial) sector. That is, they trained more apprentices than they needed because it was relatively cheap for them to do so, and they retained fewer than one-half of those youth they trained, on average. The retention data from companies in this group clearly suggest that they were not making a heavy net investment in general skills through youth training contracts.

The independently owned firms in table 3.6 are divided into two groups. The first group of ten firms consists of companies from across France; the second group includes only companies from the Valley of the Arve. In the first group, there are only three companies that trained within the target range and that retained a high proportion of those they trained. Each of these firms invested heavily in training apprentices, but each was the only one in its region to do so. These companies were models of the sort of training behavior the French government attempted to encourage through its training reforms, but they were lonely models. Their training did not appear to convince other firms in the region to train.

Why did these three invest heavily in training, given the threat of losing apprentices to the large majority of other firms in their regions that did not train and that could poach them? It appears that FSME12 and FSME13 were similar companies, and similarly unusual with respect to the rest of the French firms I studied: they were committed believers in the importance of long-term youth training, despite the acknowledged risk of having their trainees poached. They were unusually persuaded of the benefits of training and had long believed in it. As the representative of one of the firms told me, "in recruiting apprentices very young, our company tries to conserve the skills of our craft, to teach it to people. . . . This company has an educational culture." The respondent at the other firm spoke in the same terms of a conviction that youth trainees "are better adapted to our needs than are people hired from other firms. Other firms do try to poach our apprentices, but we always intend to train apprentices." Both firms received subsidies to train (as did all French firms), but both would continue training without these subsidies. In the language of chapter 2, these two firms have very low thresholds of cooperation and would train in almost any conceivable situation. But they are a small minority among French SMEs.

The third firm with a high training ratio and retention rate is a curious case, in that its manager was not persuaded of the benefits of an investment in general skills training. This company (FSME11), which was going through a period of rapid growth at the time of interview, had hired twenty-five new employees in the previous two years. Of these, two-thirds had come directly from the labor market and one-third had been hired in training contracts. In this phase of growth, youth training contracts appear to have been used by the firm as a cheap way to attract good applicants (who were later hired in regular contracts) rather than because the company was persuaded of the value of training over the long term: "it is not necessary that the trainees be very productive, since they cost so little. There are so many financial advantages that it makes sense to train, if the person is good. . . . With this system of subsidies and tax breaks, one can take risks on youth trainees; without the subsidies, one cannot afford to risk hiring a young trainee, it costs too much." This firm was rapidly expanding, so the available subsidy programs made these training contracts an efficient way to attract workers. There is no evidence that the experience of training through the subsidy program had changed the mind of the manager of this firm—despite three years of increased youth training through the *alternance* contracts, he thought it too risky to continue training without subsidies.

Two firms in this group (FSME9 and FSME10) probably could be classified as waverers, but they had remained unconvinced by the current policy mix to invest much in training. Both expressed a pressing need to "reinforce the gray matter" of the company's workforce, but neither used the youth training contracts as much as they had used the external labor market to seek new employees. One reason was the uncertainty caused by the potential for poaching. "It happens," noted a representative of FSME10, which had both poached from others and had employees poached. "It is a risk," concurred his counterpart from FSME9, who admitted that the firm had "hesitated" to train, confronted with this risk. The latter, whose company was a supplier in the bar-turning industry in the Vimeu, professed ambivalence about the potential for using youth training to upgrade skill levels: "We want to develop our bar-turning workshop, and we needed competencies and young people. That said, training is no miracle solution. A young person cannot immediately perform the tasks that an older worker can, it is also an investment in the future." For these companies, willing to consider the possibility of training but cognizant of the risks entailed, the available subsidy programs were regarded as "insufficient to incite companies to hire trainees." Although both had taken subsidies to train, the subsidy programs had done nothing to reduce their uncertainty about the benefits of training in youth contracts.

This contrasts with the observed behavior of the final group of firms in the table, all of which are located in the Valley of the Arve. Two of these five firms had a training ratio within the French target range and a retention rate of 100 percent; a third was training above the target range, but its retention of 100 percent is evidence that it was undergoing rapid growth rather than investing little in apprentices. This evidence from my sample is buttressed by data collected by the employers' organization in the Valley of the Arve. In 1998, the association conducted interviews with seventy-three of its companies that had trained through the qualification contract and found a retention rate of 77 percent among those companies (Int FRE8). (See app. C for an explanation of the interview codes.) This is almost ten percentage points higher than the western German industrial company average (Pfeiffer 1997, 15). In comparison with the group of independently owned firms from the rest of France, these training ratios and retention rates demonstrate that companies located in the Valley of the Arve were far more likely than their counterparts elsewhere to invest in training in general skills.

This evidence is further reinforced by a comparison of the educational levels of trainees in the two groups. Trainees with lower educational levels were often used by companies that wished to underwrite a cheap labor contract by adding some basic training; the presence of trainees with high educational levels in firm training contracts would be consistent with a higher level of firm investment in skill provision. And indeed, 70 percent of the trainees in the Arve Valley firms had least a bac and over half of those had two additional years after the bac. By comparison, among the second set of firms in Table 3.6, 65 percent of trainees had qualifications below the bac level.

What distinguished companies in the Arve Valley from those in the rest of France was the qualification program pursued by the employers' association located in the valley. In eastern Germany, the key determinant of the difference among SMEs was the nature of the subsidy programs available; but in France, the important subsidy programs were national and did not vary by region. As indicated by the comments of representatives of the two wavering firms (FSME9 and FSME10), these subsidies, were on their own, not enough to convince waverers to invest heavily in training. What differed in the Arve Valley was the program designed by the local employers' associations to encourage firms to train 1,000 technicians between 1990 and 2000. The association was able to use public subsidy money to underwrite the investment in new machinery for the technical center and then to craft the 1,000 Technicians program so that it would especially appeal to firms wavering on the border between cooperation and defection. Like the *Verbund* aid in Saxony, the 1,000 Technicians program used public subsidy money to give smaller companies access to a broad range of machinery that they could not afford to provide on their own, which in turn allowed them to train in broader qualifications than were strictly necessary for their own firm. And as in the Saxon case, this material aid was provided in a context (a joint training center) in which firms witnessed other firms training and talked to their training personnel, thereby conducting an extended conversation on the merits of apprenticeship training. This assurance that other actors would also cooperate was the key to coordinating on a regional high-skill equilibrium.

How did the 1,000 Technicians program succeed at convincing potential waverers where other programs failed? It appears to have circulated information about the benefits of training compared to those of poaching. One of the firms from the Arve Valley gave the following response to my question of whether poaching was a general problem for the firm: "[Poaching] was common practice around here five years ago, and the Swiss bar-turning industry runs the risk of having this problem in the future, because they have not prepared to fight the problem of a lack of skilled workers. The 1,000 Technicians program was important for this reason, and I think we need to continue it. It is less of a problem now, this poaching between firms; I have the impression that the other firm managers in the area have realized that this is not the best solution to solve the problem of a skill labor shortage." (Why the 1,000 Technicians program succeeded in convincing companies to move toward a high-skill, low-poaching equilibrium—while so many other areas in France failed to do so—is explored in chap. 5.)

THE PUZZLE OF REGIONAL VARIATION

The high-skill equilibrium has not become a reality for either the eastern German or the French economy. The overwhelming proportion of the youth training that took place was still subsidized by national or regional governments. Among eastern German companies, large private firms were on the leading edge of the move toward the high-skill equilibrium. They invested heavily in the general skills of their own workers, and they assisted smaller companies in developing long-term apprenticeship programs. Large firms in eastern Germany were fervent supporters of training not because of any sense of altruism or duty, but because this strategy was most consistent with their long-term interests. Large German companies could maintain their edge in export markets only if they were able to rely on the strategies of incremental innovation that demanded the general skills taught through the dual apprenticeship system (Streeck 1997). One of the great difficulties facing the eastern German economy was, and continues to be, that there are not enough of these large privatized firms to generate the positive externalities that could make high-skill training easier for firms in the eastern German *Mittelstand* (Carlin and Soskice 1997).

French large firms stood at the opposite extreme with respect to the training reforms. It would almost never make sense for these firms to invest heavily in general skills training through the *alternance* contracts. Their dominant production strategy did not depend on having the sort of broad general training that is the foundation of the German dual system (Regini 1997a). Moreover, the French educational system gave them alternatives for seeking skilled workers when they did adopt technological changes that required higher skills on the shop floor. The weakness of the French unions meant that the CQs, whose content was intended to be general, could be tailored by large firms to their specific needs. The French large firms, in essence, succeeded in inverting the logic of Gary Becker on general and firm-specific skills. Becker's (1964) classic analysis of skill provision suggests that companies will only invest in firm-specific skills, leaving individuals and the state to invest in general skills. The French government established the CQs as a way to persuade firms to invest in general skills, hoping to overcome problems of market failure in skill provision. But in a neat reverse, the French large firms succeeded in using the CQs to procure government subsidies for training in firm-specific skills in which (according to Becker) they should have been willing to invest on their own.

Ultimately, the fate of the training reforms in France and in eastern Germany rested not on what the large firms did, but on what the SMEs did. And on this question, this chapter has documented some interesting variations in training practices. SMEs in Saxony adopted training practices that were much closer to those of western Germany than did the firms in Saxony-Anhalt. Similarly, the SMEs in the Valley of the Arve were significantly more likely than their compatriots to adopt high-skill training practices. In all these areas, we have observed some firms wavering between the choice of whether to coordinate on a high-skill equilibrium or to maintain their existing practices. Uncertainty, both analytic and strategic, was a common element limiting the willingness of firms of this size to invest in general skills provision through training contracts. Yet firms in Saxony and in the Valley of the Arve were better able to overcome this uncertainty than were similar firms outside these regions. The next two chapters explore how these areas developed distinctive programs aimed at SMEs, and why these programs were relatively more successful in coaxing firms to set out on the road to a high-skill equilibrium.

CHAPTER FOUR

Embedded Policy-Making and Decentralized Cooperation in Eastern Germany

The state of Saxony developed policies that were far better at persuading wavering firms of the benefits of apprenticeship training than were the policies adopted by the neighboring state of Saxony-Anhalt. In this chapter, we explore why Saxony succeeded while Saxony-Anhalt failed. The answer to this puzzle turns out to be the different way policy was developed and implemented; as a result, public officials in the two states had access to different sorts of information. The information available to policy-makers shapes the way they conceive policy solutions because it influences how they construe the problems that public policy is trying to address. Governments in the two states employed different strategies to acquire information about the state of the apprenticeship market. The Saxon government gave employers' representatives and unions an important voice in proposing solutions to the shortage of apprenticeship places. The government in Saxony-Anhalt, on the contrary, designed its apprenticeship policies with minimal consultation with the social partners. The Saxon government therefore had access to the relational information held by employers' associations, whereas the government of Saxony-Anhalt could rely only on information collected through bureaucratic channels.

Bureaucracies are quite skilled at counting things: How many trainees are there in a given region? What proportion of them are female? How many training centers meet certification requirements? This is how government statistical offices make the world comprehensible, and it is on the basis of such information that governments and bureaucrats typically design their policy proposals. However, there are some types of information states are not good at gathering—information about the cooperative thresholds of private actors, for example. States measure what they can easily see, count, and categorize; they are at a disadvantage when trying to gather either private or local information (Scott 1998, 316). The more contextual the information, the more likely state methods of measuring it will break down or at least possess ever greater proportions of measurement error.

If we imagine a state agency trying to devise a policy to encourage firms to begin investing more heavily in apprenticeship training, its algorithm would look something like this: "measuring the investment of firms in apprentices is extremely difficult, but counting the number of apprentices trained and their demographic characteristics is easy. And, although we have no good metric for the quality of training, we can set baseline standards that firms or training centers have to meet and verify those using a corps of inspectors." Just doing these things generates a wealth of data about training patterns. Yet it tells policy-makers little about the internal motivations and long-term strategies of the firms that are training and even less about how to convince the firms that are most interested in investing heavily in general skills to begin doing so.

This is a firm's private information, which it will hold very close to its vest. It has little incentive to reveal this information to the state. First, companies distrust the state and worry that inside information could be used against them or shared with competitors. And second, firms have an incentive to misrepresent their true preferences if they observe that the state is in the mood for giving subsidies. Thus, in developing a transitional policy, states face a problem of asymmetric information.

As I argue in chapter 2, firms are less averse to sharing such information about their internal preferences with a trusted intermediary, such as the association that represents them. If an association has the capacity to acquire detailed information like this from member companies and then to facilitate collective discussions about the concrete measures that would help those firms hovering on the cusp of cooperation to begin cooperating, it has something that state bureaucracies are unlikely to have: high-quality relational information. Because this information differs from the information normally available to states, I hypothesize that policies made in collaboration with private-interest associations will look different than policies made unilaterally by a state. State policies will target only what the state can observe: the number of total apprenticeships, regions particularly hard hit by shortages or problems for particular subgroups of the population, or whether training centers meet observable standards. States that delegate some power to capable private-interest associations in the policy-making process can be expected to develop a dimension of public policy that specifically targets those companies most likely to be convinced of the value of investment in apprenticeship training. Without access to private information, it is very difficult to make such policies, and (from the state's perspective) it may well seem as if the state is merely paying rents to opportunistic companies.

This chapter begins with a description of the architecture of the system that the German government exported to the east: the western German system of private-interest governance of apprenticeship training. I then present evidence on the success of the transfer of these private-interest organizations to eastern Germany after 1990. Although all the major organizations involved in the German training system faced stiff organizational challenges in the new federal states, they nonetheless succeeded in assuming both the formal legal functions of private-interest governance of the training system and the organizational capacities necessary to deliver the level of employer coordination that is required in the western German model. The chapter then turns to address the role of these private groups in designing policies to encourage apprenticeship training in eastern Germany, discussing the evolution of federal training policy since unification and highlighting the divergence of preferences between the federal government and the social partners, despite their shared objective of a system based on company responsibility for training. I contrast the policy-making processes of Saxony and Saxony-Anhalt, illustrating the difference between embedded and autonomous modes of policy-making, ask why some policies work better than others in convincing waverers to begin investing in training, and consider alternative explanations of the different choices of the state governments in eastern Germany, as well as considering how Saxony might have differed from Saxony-Anhalt in ways that influenced the probability that decentralized cooperation could be secured there.

ASSOCIATIONAL CAPACITIES IN THE WESTERN GERMAN MODEL

To convince firms to make substantial uncovered investments in the training of their apprentices, the German dual system depends on the existence of strong organizations of employers and labor (Streeck et al. 1987; Soskice 1994). The institutionalized role of the representatives of potentially competing groups allows these groups to ensure that the skills certified are both general and relevant for production. Employers advocate the inclusion of skills that they judge important for their future productive needs, and the presence of labor representatives prevents employers from creating skill certifications that are merely firm-specific in their content. The federal and state governments also fulfill an important function in the governance of the training system, particularly with respect to the one or two days per week that apprentices spend in public vocational schools. The control and funding of the schools is a responsibility of the individual states (*Länder*), and the details of the national curriculum are resolved through the negotiation of the conference of state ministers for education and culture (Münch 1991, 51, 98). For questions related to the firm-based aspects of training, however, the federal and state governments rely heavily on the representatives of employers and labor. It is uncommon for federal or state political

Table 4.1 Architecture of Interest Intermediation in the German Metal Sector[a]

	Employers' Associations	Unions	Chambers
Sectoral	Gesamtmetall	IG Metall	
Intersectoral			
Directly involved in training system	BDA	DGB	IHK (industry) HWK (crafts)
Involved in training-related political issues	BDI DIHT		

[a] This table presents only the major players in interest intermediation in the metal and electronics sector; it excludes some actors that may be involved in the corporatist bodies that oversee German training, but that have little impact on this particular sector. Except for the Chambers column, this list also omits organizations representing the crafts sectors.

authorities in western Germany to undo the compromises forged by the representatives of these groups on issues having to do with occupational skill certification.

The social partners dominate the national and sectoral levels of governance of the dual system, which in times of normal functioning are the most important areas of negotiation. Regional politics is usually a domain of lesser importance for the social partners; at the regional and subregional levels, regulatory oversight is almost always the responsibility of the chambers of industry and commerce or of crafts. At the firm level, the works council serves a watchdog function: it monitors training practices and provides a forum for complaint, and in large enterprises it sometimes plays an active role in ensuring that a company pursues high-level training practices (Streeck et al. 1987; Soskice 1994).

To understand the interest group system that the German government wanted to transfer to the east, we need to familiarize ourselves with these organizations as they function in western Germany (see table 4.1). On the employer side, there are the sectoral employers' associations and the peak association of sectoral and regional employers' associations, the Bundesvereinigung der Deutschen Arbeitgeberverbände (BDA).[1] The

[1] The Bundesverband der deutschen Industrie (BDI), which is the peak federation of industry associations, does not play an important role in the governance of training policy in Germany. In recognition of this fact, and to cut costs, the BDI has withdrawn from the umbrella organization of employers concerned with professional training, the Kuratorium der deutschen Wirtschaft für Berufsbildung (KWB).

BDA has affiliates in every federal state (*Land*); these affiliates are generally dependent on and share the same personnel as the regional affiliate of the strongest sectoral association. In most cases, the *Land*-level representation of the BDA is organizationally combined with the regional affiliate of the association of metal and electronics employers (Gesamtmetall). The labor counterparts of the sectoral and intersectoral employers' associations are, respectively, the sectoral unions and the peak union confederation, the Deutscher Gewerkschaftsbund (DGB). As is true on the employer side, the leading sectoral member of the DGB comes from the metal and electronics industry. The IG Metall is widely acknowledged to play a central role in coordinating the union movement, and its wage negotiations with Gesamtmetall set the informal benchmark for the German economy overall (Thelen 1991; Hall 1994). Together, employers and unions discuss and propose revisions to the requirements for new skill qualifications, and they advise state and federal governments on training policies.

More important in the nuts-and-bolts oversight of training regulations are the local chambers. Most of the apprenticeship certifications in Germany fall either to the chambers of industry and commerce (IHKs) or of crafts (Handwerkskammer, HWKs).[2] The chambers have responsibility for the registration of apprenticeship contracts, the counseling and approval of companies wishing to hire apprentices, the administration of all examinations of apprentices, and the certification of trainers to supervise apprentices in firms. Both the IHKs and the HWKs have national peak associations that lobby for the concerns of the chambers in national politics—for the IHKs, the peak association is the Deutscher Industrie- und Handelstag (DIHT), and for the HWKs the peak association is the Deutscher Handwerkskammertag (DHKT). Given the central place of the IHKs in training in the German industrial and service sectors, I concentrate on them when discussing the role of the chambers in overseeing the functioning of the dual system.

Informational and Dialogic Capacities of Western German
Employers' Associations
In western Germany, Soskice (1994, 1999) has argued, the associations and chambers together provide employers with a capacity to coordinate

---

[2] The organizational districts of the chambers—there are eighty-three IHKs in Germany—cover geographical areas smaller than the *Länder*, except in the case of city-states such as Berlin. The chambers are public law bodies to which all firms must belong, and they are charged with the representation of the broad interests of the private economy in their districts (Henneberger 1993).

their actions, thereby allowing them to overcome certain collection action problems that plague employers in LMEs. I first enumerate the separable elements of such a coordinating capacity at a theoretical level (i.e., what would such a capacity entail, if western German associations indeed had it?). I then show what capacities they do in fact possess.

With respect to vocational training, we can specify four levels of coordinating capacity of employers' associations, each of which involves a progressively stronger role for the associations in facilitating coordination. The most basic level of coordinating capacity is information circulation among firms and between firms and the association. The information required relates to the functioning of training practices: Which other firms participate in apprenticeship training? How are existing requirements being taught through in-firm practice? What requirements in the system of training regulations need to be updated to take account of new skill demands in production? What aspects of the system need to be changed through political lobbying? An association needs to be able to obtain this information from a wide base of member firms to facilitate collective exchanges about the manner in which the system functions and to create or modify new qualifications. Likewise, the association must be able to diffuse information back down to member companies so they are aware of new training regulations and practices, as well as of subsidies or other advantages from which they can benefit.

A second level is dialogic capacity. This requires a mechanism for members and associational staff to use the information collected to brainstorm about the best potential strategies to follow to achieve their goals. For example, they need to figure out which changes to pursue in a system of qualifications and how best to achieve these changes through negotiations with representatives of labor and the state. Dialogic capacity presupposes a forum for negotiation where members with different interests can bargain over outcomes that will favor some actors more than others (Scharpf 1997, 74–75). Employers use the association not only to resolve their internal conflicts, but also to devise, through collective discussion, the best ways to achieve agreed-on goals. The association must balance the sometimes competing interests of its different members in a context in which the outcome of any given strategy is uncertain ex ante. Thus, dialogic capacity entails more than just bargaining, although it includes a bargaining component. Information circulation is the prerequisite of a dialogic capacity, but it is readily apparent that an association may be able to facilitate the exchange of information without being able to promote problem-solving discussion.

The third and fourth theoretical levels of employer coordination are the capacity to monitor the activity of companies and the capacity to sanction those not in compliance with official positions of the association. Information circulation may already encompass access to potentially sensitive information, which companies are willing to share with their association because the association is considered trustworthy and not likely to use it against them (Finegold and Soskice 1988, 47–48). But monitoring only has meaning when the association has regularized access to information about company compliance with some regulations or policies for which it is responsible—that is, information that it will use to try to exact compliance from companies. If companies can and do successfully withhold information in a given domain from the association, then the association cannot be said to possess a strong monitoring capacity in that domain. Monitoring usually occurs in a context in which sanctions are exacted for noncompliance. Sanctioning obviously requires that the association can credibly threaten to deprive firms of something that they value. For a voluntary organization, this is not easily done; but when it is available, sanctioning is the highest degree of coordinating capacity.

In the area of human capital policy, employers' associations in western Germany are only able to circulate information and promote problem-solving dialogue. The twin structure of the chambers and the associations achieves this goal through a division of labor summarized by Soskice (1994, 28): "The main roles of the employer associations are in developing new apprenticeships and modifying existing ones, as well as advising larger companies; the chambers are responsible for organizing the local apprenticeship system, approving and monitoring company training, and running the examination system." A national representative described the division of labor between the regional and national working groups of Gesamtmetall: "in the national working group, we work on strategic questions of training policy, e.g., is the broad first year of training a good thing to have, or how can we get more companies to offer more apprenticeship places? These are questions of training politics. . . . The exchange of technical information occurs only through information exchange at the level of the regional associations, or when we run expert seminars there. . . . The firms learn from each other in the apprenticeship working groups of the regional associations" (Int WNE4). German employers possess through their sectoral associations the ability to circulate information, technical and political, about what they collectively require in the area of skill provision. Moreover, the associations provide a forum for regular dialogue in which members and staff can craft strategies to assure the responsiveness of the German dual system to the needs of companies.

The formal monitoring capacity of the German employers is limited and is aimed at those companies on the margin of meeting training requirements; this is the bailiwick of the chambers (Streeck et al. 1987).[3] For large companies, with established training facilities, this supervisory right is pro forma because they are not likely to fall below the minimal training requirements regulated by the chambers. Large companies voluntarily share basic information about their training with the chambers and the employers' association, and they are willing to share sensitive information with the association. However, contrary to the implications drawn by Finegold and Soskice (1988, 29) and Soskice (1994, 34), the association does not have the capacity to extract this information from large companies when they do not want to reveal it. Employers' organizations in western Germany have access to private information about the quantitative level of training taking place in member firms and their likely future training practices, which is relational information to which the state does not have access. Yet the associational capacity for monitoring is limited to the ability of the chambers to ensure that all companies training apprentices stay at or above the minimal requirements established by collective agreements. Similarly, the only sanction possessed by organizations of employers (the chambers) is the capacity to remove a company's approval for training. Although this constitutes an important constraint on smaller companies, this sanction does not extend to larger companies.[4]

The de facto governance of training regulations by private groups— preeminently, employers' organizations—has provided western German companies with a decisive voice in determining the content of skill certifications, and this institutional feature has persuaded them to invest heavily in apprenticeship training in western Germany (Soskice 1994; Wagner 1999). The success of the transfer of the dual system of apprenticeship training to eastern Germany depends on the capacity of new or newly constituted private groups to assume the functions they play in the west.

[3] Depending on the training area, this authority falls on the relevant responsible actor (*zuständige Stelle*). For most apprentices, this actor is the IHK or HWK (see Münch 1991 for a discussion).
[4] The Gesamtmetall official responsible for training policy during the mid-1990s emphatically denied the existence of such sanctions in western Germany in an interview with the author: "in the case of poaching, Gesamtmetall has no legal means to punish firms. [Our members accept] no such restrictions. But we do have moral authority that we can try to use, appealing to a company's management." The claim made here is that western German associations possess weak monitoring and no sanctioning capacities. This ignores the secondary supervisory role played by unions in the bodies of codetermination and of works councils at the plant level, which together provide a check on employer action without being in any way controlled by the organizations of employers.

ASSOCIATIONAL CAPACITIES IN EASTERN GERMANY

Despite the real organizational difficulties facing employers and unions in the newly united Germany (Silvia 1997; Hyman 1996; Fichter 1997), the eastern organizations succeeded by and large in carrying out both the legal and the practical functions delegated to them in the coordinated market economy. The eastern German employers and unions had by the mid-1990s established and staffed their organizations in all of the new federal states in the east. Moreover, despite significant defections from collectively negotiated wage agreements, eastern German employers' associations exercised a coordinating capacity in the area of vocational training that was essentially equivalent to that exercised by employers in the west. Across eastern Germany, it appears that employers' associations were capable of promoting information circulation and problem-solving dialogue among their members. They were able to exercise these capacities because their largest members relied on them to sustain the coordinating functions that would allow them to pursue a strategy of DQP. Yet the dominance of the large companies in eastern German employers' associations provoked significant discontent among smaller companies belonging to the association, as we shall see later.

Organizational Transition in the East

The principal associations of employers and of labor, as well as the chambers, transferred the western model of organizations wholesale into eastern Germany.[5] The BDA affiliates sent personnel eastward and brought new eastern personnel to sites in the west for training. Employers' associations set up partnerships between the new regional affiliates and existing associations in the west, such that the personnel in each of the new associations had designated western interlocutors for questions of legal advice and wage-bargaining procedures.[6] Yet many of the staff of the eastern association were themselves western Germans; Henneberger (1993, 668) reports that half their important decision-making posts were filled by *Wessis*. This pronounced western orientation detracted from the ability of the associations to attract new members in the east (Silvia 1997).

The DGB followed a similar model of expansion, hewing closely to the western organizational chart rather than trying to incorporate the

[5] On the organizational strategy of employers in eastern Germany, see Henneberger (1993); on labor, see Fichter (1993, 1997).

[6] The metal and electronics employers' associations, which are generally also the regional BDA affiliates, established the following partnerships: Saxony with Bavaria, Saxony-Anhalt with Lower Saxony, Mecklenburg-West Pomerania with Schleswig-Holstein, and Thuringia with Hesse. The Brandenburg association merged with that of Berlin to become a single association (Henneberger 1993).

form of the existing eastern German unions. Unlike the employers, western unions were confronted with a large preexisting federation that had represented workers in eastern Germany, the Freier Deutscher Gewerkschaftsbund (FDGB).[7] Most of the DGB unions, including the IG Metall, did not take staffers of the old union on as a matter of course; they did so only after a period of individual selection, aimed at weeding out lackeys of the former GDR government (Fichter 1993, 23–25). In tandem with this personnel choice, the western union leadership decided to incorporate much of eastern Germany into western German administrative districts.[8] Although it taxed the resources of the unions, this strategy enabled them to complete the expansion of the DGB to the east by fall 1991 (Fichter 1997). The strategy of the western leaders of the employers' and labor federations allowed them quickly to establish an organizational model of private-interest governance similar to that of western Germany, and the personnel support provided to the eastern associations allowed them to assume the parapublic functions entailed in German corporatist governance.

All was not smooth sailing for the western associations in eastern Germany, to be sure. The employers' associations were largely unsuccessful in attracting new SMEs as members (Ettl and Heikenroth 1995). Meanwhile, the continuing high unemployment in the eastern German economy contributed to declining union membership, and the working relationship between works councils and unions was fraught with more tension in eastern than in western Germany (Fichter 1997; Hyman 1996, 27). These organizational pressures on employers and labor created the possibility that the institutions of private-interest governance might eventually function less effectively in eastern than in western Germany. So far, however, the institutional transfer had been largely successful; the eastern affiliates of the BDA and the DGB could play the legal role delegated to them in the western German system of private-interest governance. But did they provide eastern Germany employers with the same de facto coordinating capacity as their counterparts in the west?

*Informational and Dialogic Capacities of Eastern German
Employers' Associations*
There is a wide consensus that the formal organizational structure of private-interest governance in western Germany was established suc-

[7] In the GDR, 98 percent of workers belonged to unions belonging to the FDGB (Lange and Shackleton 1998).

[8] The IG Metall, for example, created only one new district in eastern Germany, in the most populous state, Saxony. In 1995, this single district was expanded to incorporate Berlin and Brandenburg (Fichter 1997).

cessfully in eastern Germany (e.g., Wiesenthal 1995; Padgett 1999, 160–65). Yet many observers claim that the institutional "hardware" of western Germany worked differently because of the different perspectives of eastern Germans toward these institutions. As Claus Offe (1997) has argued, the cognitive "software" demanded to run the system may be different in eastern Germany.[9] These categories are difficult to measure and document empirically, and the import of such differences clearly depends on what we are trying to explain.[10] Our interest here is in knowing if the tools of private-interest governance of apprenticeship training fulfilled the functions in eastern Germany that they played in the western German model. These judgments are based on data collected through interviews with representatives of thirty-four industrial and craft firms in the eastern and western Germany.[11] I supplement this evidence with information from twenty-eight interviews with the relevant associational and governmental agency representatives in eastern and western Germany.[12] In order to convince employers to invest in the general skills of their apprentices, the private-interest governance architecture established in eastern Germany had to reassure those employers that the training system was responsive to their needs. Because the firms themselves invested in the costs of training, I focus on the role of their representatives—the employer associations and the IHKs.[13]

In eastern Germany, the evidence from my interviews clearly suggests that the institutions of information circulation among employers were functioning as they did in the west. A higher proportion of large firms than of small firms belonged to the employers' association, and large

[9] Fichter (1993, 1997) and Locke and Jacoby (1997) have also argued in this vein.

[10] One of the most systematic studies of the different functioning of institutions in eastern and western Germany—in this instance, institutions of local government—is that undertaken by Thomas Cusack and his colleagues. Cusack (1997, 25) finds that "appropriate institutional design need not fail in the context of low stocks of social capital," which certainly suggests that well-designed "hardware" can function with suboptimal "software."

[11] The total number of firms (thirty-four) exceeds the slightly smaller firm sample used in the analysis in chapter 3 because it includes western German firms and several firms from the crafts (rather than the industrial) training sector in eastern Germany.

[12] These interviews included representatives of sectoral and intersectoral employers' associations, IHKs, employment offices, and state policy-makers responsible for apprenticeship training. I interviewed regional representatives from Berlin and Brandenburg, Saxony, Saxony-Anhalt, and Rhineland-Palatinate, as well as representatives of all the national employers' associations.

[13] When discussing the capacity of employers' associations, I refer throughout this chapter to the sectoral associations of the metalworking industry. In actual fact, these organizations also doubled as the affiliates of the BDA in Saxony and Saxony-Anhalt, with the same personnel and the same political stances. The story of metal employers in eastern Germany is to a large extent the story of the collective capacities of eastern German employers.

firms played the most active role in associational politics (Ettl and Heikenroth 1995). With their large personnel staffs and dedicated training facilities, large firms were the companies most likely to be involved in trying to change training regulations to take account of their new skill requirements. Moreover, if the interest analysis of chapter 2 is correct, large companies should have been heavily involved in trying to establish the collective capacities of the association because they depended on them most. Apprenticeship training had for them the structure of an assurance game: they wanted to invest in general skills if other large firms also did so, in order to permit them to follow their preferred production strategy of DQP. Thus, they had the incentive to see that the association developed a capacity for information circulation so that they could coordinate on their preferred equilibrium point, characterized by high investment in training and low poaching. Simultaneously, they had reason to try to endow the association with a problem-solving capacity to develop a strategy to attract more small companies to train because the survival of the dual system in eastern Germany depended on the SMEs. Given these incentives, the perspective of training personnel in large firms from my sample of industrial firms is especially important in assessing how the association fulfilled its information circulation and dialogic functions.

Only four of the privately owned firms in my sample had more than five hundred employees: two were in Saxony, one was in Saxony-Anhalt, and one had plants in both states. They each described the activities of the association in similar terms and in terms that make sense in light of the incentives of large companies for apprenticeship training. "The role of the association is to seek additional apprenticeship places [in smaller companies], and to allow things to be coordinated among firms. For example, it might be used to analyze and propose changes to a given profession" (Int EGL5). Or, as a representative from firm EGL4 succinctly noted, "the association makes strategy for the companies in a sector." Representatives of EGL3 and EGL5 were both involved, at the time of interview, with discussions through the association to propose reforms to the theoretical requirements involved in general training. And as the representative of EGL5 added, "we do not really have a problem sharing information with the association." Large firms perceived the association as their strategy-making tool, and good information allowed it to do its job more effectively. One of these jobs was to improve the participation of SMEs in the dual system. According to a representative of EGL4, "In the association, we are all interested in ensuring that every firm trains well." Three of the four were assisting apprentices from smaller firms through use of their training workshop, and the fourth had let it be known among local small employers that it was ready to help local companies through a *Verbund*. As far as these large firms were concerned, the eastern German system of employer coordination was functioning very well.[14]

My evidence further suggests that there was no difference between the capacities of associations in Saxony and Saxony-Anhalt: both could circulate information and promote discussion to develop collective problem-solving strategies.[15] The training manager for the firm with establishments in both states evinced satisfaction with the general operation of the associations in the states where the firm was active. This finding is supported by other research as well.[16] The capacity of employers' associations to facilitate the coordination of firm practices appears to have been evenly distributed across the new federal states of eastern Germany.

Yet all was not well for eastern German employers' associations. The overwhelming problem for the future of the employers' associations in the east was, and is, an increasing tension between their large well-capitalized members, often with western ownership, and the new eastern German–owned *Mittelstand* (Henneberger 1993; Ettl and Heikenroth 1995). The divergent interests of firms of different sizes was also felt in the west (Silvia 1997), but the greater disparities between firms in different size and ownership categories exacerbated the problem in the east.[17] However, inasmuch as coordinating capacity had always reflected most prominently the ability to circulate information and foster collective discussions among its large members, employer coordination was functioning across all the regions in the east. Certainly, this is the conclusion of my interviews with firms in Saxony and Saxony-Anhalt, a conclusion supported by the survey data of Ettl and Heikenroth (1995). The threat to employers' associations in the east posed by the heterogeneity of the eastern economy is real, and in the long-term it could erode these capacities. That has not happened yet.

However, like the western associations, the eastern employers had a limited ability to monitor and an even more limited ability to sanction large member firms that chose not to cooperate with the association.

[14] Large firms acknowledged the role of the IHK in the system, but only as a source of support to and supervision of the smaller firms.

[15] Indeed, the two metalworking employers' associations joined in 1998 with the association in Thuringia to form Ostmetall, a joint association whose role was to strengthen their negotiating power against the IG Metall (Bluhm 1999, 230).

[16] Based on a survey of eastern German companies conducted in 1994, Ettl and Heikenroth (1995) find that there was no statistically significant difference among the eastern German regions in the behavior of companies vis-à-vis their associations.

[17] Associations in eastern Germany responded to the dissatisfaction of members in the *Mittelstand* by increasing their provision of services for firms of this size (Bluhm 1999, 243–45).

As in the west, the IHK regulations set the ground rules to which smaller firms had to adhere. The IHK was in a position to monitor their compliance with minimal standards, and it had the sanction of not allowing firms to train if they did not meet those standards.[18] However, for larger companies neither capacity had a real effect: these companies easily satisfied the minimal training regulations of the IHK, and the association had no sanction it could effectively threaten to use against them. The representative of one large firm in eastern Germany (EGL3) agreed that the information exchanges with other colleagues were an important function played by the eastern association, but indicated that the firm did not give the association carte blanche to monitor its training: "our competitors are there, so there is information that we hold back." The same firm joined other large companies in dismissing the idea of sanctions in the case of delinquent behavior by other large member firms. Faced with the poaching of its workers by western German firms in 1991, its only recourse was to raise its wages to parity with the western rate; the association could provide no sanction that would prevent the poaching. Like employers in the west, eastern employers demonstrated an ability to circulate information and to develop collective strategies effectively, but they did not have effective monitoring or sanctioning capabilities.

If eastern Germany had been in a situation of political and economic equilibrium, employers' associations and unions would have been the predominant players in regulating the functioning of the apprenticeship system. That is the role they play in western Germany. But eastern Germany in the 1990s was an economy in transition, and its apprenticeship market was dysfunctional. There were far more youth seeking apprenticeship jobs than there were apprenticeship places available in companies. Faced with this situation, the federal and state governments stepped in to develop policies to cope with the mismatch between supply and demand in the eastern German apprenticeship market. These governments thereby became important players in the apprenticeship system, even as the eastern German social partners continue to be responsible for most of the firm-related aspects of the dual system.

FROM NATIONAL NEGOTIATIONS TO REGIONALLY EMBEDDED POLICY-MAKING

Compared to adopting a new currency, building new regional governments, and privatizing a state-controlled economy, apprenticeship policy

---

[18] Given the shortage of apprenticeship places in the east, the IHKs with whose representatives I spoke seemed extremely reluctant to deny firms the right to train. But they did possess the sanction, and some firms did not train in anticipation of not being able to meet the guidelines of the IHK.

was a low-visibility political issue in eastern Germany in 1990. Yet the development of policy-making in these other, more prominent political fields paralleled and influenced the way in which eastern German training policy evolved. The extraordinary political dynamic triggered by the fall of the Berlin Wall provided a brief moment during which national policy was largely unconstrained by the dense network of parapublic institutions that had dictated the normally glacial pace of political change in the days of the Bonn Republic (Katzenstein 1989, 333). The administrative model of privatization conducted by the Treuhand coupled with the shock of immersing eastern Germany in the western German market economy, soon created a backlash from newly established governments and social partners in eastern Germany (Stark and Bruszt 1998, 175–79).[19] The privatization policies of the Treuhand, like the economic policies of the government of Helmut Kohl, reverted in short order to being discussed with the social partners rather than being foisted on them. However, the national discussions with the social partners—through the institution of the *Kanzlerrunde* (chancellor's round tables)—were largely a government briefing for employers and unions rather than a forum for serious negotiation with them (Padgett 1999, 153–56). Regional governments and regional social partners, faced with daunting tasks of economic reconstruction, had similar concerns, whereas the federal government had to balance these concerns against the less acute, but still pressing problems of running Europe's largest economy and polity. As a result, the practice of embedded policy-making—which had been the major characteristic of preunification Germany—shifted somewhat after unification away from the federal government and in the direction of the *Länder*. However, not all regional governments in eastern Germany adopted the model of embedded policy-making, and this choice had important consequences for the development of apprenticeship policies.

Employers' associations and federal policy-makers agreed on the major objectives involved in transferring the dual system to eastern Germany, but their preferred policy strategies to achieve these objectives diverged over the course of 1990s. Two imperatives drove the development of training policy for eastern Germany: ensuring the successful establishment of a dual system in which companies paid the costs of in-firm training and minimizing eastern German youth unemployment. On the one hand, the federal government was clear and consistent in

---

[19] "The signs [of political crisis] were soon manifest: the assassination of the Treuhand's chief executive, demonstrations in the city seats of *Länder* parliaments, and strike waves in the East, where workers held dozens of factories and occupied the state parliament in Schwerin, capital of Mecklenburg-Vorpommern" (Stark and Bruszt 1998, 176).

its policy of not wanting to subsidize in-firm training, so as not to under-mine the principle of company responsibility for apprenticeship. On the other hand, the government wanted to keep young people out of unemployment, for fear of the political consequences massive unemploy-ment could create.[20] Employers' associations accepted the importance of keeping youth unemployment low, and they wanted to ensure the prin-ciple of employer responsibility for the costs (and control) of the training system. Given the durability of the problems of the apprenticeship market, both sides agreed that subsidies were a necessary transitional measure. Yet the sort of subsidies preferred by the two sides differed: the federal government adopted a rigid policy of refusing to subsidize in-firm places, whereas employers insisted that subsidies would be better used in developing the in-firm training system rather than in support-ing training that did not take place in real companies. As a result of the split, employers' associations eventually moved to influence the nature of subsidy programs at the state, rather than the federal, level.

The evolution of eastern German policy for apprenticeship can there-fore be characterized as having three distinct stages. In the years imme-diately after unification, from 1991 to 1993, apprenticeship policy was subordinated to larger problems of the immediate transition to the market economy. The federal government used its privatization agency to maintain an artificially high number of apprentices while companies were reorganized. Employers' associations and unions were, during this time, largely devoted to the tasks of organization building (described in the previous section) rather than to proposing ways to improve the training system. During the second phase from 1993 to 1995, state and federal governments, along with the social partners, began to develop different policy preferences—the federal government established a program to subsidize out-of-firm training, the states indiscriminately subsidized in-firm training, and employers' associations criticized both strategies. The third period, from 1995 to 2000, was marked by the

---

[20] Youth unemployment was, obviously, a general electoral liability, but there was also the risk that unemployed youth would be attracted to the parties or ideas of the radical right. The political salience of this fear in modern Germany is undeniable, but existing research has only partially confirmed the connection between youth unemployment and the radical right. A panel study of 2,000 eastern German school-leavers, conducted by researchers from the BiBB between 1992 and 1996, found that young people who were unemployed or had been unable to find an apprenticeship place were no more likely than those who had found an apprenticeship to voice "authoritarian-nationalist tendencies" or to agree with xenophobic propositions. Those without an apprenticeship were, however, 10 percent more likely to respond that they would resort to violence faced with certain political outcomes, such as a rise in the proportion of foreigners in the population (BMBW 1995; Schweikert 1999).

preeminence of the eastern state governments rather than the federal government in developing different policy strategies to promote general skills investment in eastern Germany. The policies adopted by the states at the beginning of this period, which coincided with the declining avail-ability of highly qualified skilled workers in the eastern German labor market, influenced the choice of companies deciding whether to begin using the apprenticeship system.

In the immediate aftermath of unification, the federal government effectively subsidized apprenticeship through its privatization agency, the Treuhand. Cognizant of the implosion of the eastern German eco-nomy and the consequent lack of training places in companies, the policy of the Treuhand was to prevent an even higher rate of youth unemployment. The agency instructed its companies to maintain exist-ing apprentices and hire new ones, even when there was no apparent future need for them in the company's employment plans. In the large state conglomerates (the former *Kombinate*), these apprentices would be concentrated in the conglomerate training center, which would then be legally separated from the rest of the conglomerate to make the other parts of the company more attractive as candidates for privatization (Johnson 1995). This policy created a new actor in the eastern German apprenticeship universe, one completely foreign to the western German system: training centers that were companies that produced nothing but trainees.[21] Once governments turned their attention to the problem of apprenticeship, these training centers became an important part of the debate about the appropriate policy for developing the dual system in eastern Germany.

By 1993, as more and more companies were being privatized, the Treuhand could no longer function as the principal vector of federal apprenticeship policy. At this point, both the federal and state govern-ments stepped directly into the void of the eastern German appren-ticeship market. Their foremost problem was what to do about the young people who were unsuccessful in finding apprenticeships. The federal government, highly concerned about setting any negative precedents for the dual system in western Germany, proposed a system of out-of-firm apprenticeship training. The policy, called the Gemeinschaft-sinitiative Ost (GIOst), sponsored apprenticeship training in the new centers that had been established by the Treuhand, aid for out-of-firm training funded jointly by the federal government, state governments,

---

[21] Training centers existed in western Germany, but they existed to assist companies in training apprentices in specialties. The training centers that spun off from the *Kombinate* established contracts with their apprentices directly—there was no connec-tion between the trainee and a company that actually produced something.

and the structural funds of the European Union. The GIOst program served three purposes for the federal government: it provided an effective way to keep youth unemployment from ballooning; it shared the financial burden with the states and the EU, thus giving state governments an incentive not to rely too heavily on the program; and it underlined the government's commitment to a dual system in which firms paid the costs of in-firm training (BMBW 1995, 15).[22]

Eastern German state governments, which were unconcerned with the precedents they might set for western states, *were* willing to subsidize in-firm training. State governments in western Germany typically played a minor role in apprenticeship policy, but the refusal of the federal government to develop subsidy policies to encourage in-firm training led the governments of the new federal states of the east to become the principal policy experimenters in eastern Germany.[23] The subsidy programs that were adopted did not vary among the eastern states to any significant degree in the early years after unification. They had in common that they took the form of simple monetary incentives for hiring apprentices; that is, a firm received a subsidy when it signed a contract with an apprentice in a given category.[24] For companies, this was a one-time payment that reduced the cost of hiring an apprentice.

In all the early state programs the eligibility requirements were based on readily observable problems of the apprenticeship market rather than on characteristics of the hiring firm. In 1993, for example, all five states and Berlin provided subsidy support for the hiring of additional apprentices (beyond the firm's own need) and the hiring of female apprentices, particularly in the technical professions (BMBW 1993, 195–97).[25] Although states employed different formulas for distributing the aid, nothing about the aid programs specified the conditions of training or attempted to target companies that would be especially likely to invest in the general skills of their apprentices. Instead, the government subsidies targeted problems that the government's statistical offices could readily observe: the lack of apprenticeship places, the underrepresentation of females in technical apprenticeships, and so on.

---

[22] From 1996 to 1998, the federal government continued the GIOst program under different names, but with the same refusal to underwrite in-firm contracts.

[23] Prior to unification, the role of the *Länder* in the politics of western German training had consisted largely of their responsibility for the vocational schools (*Berufsschulen*).

[24] The subsidies ranged from 2,500 to 8,400 DM ($1,150 to $3,900) per apprentice in 1993.

[25] Which apprentices were "additional" and therefore made the firm eligible for the aid was sometimes left undefined in the subsidy program. Saxony limited the aid to companies with a training ratio over 10 percent, and Thuringia and Mecklenburg-West Pomerania chose a threshold training ratio of 8 percent.

In this sense, the state aid was an indiscriminate side-payment, available to any firm that could meet the minimal training requirements of the IHK.

Employers' associations in the east, which were well established on the ground by 1993, objected to both strategies. The GIOst program of the federal government comprised two elements abhorred by the employers: it supported training in out-of-firm centers rather than directly in firms under a work contract and it provided public support for training places rather than having firms pay for their own trainees. Employers' representatives repeatedly denounced out-of-firm training as a second-best solution because the apprentices did not gain the actual experience of work in a firm. The practical consequences of removing the apprentice from the firm included drastically lower rates of employment for out-of-firm than for in-firm apprentices and a presumption of lower quality of the training received (Schober and Rauch 1995; Ulrich 1995). Employers favored some form of in-firm subsidy, but they were critical of the subsidies of the state governments, deriding the "watering-can principle," by which states sprinkled money indiscriminately over all firms that hired apprentices rather than focusing their subsidies on the needs of those private firms most likely to be convinced of the long-term value of training (VSME 1995, 10).

Eastern employers' associations advocated instead a *Verbund* (alliance) policy of the sort discussed in chapter 3. In 1991, the Berlin metalworking employers' association had already begun to alert other members of Gesamtmetall that out-of-firm training was not meeting the goals of the dual system. By 1993, the Berlin employers' association and the state affiliate of IG Metall had agreed on the desirability of the *Verbund* subsidy (Int ERE8). The idea of firms training in subsidized partnership was adopted that year, in limited form, by the Berlin state government (BMBW 1994, 195–96). Eastern associations adopted the idea of the *Verbund* because they knew it would appeal most to firms that were interested in investing in in-firm apprenticeship training rather than further developing out-of-firm training centers. The *Verbund* represented a solution to the problem of how to use subsidies to convert waverers to cooperators rather than to attract committed defectors who merely liked the idea of acquiring subsidy money. Thus eastern associations pushed the national peak associations to pursue the policy, and the national associations worked together with the Federal Institute of Vocational Training (BiBB) to make the policy more widely known (Int ERE10). Moreover, the *Verbund* allowed the associations to show their SME members that they were engaged in bringing government policy closer to firm needs, not merely catering to the needs of the large firms (VSME 1995, 10). Large firms, meanwhile, having benefited from the

Leitbetriebe investments to their training workshops (see chap. 3), wanted to use the alliance policy to ensure their new training facilities were used at close to capacity levels. Forming partnerships between these two groups of firms, the two political constituencies of the associations, also established informational linkages among new training companies and experienced training companies, linkages that would endure over the 3.5-year life of the apprenticeship contract.

The original policy mix employed by the eastern German states reflected a response to the information they had available: the aggregate number of apprenticeship places (which was insufficient, leading them to create incentives for firms to train additional apprentices) and the problems facing specific demographic groups (notably, young women) on the apprenticeship market. With only this aggregate information, it is not clear why the *Verbund* policy would appear preferable to a state policy-maker trying to act on the problem of creating apprenticeship places. But for actors with information sources closer to the shop floor, such as employers' associations and unions, it became increasingly clear during the early 1990s that indiscriminate subsidies for companies, and especially the federal subsidies for out-of-firm training places, were not encouraging firms that were most likely to become voluntary participants in an eastern German high-skill equilibrium to train (BMBW 1996). Despite the joint efforts of employers and unions to shift the focus of federal policy by using the *Verbund*, the government in Bonn was unwilling to use subsidy money to support in-firm training. The breaking point was the *Kanzlerrund* of March 1995, when the federal government explicitly rejected the *Verbund* policies and instead exhorted employers to create more apprenticeship places on their own.[26] At this juncture, associations turned their attention to state policies.

In 1995, employers and unions successfully persuaded state governments in Saxony, Berlin, and Brandenburg to adopt a state-subsidized *Verbund* program.[27] Saxony-Anhalt rejected the phased *Verbund* measure

---

[26] In a letter to the leaders of Gesamtmetall, Education Minister Jürgen Rüttgers dismissed the *Verbund* proposal on the grounds that it might cause "some firms to lose interest in investing their own apprenticeship training" (1995, 2). The western German leader of the BDA, Klaus Murmann, pledged that firms in the private economy would create 600,000 places in 1995 (an increase of 33,000 over the previous year), which they predictably failed to do; at the time of this pledge, it was apparent to associations in the east and west that private companies would not create this many places on their own (Int WNE1; ERE6; ERE8).

[27] Saxony and Berlin adopted similar *Verbund* support programs phased over three and one-half years. This represented a substantial expansion of Berlin's earlier partnership program. Brandenburg's *Verbund* support program provided support exclusively for the first year of training (BMBW 1996, 192–94).

and continued with its more traditional measures to support apprenticeship training. The principal reason for these different policy approaches lies in the extent to which state governments involved employers' associations in the development of regional policy. In other words, the states that constructed informational links to the private networks were those that developed these distinctive sets of policies, whereas those that refused to do so continued with the traditional set of indiscriminate subsidy policies.

EMBEDDED VERSUS AUTONOMOUS POLICY-MAKING IN THE EASTERN GERMAN STATES

What most distinguished the human capital policies of Saxony from those of Saxony-Anhalt was the extent to which governments in the two states developed the practice of embedded policy-making. Throughout Germany, the formal body through which the social partners deliberate in order to advise state policy-makers is the Landesausschuß für Berufsbildung (LAB), which comprises equal tripartite voting representation of the employers, employees, and public authorities. The LABs did not play an important role in shaping apprenticeship policies in the western states before 1990, because the ambit of *Land* intervention in this policy domain was relatively constrained; the social partners were more likely to wield their influence at the national or sectoral level (Streeck et al. 1987). However, with the active participation of eastern states in subsidizing in-firm training, the LAB became an actor with significant influence in some eastern states during the 1990s. Legally, its role was only advisory, so its de facto importance depended on the extent to which regional governments deferred to its suggestions. Some regional governments also named smaller working groups, made up of representatives of employers and unions, which could advise governments on specific policy problems. In the case of subsidized apprenticeship alliances in Saxony, the familiarity of employers' representatives with the problems that prevented companies from hiring apprentices enabled the social partners to convince a reluctant government to pursue such a policy. The Saxon-Anhalt government did not generally solicit the input of the social partners, and the policies that emerged there, correspondingly, reflected a different set of informational inputs.

The creation of a special LAB working group in Saxony, devoted to combating weaknesses in the apprenticeship market, gave the Saxon Economics Ministry a source of proposals different from the standard palette of subsidies offered by the other eastern states. Starting in 1993, the Saxon Federation of Employers' Associations (VAS) collaborated with the local affiliate of the DGB to urge state aid for training through a

Verbund arrangement (Int ERE 10; ERU3). In mid-1994, before the failure of the 1995 chancellor's round table, the Saxon government rejected the private actors' push to subsidize a "blanket conception of an apprentice-ship *Verbund* for all of Saxony" (SSWA 1994, 4). Yet the working group, which comprised employer and union representatives alongside bureau-crats, agreed to establish three experimental *Verbünde* in structurally weak regions, mandating that these pilot projects "be able to function as a model for other regions in future" (SSWA 1994, 5). The expressed pref-erences of the Saxon government—a CDU majority government led by Kurt Biedenkopf—were not fundamentally different than those of the federal CDU/CSU government of Helmut Kohl. Both governments wanted to minimize youth unemployment while reinforcing the principle of company responsibility for apprenticeship training. But the Saxon state's sponsorship of the *Verbund* pilot project enabled it to gather further information on a project about which it was initially skeptical.

When the federal government again rejected the *Verbund* at the national level in 1995, the Saxon government had already established links to a set of informed private actors and an experimental *Verbund* model. In the employers' associations and unions that were active in the working group of the regional economics minister, the government had a group of proponents well versed in the problems of SMEs. As volun-teered by the head of the training department in the Saxon Economics Ministry, state policy-makers were "initially dissatisfied" with the way in which the *Verbund* aid was concentrated during the first year of an appren-ticeship because this was costly for the state and appeared to allow com-panies to avoid investing their own money in training. He acknowledged that this feature, which dismayed state policy-makers, was exactly the feature advocated by employers' associations. The associations knew that the costs of first-year training were dissuading some of the companies most likely to be persuaded to train (the waverers) from hiring appren-tices. "The chambers and employers' associations, they liked this aspect [of the *Verbund*], because they know how things work in their firms" (Int ERG8). Employers had better information than state policy-makers about the obstacles that prevented wavering firms from training appren-tices, and this relational information was only available to the state because it relied on the proposals of these employers' groups.

The federal government in Bonn worried about setting precedents under which western German firms would stop investing in their own training. The major concern of the Saxon state government was, in the words of Economics Minister Kajo Schommer, to develop a policy that would "put the responsibility for apprenticeship training back where it belongs: with the firms of the private economy" (SSWA 1995, 3). The difference between the federal and state governments was one of means:

the federal government viewed subsidies for in-firm training as a slippery slope to a state-funded system, which would undercut the principle of firm responsibility that underpins the high-skill equilibrium. The Saxon state government agreed with this proposition. However, given that some subsidies were inevitable, the state government wanted to adopt policies that were most likely to be consistent with developing company investment in apprenticeship training. Given the state government's rejection less than one year earlier of the utility of a blanket *Verbund*, it was very unlikely that Schommer would have adopted the policy on his own. Yet because he continued to use the working group of unions and employers to draft policy alternatives, Schommer had access to well-informed advocates of the *Verbund* policy as he was becoming disillusioned with the existing mix of policies employed by the federal government.

In addition, once the new subsidy was adopted, the information-circulation and mobilization capacities of the employers' association in Saxony became important assets, because the association was able to diffuse information about the new program to member firms immediately and to lobby them to use it. A representative of one of the Saxon firms in my sample commented on why she chose the *Verbund*, stressing exactly these aspects of associational involvement: "The policy was pushed by the VSME (employers' association), which had gathered information about the training needs of firms [to develop it]" (Int EGSME13). The ability to mobilize firms to participate was important, given that it asked potentially competing firms to cooperate with each other. This concern is reflected in the minutes from the discussion of the *Verbund* policy by the LAB's apprenticeship working group, which show that "doubts were expressed about the possibility of attracting firms to participate in such a training *Verbund*, since competing firms would, unusually for them, have to cooperate with each other" (SSWA 1994, 4). The Saxon metal employers hailed the new policy as a welcome departure from the indiscriminate spending of the state on apprenticeship studies, promising members efforts on its part to "create further incentives for companies themselves to train" (VSME 1995, 10). Their network of large firms, which had been specially subsidized to revamp their training facilities (*Leitbetriebe*), gave the employers' association a group around which to mobilize support for the *Verbund* among SMEs. The employers' associations not only provided crucial information for the government in developing the *Verbund* policy, but they were also effective in diffusing information about it and mobilizing wavering SMEs to participate in it.

In contrast to Saxon policies, the composition of apprenticeship policies in Saxony-Anhalt was a product of the autonomous policy-making model pursued by the red-green government between 1994 and 1997. Both the employers' associations and the regional IHKs decried the lack of consultation established by the government with the private economy (Padgett 1999, 159). In its August 1995 newsletter to members, the Saxon-Anhalt metal employers' association excoriated the state government for proposing changes to the regional education system without consulting it or going through the advisory group of state school experts: "as an employers' association we are astonished that an expert commission, which will draw up the state of affairs in education policy for the political decision-makers, has been set up. We were neither officially informed of the putting together of this expert commission, nor was our participation solicited" (Schramedei 1995, 1). In the same vein, a representative of the IHK in Halle complained that the state government tended to "bypass" the employers' organizations in the policy-making process (Int ERE2). Whereas the government in Saxony relied heavily on standing working groups to design both the broad outlines and details of implementation of a *Verbund* policy, the Saxon-Anhalt government did not set up a *Verbund* working group until the end of 1998—four years later—by which time every other eastern state was aggressively pursuing a *Verbund* policy (Int ERG7).

Consequently, the Saxon-Anhalt program for supporting training partnerships was less attractive to companies than was the Saxon *Verbund* policy. Until 1997, and in spite of the fact that the state DGB affiliate and the regional employers' association both advocated the use of state subsidies for training alliances, the state government had not developed a program that included the two defining elements of a *Verbund*: support for multifirm cooperation and phased support focused especially on the first year.[28] Instead, Saxony-Anhalt continued to rely on the traditional subsidy measures based on government-perceived shortages in the apprenticeship market. And recall from chapter 3 that *none* of the firms in my sample from metalworking industry in Saxony-Anhalt had been persuaded to invest in general skills by the existing state subsidies. Although the Saxon-Anhalt government maintained the same formal structures of private-interest governance as the other new federal states, its unwillingness to accord employers' representatives any substantial

---

[28] The only subsidy available for small firms to train in partnership with another firm provided support only for up to twelve weeks, at a weekly maximum of 100 DM, making it the smallest apprenticeship subsidy available in Saxony-Anhalt. This subsidy could not set up the multifirm groups of the *Verbund*, nor were the administrative costs of host firms defrayed. For comparison, the Berlin and Saxony programs, which were both phased over 3–4 years, provided thirty weeks and fifty-two weeks of support, respectively, in the first year alone; and weekly support amounted to 225 DM in Saxony (plus administrative costs for the *Verbund*) and 350 DM in Berlin.

voice in the shaping of state policy left the state with a policy mix that was necessarily based on the information that its bureaucracies could gather. And policies based on this information alone did not resemble the mix adopted when the social partners had a more significant voice in the making of state policy.

Was the autonomous method of policy-making in Saxony-Anhalt idiosyncratic to apprenticeship policies, or did it extend beyond this policy area? Part of the problem might have been due to a difference in administrative structure in the two states: in Saxony the Economics and Labor Ministry was primarily responsible for training policy, whereas in Saxony-Anhalt the Culture Ministry played the preeminent role.[29] The practice of coordination with social partners may come more easily to an economics than a culture ministry in Germany. An official of the Saxon-Anhalt Culture Ministry agreed in an interview with the author that his office had only limited contact with the private economy through formal bodies of consultation—notably, the LAB—but claimed that he maintained frequent contact with its representatives on an informal basis. When asked for an example, however, he could not name a single informal contact that had been relevant in the crafting of state policy relative to vocational education and training (Int ERG3).

Yet the division of labor between state ministries is only part of the story. A representative of the employers' association in Saxony-Anhalt said that employers "had never had much luck" persuading the economics minister to listen to them (Int ERE7). In his study of interest groups in eastern Germany, Stephen Padgett argues that the pattern of autonomous policy-making broadly characterizes state-employer relations in Saxony-Anhalt: "In Sachsen-Anhalt, employer and business groups ascribed difficulties in their relations with the minority Social Democrat-led coalition formed in 1994 to political instability and policy uncertainty" (1999, 160). Padgett notes that the lack of partisan affinity did not appear to be the major reason for the pattern of autonomous policy-making. Instead, he finds that patterns of embedded policy-making were most pronounced in states with stable single-party majority governments, whether of the right (Saxony) or the left (Brandenburg).

Evidence on apprenticeship policy-making in other eastern German states likewise disconfirms the proposition that differences in either policies or patterns of policy-making were driven by political partisanship. The partisan composition of government seems like a viable explanatory candidate (Boix 1998), because governments of particular stripes

---

[29] Regional culture ministries in Germany have responsibility for questions of education, including the management of *Berufsschulen* for the apprenticeship system.

might be more likely to invite their preferred private-interest group into policy-making (Peterson and Walker 1991). I have especially focused on the capacities of employers' organizations, so we expect that governments of the right would have been especially likely to give employers' associations a privileged role in policy-making.

However, studies of the policy-making process in Berlin and Brandenburg, where governments also adopted a *Verbund* policy, do not support the partisan explanation. In 1995, the government in Berlin was a grand coalition between the major parties of the right (CDU) and the left (SPD). The Berlin government, like the Saxon government, established a special working group devoted to the problem of resolving the disequilibrium on the apprenticeship market. The commission included not just employer and union representatives, but also members of the government, including Mayor Eberhard Diepgen of the CDU and Ingrid Stahmer, leader of the state SPD and the Berlin minister for social affairs. As in Saxony, it was the metalworking employers and unions that led the push for the adoption of a *Verbund* phased over the life of an apprenticeship contract, with the bulk of support coming in the first year. Because the employers' association in Berlin had established its own out-of-firm training center using spare firm capacity, it was able to provide detailed cost estimates to the Berlin government showing that *Verbund* training was actually cheaper than out-of-firm training to the public authorities (VME 1995; Int ERE8). Following the joint recommendations of the employers and the unions, the Berlin government coalition adopted the program for the metal and electronics industry and made it public in September 1995, immediately before the start of the new apprenticeship year.[30] In Brandenburg, which was governed at this time by a single-party majority of the SPD, Manfred Stolpe's government also brought private-interest actors into its policy-making process and adopted a *Verbund* in 1995.

Across the political spectrum, eastern German states that incorporated private associations into the policy-making process were more likely to adopt a phased *Verbund* policy, regardless of their partisan character. Recall also that it was a federal governing coalition of the right (CDU-FDP) that rejected the joint recommendation of Gesamtmetall and the IG Metall to adopt the *Verbund* at the national level in 1995, spurring the flurry of regional *Verbund* policies. This policy was not

[30] Even the timing of the adoption of the policy was also explicitly recommended by the unions and employers in a joint letter to Diepgen in May 1995. They proposed that the government only announce the program just before the start of the new apprenticeship year to avoid having companies use it that would have trained apprentices anyway (Kleiner and Bretz 1995).

uniquely adopted by governments of the right because it was not a policy that divided eastern German parties of the right and the left. In all of these states, as well as at the national level, the employers' associations and the unions both agreed on the desirability of the *Verbund* policy. The government in Saxony-Anhalt was, therefore, also spurning the unions in not incorporating a serious phased *Verbund* policy. Although partisanship may influence the individual policies chosen by states or regions, it does not explain why states do or do not develop the practice of embedded policy-making.

THE COSTS OF AUTONOMOUS POLICY-MAKING

Recall from chapter 3 that the *Verbund* was far more effective than any other policy in convincing wavering SMEs to adopt training practices consistent with those of the western German high-skill equilibrium. Findings by researchers at the Center for Social Research in Halle, in a report commissioned by the government of Saxony-Anhalt, confirm this result. Despite the high level of spending by the state government on training subsidies, the apprenticeships that grew most quickly in Saxony-Anhalt were those "whose productive potential and breadth of applicability are rather low, and which are characterized by low, if not negative, training costs; for such jobs, therefore, additional apprenticeship places can quickly be created" (Lutz and Grünert 1999, 81–82). By contrast, apprenticeships in sectors with high net investment per apprentice, such as industrial metalworking and banking, have declined. To counter this negative trend, Lutz and Grünert recommend strongly in their final report that the state gradually reduce its overall subsidy programs, while emphasizing that a few select policies should be strengthened because their "financial, organizational, and conceptual support . . . can be expected to provide a positive impetus for the consolidation of the dual system of apprenticeship training" (1999, 105). Foremost among the policies recommended to achieve this end is the *Verbund*.

What was it about the *Verbund* that was particularly likely to attract those companies most inclined to invest in high-quality training? This training alliance gave companies in the Saxon *Mittelstand* access to the machinery and use of other (larger) company trainers that allowed them to fulfill the IHK requirements, which they perceived as onerous. In so doing, the policy not only allowed these firms to meet these material requirements; it also established informational linkages among these training companies, giving the companies access to information that could reinforce their confidence that they could use the training system effectively, while simultaneously providing them with demonstration effects of the benefits of training at other companies. Thus, managers from these wavering companies were put together with representatives of large companies, whose workshops the alliances often used. The people these managers then turned to for information about training investments were therefore far more likely than the average company manager in eastern Germany to be convinced of the value of apprenticeship training. The discussion created through the training alliance was likely to be biased in favor of the advantages of training, and the dynamic of group polarization (discussed in chap. 2) was able to come into play. One advantage of the *Verbund* was the fact that it married financial aid and technical assistance with a three-year conversation among company managers who were likely to believe in the value of apprenticeship training.

The associations that influenced Saxon policy understood the coexistence within the SMEs of both strategic and analytic uncertainty. Recall from chapter 3 that these companies worried about the possibility of poaching, but they were also uncertain about the returns on investing in the general skills of their trainees, even if the trainees were not poached subsequently. The design of the *Verbund* disproportionately attracted waverers because it focused the aid on the specific obstacles they faced: uncertain returns on their training facilities and a lack of information about training practices. One objection to the argument based on analytic uncertainty runs as follows: If the chambers and associations were well established in eastern Germany and capable of information circulation, why were they not capable of directly providing information to firms to overcome their analytic uncertainty? The flaw here is missing the importance of direct interorganizational information exchange within the context of a multifirm training alliance. A representative of one firm in my sample from Saxony, when asked how important or useful she found the information on apprenticeship provided by the local IHK, responded dismissively, "yes, I can get information from the IHK, but that is only theory. One really needs to speak directly to people from other firms [to get useful, practical information]." By virtue of participating in a *Verbund*, she was likely to turn for advice to training personnel of the large firm around which the training alliance was constructed—and such personnel were very likely to be believers in the value of investment in the general skills of apprentices.

Policy-makers in Saxony-Anhalt lacked the private information in 1995 that would have made them especially likely to adopt a *Verbund* subsidy program. Evidence from my own sample of firms, assembled shortly after the introduction of the Saxon program in 1995, shows clearly that the *Verbund* was more effective than the traditional measures in Saxony-Anhalt in persuading firms to begin adopting high-skill training practices. Yet the advantages of the *Verbund* have been noted by other researchers, and the experience of states that did adopt a multifirm

Table 4.2 Places Created by *Verbund* Policy in Saxony and Saxony-Anhalt[a]

	Year 1	Year 2	Year 3	Change in 1 year (%)	Change, Cumulative (%)
Saxony	500 (1995)	1,012 (1996)	2,032 (1997)	102	306
Saxony-Anhalt	400 (1997)	409 (1998)	281 (1999)	2	−29

[a] Source: Data for Saxony are from the state Ministry for the Economy; data from Saxony-Anhalt are from the state Ministry for Economy and Technology.

Verbund in 1995 are observable. So the question becomes whether Saxony-Anhalt could subsequently adopt a *Verbund* subsidy and thereby achieve better results among its SMEs.

In 1997, two years after Saxony adopted its *Verbund* program, Saxony-Anhalt transformed its old partnership subsidy in a way that more closely matched the Saxon program: it increased the amount of the subsidy; phased it over the life of the contract, concentrating the money in the first year of the apprenticeship; and it permitted multifirm alliances. Yet this program appears to have been much less attractive to companies in Saxony-Anhalt than elsewhere. In the first three years of its operation, the number of apprenticeship places created by the policy grew very little, whereas the Saxon program exploded in popularity with employers over its first three years (see table 4.2). Given the clear success of the *Verbund* in other eastern states, this is puzzling: "since apprenticeship *Verbünde* could be extremely important in securing higher quality training in an overwhelmingly small-firm economy, it is recommended that the state [of Saxony-Anhalt] look into the low utilization of this policy—especially in comparison to neighboring states—and seek a remedy for it" (Lutz and Grünert 1999, 106).

Why was the Saxon-Anhalt subsidy markedly less successful in attracting firms than the Saxon program that preceded it? Two factors seem to have played a role. First, unlike the Saxon program, which was developed with the close input of employers' groups, the policy in Saxony-Anhalt did not pay the administrative costs of the large companies that agreed to serve as a central node for several smaller firms that wanted to train together. This might have dissuaded large companies from agreeing to serve as the center of a *Verbund* (Lutz and Grünert 1999, 75). Large companies were particularly important to the alliance policy, both because they were likely to have state-of-the-art training workshops and because they were committed cooperators who could convince wavering firms of the value of investing in apprenticeship training. Second, the timing of the policy might have been extremely important, based on when eastern German companies first began to choose strategies for acquiring skilled labor. In the early years after unification, many highly skilled workers were unemployed because of economic restructuring, and available government subsidies often made those workers more attractive to hire than apprentices (Wagner 1999). Yet the availability of these skilled workers declined over time, as the best workers were gradually rehired. In 1992, a survey of companies in eastern Germany showed that the abundant supply of skilled labor was the reason most frequently cited by companies for not training apprentices, an answer given by one-third of those companies (von Bardeleben 1993). In 1994, this answer was the fourth most frequent, given by only 17 percent of companies (von Bardeleben 1995). By 1996, one year after the start of the Saxon program and one year before the introduction of the Saxon-Anhalt subsidy, a poll of those working for the chambers to promote the hiring of apprentices cited the supply of skilled labor on the labor market as only an occasional obstacle for companies' hiring of apprentices (in seventh place on the list of ten potential obstacles) (BMBW 1997, 33). In other words, the adoption of the *Verbund* in 1995 was roughly simultaneous with the decrease of the alternative sources of skilled labor available to SMEs in eastern Germany. By adopting the policy two years after Saxony, the government in Saxony-Anhalt may have missed its chance to use the subsidy to persuade waverers to begin investing in apprenticeship because they had already decided to seek their skilled workers by other means.

Although the data are not available to test rigorously this proposed explanation of the failure of Saxony-Anhalt's later program, a comparison of two of the firms in my sample suggests the plausibility of the claim. These firms were interviewed at the end of 1995, and both produced primarily for export markets: company EGSME13 (in Saxony) and company EGSME16 (in Saxony-Anhalt). Although both trained below the target range in 1995, EGSME13 had just begun training as a result of the *Verbund* program. All of its apprentices were in the first year of training, and the firm had definite plans to continue, once they had begun. Their personal director explained why: "we needed to develop a younger workforce, [as] the average age of our workers is 47. [However,] we would not have trained this year without the *Verbund* aid; we could not have begun training until next year."[31]

---

[31] When contacted again in 2000, the firm's training ratio (4.4 percent) and its retention rate of apprentices who had finished the previous year (100 percent) both indicated a training investment at western German levels.

Contrast these sentiments with those of the personnel director of firm EGSME16 in Saxony-Anhalt. This company was desperate for workers—in 1994 and 1995, the company had hired ten times as many workers directly from the labor market (forty)[32] as it had hired its own apprentices (4). The firm was clearly not prioritizing apprenticeship training to get skilled workers; why not? "We would have trained more [apprentices] if the policy of the state government were reasonable. The policy [in Saxony-Anhalt] is to base aid on the number of apprentices trained last year. So, if we had 6 apprentices in the third year in 1994, we would have received state aid only if we created 7 new places, i.e., supplementary places. This is stupid!" In the previous year, this firm had joined other companies in the area to lobby the state government to subsidize a partnership along the lines of the *Verbund* model, but the state had not adopted such a policy and the would-be partnership collapsed. The fact that Saxony-Anhalt waited two years before adopting a *Verbund* policy may well have led a significant number of SMEs to dismiss apprenticeship and instead choose alternative ways to find skilled labor.

ALTERNATIVE EXPLANATIONS FOR GOVERNMENT STRATEGIES

The organization of the empirical material in this chapter has followed the two-stage explanatory logic of the theoretical framework developed in chapter 2. First, I have shown that employers' associations in Saxony and Saxony-Anhalt both established the informational and dialogic capacities characteristic of western German associations. In spite of the similar capacities of their associations, governments in the two states developed different modes of policy-making. Saxony practiced embedded policy-making, devolving an extensive role in policy design and execution to private organizations, especially the organizations of employers. In Saxony-Anhalt, by contrast, the government practiced autonomous policy-making, delegating little real authority to private associations. I have demonstrated that these differences led to the differential development of apprenticeship alliances in the two states. Then, returning to the data presented in chapter 3, in the second stage of the argument I have shown how the structure of the *Verbund* policy succeeded in attracting waverers and convincing them to model their training on western German practices. I claim that it was the heavy use of the phased *Verbund* in Saxony, and its absence in Saxony-Anhalt, that explains the differences in the investment of SMEs in human capital development documented in chapter 3.

This causal account is open to challenge on two fronts. First, we could contest the claim that the embeddedness of public policy-making in

[32] Thirty of these were skilled workers; ten were semiskilled.

private networks in Saxony, and its absence in Saxony-Anhalt, explains why the two states pursued different policy mixes. Second, we could challenge the claim that the existence of this policy (rather than other differences between the two states) explains the real difference in the levels of cooperation observed in Saxony and Saxony-Anhalt. This is a more credible objection than the first, although it is not without problems. Indeed, this thought has probably already crossed the mind of readers who know a lot about Germany because the history of industrial development in Saxony should clearly be more propitious to the emergence of decentralized cooperation than that of Saxony-Anhalt.

Table 4.3 lists variables that might plausibly account for the difference in outcomes between Saxony and Saxony-Anhalt: partisanship, political entrepreneurship, the dialogic and sanctioning capacities of employers' associations, and the practice of embedded versus autonomous policy-making. The final column shows which states adopted a *Verbund* policy in 1995, following the federal government's rejection of the policy. In order to increase comparative leverage, I have included the eastern German states of Berlin and Brandenburg in the table.

The first variable reminds us graphically of what we have already seen in the previous discussion: political partisanship cannot account for the variation in the observed policy outcomes among the eastern German states. Parties of the left, parties of the right, and coalitions of both left and right all adopted phased *Verbund* subsidy policies in 1995.

Perhaps powerful political entrepreneurship is necessary for a state to develop an innovative policy by using private information (cf. Kingdon 1984). This is somewhat difficult to test, but I have used my knowledge of the regional political backgrounds to try to classify the potential entrepreneurs in the area of youth training.[33] By this standard, both Saxony (Kajo Schommer) and Saxony-Anhalt (Reinhard Höppner) had powerful political entrepreneurs interested in youth training. It is clear that Schommer tried to incorporate private associations into regional policy-making and that Höppner made an equally sustained effort to create the "possibility of an apprenticeship" for all youth in Saxony-Anhalt.[34] In Berlin and in Brandenburg, conversely, there was no

---

[33] My standard for classification is a thought-experiment: Given the statements made in the press and party programs, was there a senior minister who would be known to all members of the training policy milieu, and to at least some members of the general public, as one who had a special interest in apprenticeship policy? Although the method is admittedly subjective, it would be surprising if knowledgeable observers were to challenge these classifications. Certainly, no one could reasonably contest the two I have classified as interested entrepreneurs.

[34] "Apprenticeship possibility" differed from the policies of many other eastern German states, because it forfeited the goal of an "apprenticeship place [in a firm]."

Table 4.3 Correlates of *Verbund* Adoption in Eastern Germany

	Government Partisanship[a]	Political Entrepreneurship	Associational Dialogic Capacity	Associational Sanctioning	Embedded Policy-Making	Adopted Verbund, 1995
Berlin	R-L		High		X	X
Brandenburg	L		High		X	X
Saxony	R	X	High		X	X
Saxony-Anhalt	L	X	High			

[a] Government partisanship refers to whether the state government is controlled by a party of the right (R), left (L), or by a grand coalition (R-L).

policy entrepreneur closely attached to apprenticeship, although both Eberhard Diepgen and Manfred Stolpe were willing to defer to their working group of employers and unions in adopting a generous *Verbund* policy. Entrepreneurship is thus neither a necessary nor a sufficient condition for the adoption of such a policy.

The evidence presented earlier in this chapter demonstrated that variation in the collective capacities of associations cannot explain the different policy outcomes because the dialogic capacity of eastern German employers was uniformly high. There is no reason to think, and no evidence from my interviews to imply, that the Saxon-Anhalt association was any less capable of facilitating information circulation and collective discussion than the other associations of the east. Likewise, the rationalist looking for sanctioning capacity to explain how these policies could lead to the emergence of cooperation will find none. None of the associations in the east had the capacity to stop poaching or other forms of free-riding. The eastern German states did not differ, in any meaningful respect that I was able to measure, in the organizational capacity of their employers.

The story of Saxony versus Saxony-Anhalt is not one of different partisan preferences, different concentration of leading politicians, or different private coordinating capacity. It is the story of the difference between policies based on publicly available information and policies based on private relational information. The German employment offices have very good data on which eastern German districts had the worst rates of unemployment for apprentices, in which sectors companies were particularly unwilling to offer apprenticeship places, and which subsets of the youth population had the most severe difficulties finding an apprenticeship. Yet companies have many reasons to withhold information about their own preferences from state agencies, and there are incentives for them to misrepresent other sorts of information to the public hand that collects taxes and distributes subsidies. In eastern Germany, as in western Germany, companies were much more willing to share information with their representatives—the employers' associations and also the chambers—than with the state. Eastern unions, too, had access to information about firms, although the strains between unions and works councils in the new federal states had considerably weakened the information resources of the unions (Hyman 1996). The private information to which these associations had access was not identical to the public information available to the state.

This difference in information resources is crucial to understanding the divergent policy mixes pursued by the state governments in eastern Germany. The states that afforded the organizations of private-interest governance a prominent role in the design of policies to cope with the lack of apprenticeship places in the east gained the benefit of the input of groups with access to private information. With excellent information about firm motives and practical problems in training, employers' associations were able to design policies that targeted the particular problems of firms that were slightly uncertain about the benefits of a training investment (the waverers). To governments without this private information, the *Verbund* looked like just one more unnecessarily experimental subsidy that was untried in the west and that promised no gains in efficiency to compensate for its increased complexity. When the Saxon-Anhalt government relegated the forums for private associational consultation to secondary status in its policy-making, it deprived itself of the benefit of this private information.

Let us now return to the claim that there are other differences between Saxony and Saxony-Anhalt that may explain why I find more cooperation in the former than the latter. Saxony was the industrial heartland of the GDR, and it was the site of early industrialization in the nineteenth century. Gary Herrigel (1996) has lucidly argued that the history of industrialization in Germany is in fact marked by the coexistence of two types of political economy, each of which developed different industrial characteristics and governance institutions. On the one hand, the area that is now Saxony-Anhalt stood in the middle of the "autarkic industrial order," characterized by large companies that organized all aspects of production within the hierarchical boundaries of the firm. Saxony, like the western state of Baden-Württemberg, was the home of a "decentralized industrial order." This second form of political economy, according to Herrigel, was dominated by the production of SMEs, and the governance institutions demanded by these firms were designed to support the active interfirm collaboration on which these regions depended for their livelihoods. It is obvious why such a political economy might have an inheritance of cooperative traditions that would make interfirm cooperation easier to initiate than the former autarkic order of Saxony-Anhalt, which had been dominated by large chemical companies during the time of the GDR.

Katharina Bluhm (1999) has produced a richly empirical study of interfirm cooperation in Saxony, in which she makes exactly this argument. Bluhm articulates a constructivist interpretation of cooperation in three economic sectors in Saxony, in which companies were able to draw on the inheritance of their common industrial history to facilitate the development of collective capacities. This common history is a helpful tool for cooperation among actors, but it is not a sufficient precondition. Bluhm's study concerns only firms in Saxony, and even within that region she rejects any model based on a controlling set of norms and values—such as social capital—that dictates the possibilities for future cooperation: "The considerable differences observed among the three sectors cannot be traced back to a different set of regional cultures in the sense of definite set of norms and values, since the regional level is [analytically] too 'thick.' Far more decisive are the differences in the micro-political constellation of actors, which have a fundamental influence on the construction and efficiency of inter-firm supportive networks" (1999, 253).[35] Bluhm's book is probably the best available empirical study of interfirm cooperation in Saxony, and she concludes that the heavy hand of history is not so heavy. This past history provides a resource for forging common identities in a rapidly restructuring economy, but it is no guarantee of success. Instead, the way that microlevel agents interact with one another appears, on her evidence, to be more important.

What the Saxon *Verbund* policy did was to promote the development of networks of actors that excluded confirmed defectors. It brought the existing cooperators from large companies together with the tentative wavering actors from SMEs. No company in my sample was convinced to invest in the general skills of apprentices by any other subsidy policy, and the participants in the *Verbünde* pointed to aspects of the policy— rather than to their common Saxon heritage—as the features that convinced them to begin training apprentices. Likewise, the personnel manager from firm EGSME16 in Saxony-Anhalt complained about the design of the policies in his state, not the lack of a cooperative industrial tissue on which to build a network of interfirm cooperation. It is true, consistent with the arguments of Herrigel and Bluhm, that there was a larger stratum of SMEs in Saxony than in Saxony-Anhalt. But, as we have seen, having too many SMEs is not necessarily a good thing for developing cooperation in human capital development. Private large firms with western German owners, which existed aplenty in Saxony-Anhalt, are a firmer foundation around which to build new cooperative networks. It may be true that a combination of the material and sociological inheritance of Saxony made it somehow easier to create cooperation there. Yet the evidence certainly suggests that the success of Saxony in apprenticeship training, like the failure of Saxony-Anhalt, is a product of current public policies more than of past industrial inheritances.

---

[35] Locke and Jacoby (1997) make a similar argument about the importance of the different functioning of micropolitical networks in apprenticeship training in the Saxon cities of Leipzig and Chemnitz.

PUBLIC POLICIES AND PRIVATE COOPERATION

Eastern German employers' associations successfully developed the same collective capacities exercised by western German associations in the apprenticeship system. There was no appreciable difference in the capacity of the organizations representing employers in Saxony and Saxony-Anhalt; both states had associations capable of promoting information exchange and collective discussion. Yet the firm-level outcomes observed in Saxony were much better than in Saxony-Anhalt. These outcomes were a product of the different sorts of subsidy policies available to waverers in the two states, and these policies were in turn a product of the distinctive way in which the two governments incorporated private associations into the policy-making process.

The Saxon *Verbund* policy worked because it was especially responsive to the problems of those SMEs that wavered on the border of cooperation. It combined a generous aid package in a phased payment plan, concentrating aid during the time when waverers needed it most—during the first year of general training, when the apprentice generates almost no returns for the firm but requires expensive machinery to be trained in all the required fields. And rather than encouraging firms to cut corners in meeting general standards, it offered them the ultra-modern training facilities of large firm partners (the *Leitbetriebe*) and the expertise of the trainers working there. These experts, who became their regular interlocutors over the three-and-one-half-year course of the apprenticeship, were committed investors in the high-skill equilibrium. The *Verbund* thus combined material advantage with a built-in mechanism for reducing analytic uncertainty. If a company were only interested in generating maximal revenue from its apprenticeship subsidies, the program would not have been especially appealing: Better to get the money yourself and have the apprentice work in your firm, where he or she can at least generate some economic return. But for a firm uncertain about its ability to produce a highly skilled apprentice, the *Verbund* was very well adapted: the apprentice was trained at good facilities and the firm did not lose money on the initial year's investment. In my limited firm sample, several companies received training subsidies—some more generous than Saxon *Verbund* aid—but only the *Verbund* aid was cited as leading eastern German firms to train, which would not have trained otherwise, at levels associated with the high-skill equilibrium in western Germany.

Policy-makers in the Saxon government did not immediately appreciate all these advantages of the new policy. Given the information available to them, it simply looked like a subsidy that covered most of the first-year training costs of companies and thus a potential target for rent-seekers. But Saxon policy-makers recognized the informational advantages possessed by employers' associations and established a model plan to test their proposed solution. Then, when the federal government failed in 1995 to announce a plan that would subsidize in-firm training of the sort Saxony wanted to encourage, the state government adopted the plan proposed by employers. The associations, having canvassed the needs of their firms, were then able to mobilize the companies they judged most likely to take part in the new subsidy plan. At both the policy-formulation and policy-implementation stages, Saxony's practice of embedded policy making gave officials greater information and greater capacity to put subsidies in place. In Saxony-Anhalt, the government's refusal to delegate a significant role to the social partners in policy development and policy implementation meant that its political leaders were blind to the advantages of the *Verbund.*

If the universe of eastern German companies were entirely composed of large firms with western German ownership, then employer coordinating capacity would be sufficient to enable these reforms to succeed. As described in chapter 2, the structural position of these large companies makes it eminently reasonable for them invest in the provision of general skills, provided other large firms will also do so. They want only assurances that they will not be alone in making this investment and that they will be able to influence the shape of skill certifications in accordance with their production needs. The nature of the training game for these companies is such that they need only this basic level of confidence in order to begin training. Functioning institutions of employer coordination—which, we have already seen, existed by 1995 in the states of eastern Germany—are the sole prerequisites for these companies to invest in high-skill training.

However, large private companies like these were a small minority in eastern Germany. SMEs were unlikely to be persuaded to begin training by the mere existence of institutions of employer coordination. The *Verbund* policy provided both the incentives for these companies to participate and the structure to convince them, during the course of the subsidy, of the continuing value of apprenticeship training.

Embedded policy-making is no panacea, and it carries its own set of risks. The worry of the state in delegating such a substantial role to private organizations is that it will be milked by the associations to provide money to firms that do not need it or that it is setting a precedent that will undermine the responsibility of companies for vocational training in the German model. There is no easy answer to this problem because the blindness of the state to different proclivities to train among firms is what requires it to seek private information from private associational actors. Over the long run, governments can benchmark against the practices of other governments, but that is a slow process. Over the short term, the state needs to construct an alliance with actors that have access to information about waverers, in order to know how to attract them to cooperate the first time, and it needs to devise ways to monitor these groups. But without the groups and their access to relational information, policies aimed at eliciting cooperation from waverers are likely to fail.

CHAPTER FIVE

French Policy Failure and the Surprising Success of the Valley of the Arve

The French reforms of vocational training, by and large, failed to convince companies to cooperate with each other in securing the provision of general skills. In this chapter, we explore why the government failed in its goal. Although the problems of the reform have been most evident at the regional level, the sheer magnitude of the failure implies that the defects of the French training reforms were not simply the fault of bumbling regional governments. The inability of employers' organizations to exercise basic coordinating capacity sabotaged regional government policies because the regions were unable to gain access to private information. However, the problem of employer coordination is not insoluble in France. We know this is true because the association of employers in the Valley of the Arve demonstrated it. Moreover, the ability of this association to design a private strategy that took advantage of national subsidies to promote decentralized cooperation provides one of the few bright spots in the otherwise grim record of human capital reform in France since 1982. How was the success of the Valley of the Arve achieved, and to what extent might those lessons be transferable to other places in France?

This chapter first describes the organizational landscape of French training, with a particular focus on how the role of employers' organizations in France differed from that of their German counterparts. Rather than focusing on the regional organizations of employers, which were clearly weak in most French regions, the second section assesses the collective capacities of employers in the strongest sector (metalworking) at their strongest organizational level—the territorial association. The evidence in this section demonstrates that even at the level of their constituent units, French employers did not generally enjoy the same level of coordinating capacity exercised by employers' associations in Germany, east and west. Yet this is not always the case. Employers in the Valley of the Arve were able to develop an unusually high level of coordinating capacity, and this anomaly had important consequences for the training practices of firms there. This chapter then shows how the weak capacity of employers undercut the ability of regional governments to make effective policy to promote company investment in general skills training. As in eastern Germany, there were regional governments that tried to incorporate private associations into the design and implementation of public policy and those that did not. Unlike in eastern Germany, there was no difference in the cooperative results achieved by the two strategies. Embedded policy-making is impossible in the absence of a viable societal interlocutor, so all French regions were forced to pursue a model of autonomous policy-making. There was, however, one French employment zone in which we do observe firms training at levels characteristic of the western German high-skill equilibrium: the Valley of the Arve. Only in the Arve did the capacity of the employers' association enable a response to skill shortage that used national subsidies to target wavering firms and incite them to invest in youth training contracts. I then consider the implications of the unique success of the Arve for the prospect of securing future cooperation in the French political economy.

EMPLOYERS AND UNIONS IN THE FRENCH TRAINING SYSTEM

Two key differences between the French and German models of employer organization were consequential for the course of training reforms. First, the political-administrative equivalent to the German *Land*—the *région*—was not a constituent organizing unit for employers in France. The training reforms of the 1980s and 1990s were constructed on the premise of delegating power to the regions, and the fact that employers and unions did not regard the region as an organizationally dominant level severely limited the ability of regional governments to rely on private-interest governance in developing policy. Second, the stakes that were centrally contested in French training policy were different; instead of fighting over the content of qualifications (as in Germany), employers and unions battled over control of the resources available to finance French training centers. Firm-based training in France takes place in private training centers instead of in state-administered schools.[1] Controlling the funding of these centers, which are financed by training taxes, was the central issue of training politics in France. This had the effect not only of fomenting discord among employers' groups, but also of further marginalizing the regional coun-

---

[1] Public vocational schools in France train only those apprentices who do not have a firm-based contract. These apprentices are publicly funded, and so their training does not raise any of the issues of employer coordination that are central to reforms based on securing decentralized cooperation.

Table 5.1 Architecture of Interest Intermediation in the French Metal Sector[a]

	Employers' Associations	Unions	Chambers
Sectoral, role in negotiating qualifications— CQ (direct) Apprenticeship (consultative)	UIMM	FTM-CGT, FGMM-CFDT, FM-FO, FM-CFTC, CFE-CGC	
Intersectoral			
Involved in training system, either through collection of funds or managing training centers	CNPF CGPME	CGT, CFDT, CGT-FO, CFTC, CGC	CCI (industry) CM (crafts)
Involved in training-related political issues	ACFCI FIM		

[a] This table includes only the major players of interest intermediation in the metal and electronics sector; it excludes some actors that may be involved in the corporatist bodies that oversee French training, but that have little impact on this particular sector. Except in the Chambers column, this list also omits organizations representing the crafts sectors.

cils, which did not participate in burden-sharing through the financing of public vocational schools for firm-based apprentices, as German federal states do.

The organizational chart of French employers' associations is similar in form to that in Germany, but the actual training functions carried out by organizations in the two countries differ substantially (see table 5.1). The sectoral employers' associations, of which the most powerful is that of the metalworking employers—(the Union des Industries Métallurgiques et Minières UIMM), had as their peak confederation the Conseil National du Patronat Français (CNPF).[2] These are the analogs, respectively, of Gesamtmetall and the BDA in Germany.[3] The UIMM

[2] This was the name of the principal peak association of French employers during the period in which the training reforms of the 1980s and 1990s were adopted, and this is how it is referred to throughout this chapter. In 1998, the CNPF changed its name to the Mouvement des Entreprises de France (MEDEF).

[3] In addition to the CNPF, which claimed to represent all firms, there was also a separate confederation of smaller firms, the Confédération Générale des Petites et Moyennes Entreprises (CGPME), which played some role in the financing of training.

comprised ninety-three territorial associations, but it had no formal regional structures. The CNPF had 120 local affiliates, over one-third of which were directly controlled by the local affiliate of the UIMM. The CNPF also had twenty-one regional affiliates, but they depended for personnel and financing on the local affiliates at the departmental level (Bunel 1995, 57–60).[4] Neither the UIMM nor the CNPF, whose organizational structure was premised on a France governed centrally from Paris, was naturally suited to serve as an interlocutor for regional governments when power over training policy was decentralized to those governments in the 1980s.

The organizational structure of French unions reflects their polarized political history. Rather than having a single peak association such as the DGB, there are three major peak union confederations in France: the Confédération Générale du Travail (CGT), the Confédération Française et Démocratique du Travail (CFDT), and the Confédération Générale du Travail–Force Ouvrère (CGT-FO).[5] Each of these union confederations has sectoral and subnational affiliates, which means that the UIMM has no single negotiating partner equivalent to the IG Metall. Instead, it has three negotiating partners, which gave the employers greater leverage to play the different federations off against one another during the course of the training reforms. Both the CGT and the FO opposed the move toward regionalization and organized on a national and departmental basis. Only the CFDT invested significant organizational resources in developing regionwide organizations, a fact that strengthened its ability to enter the regionalized debates on policy-making that followed passage of the Five-Year Law in 1993. Yet, even in its strengthened state, the position of the CFDT cannot be equated with the position of the IG Metall in Germany, which is the inevitable partner of Gesamtmetall in any negotiation.

In Germany, the principal subject of negotiation between the social partners in vocational training related to the content of occupational certifications. In France, this was not the case, partially as a result of the bifurcation of the French training system between the apprenticeship contracts and CQs. An actor that was much less present in federalist Germany dominated French apprenticeship: the national Ministry of Education. Attached to the Ministry of Education were parity boards

[4] The Rhône-Alpes region was unusual in this regard; the regional CNPF affiliate had its own buildings and personnel and thus a certain independence (Bunel 1995, 60).

[5] Two other unions that had smaller overall membership but are usually included in collective negotiations were the Confédération Française des Travailleurs Chrétiens (CFTC) and the Confédération Générale des Cadres (CGC). For a thorough analysis of the structure of French unions, see Howell (1992); for union perspectives on training, see Dubar (1995).

(commissions professionnelles consultatives, CPCs) that brought together sectoral representatives of the professional world in a consultative role only (D'Iribarne and Lemaître 1987). These groups had no
decision-making power. In Germany, the content of apprenticeship
qualifications was determined by negotiations between employers and
employees and consequently depended on debates among experts on
the qualifications for the skilled worker. The role of the professions in
French apprenticeship was far more limited (Jobert and Tallard 1995;
Int FNG6). The dominant voice in French apprenticeship is a Ministry
of Education that traditionally was more concerned with the general
education of French citizens than with their training as skilled workers.

The lack of real power accorded to the French social partners in
apprenticeship decision-making was one of the factors that led to the
development of the youth *alternance* contracts—most importantly, the
CQ—in the 1980s. In the metal and electronics sector, the definition of
the content of the qualifications awarded at the completion of qualification contract—the Certificat de qualification professionnelle de la
métallurgie (CQPM)—was dominated from start to finish by the UIMM.[6]
The CQPM qualifications were designed by companies and technical
experts associated with the UIMM, sometimes in informal consultation
with local representatives of the education ministry. There was no set
duration for the CQPM; it could last from six months to two years. In
theory, the CQPM had to be ratified by a collective agreement signed
by at least one of the representative unions, but "in practice this negotiation is not systematically understood by all the sectors as a procedure
to be realized simultaneously with the construction of the qualification.
This [delay of the approval by collective agreement] can sometimes take
up to several years" (Charraud 1995, 124). Rather than being a product
of negotiation between the experts of the unions and the employers'
association, the CQPM was the product of experts primarily associated
with the employers, which only later was presented to the unions for
ratification. As a result of the imbalance of power between employers
and unions in its definition, the CQPM was quite likely to result in a
firm-specific training qualification, without a much wider transferability
of those skills (cf. Charraud, Personnaz, and Venau 1996).

Whereas the premier political issue of German apprenticeship was
skill content, the politics of French training revolved around the ques-

[6] There are in fact three possible ways of certifying training received by means of a
CQ. Here I discuss only the method widely used in the metal and electronics branch. See
Charraud (1995) for a comparative discussion of the three approaches. In the remainder
of the chapter I use the abbreviation CQ to refer both to the general contract and to the
certification awarded at the end of this contract.

tion of training taxes and their collection.[7] Employers' organizations challenged one another for the right to control this money, uniting only to block the labor unions' attempts to acquire a voice in the use of the training funds. The total stakes involved were high: in 1993, the apprenticeship tax brought in 3.3 billion FFr from firms and the portion of the continuing training tax on enterprises earmarked for youth training brought in 5.4 billion FFr (Bertrand 1996, 11). Before the reform of 1993, French employers' associations maintained training centers eligible to collect the payroll tax for continuing training (although not the tax for apprenticeship).[8] The control of these resources represented a major bone of contention between the associations and the other employer representative involved in French training—the chambers.

Unlike those in Germany, the French chambers were not at all involved in approving firms to train apprentices or in testing apprentices to achieve their final certification.[9] Instead, their role in the training system was limited to sponsoring training centers, which played a role equivalent to that of German vocational schools. French firms belong to either the chambers of commerce and industry (CCIs) or the craft chambers.[10] There are 161 local CCIs and 22 regional chambers. The regional chambers are merely coordinating bodies for the local chambers at the regional level and have no independent power (Bunel 1995, 33–42). The peak associations of the two bodies, which lobby for their interests at the national level, are the Association des Chambres Françaises de Commerce et d'Industrie (ACFCI) and the Assemblée Permanente des Chambres de Métiers (APCM). The CCIs carried out two important functions in the apprenticeship system: they collected the apprenticeship tax from companies and they had 107 of their own apprenticeship centers. Indeed, the CCIs and the chambers of crafts were the two largest single operators of apprenticeship training centers in France during the 1990s (Huré et al. 1995, 7). The apprenticeship training centers of the CCIs drew over 40 percent of their income from

[7] No such levy exists in Germany, except in the construction industry.

[8] The tax for continuing training was raised to its current level of 1.5 percent of the gross payroll of a firm in 1993, of which 0.4 percent was earmarked exclusively for the alternating training programs for young people.

[9] This is true except in Alsace and in the Moselle department, where the chambers maintain a special status as a result of their having once been part of the German system.

[10] As in Germany, membership in the chambers is mandatory, and is financed by a tax (the *taxe professionnelle*). However, the main statutory tasks of the French CCIs are the promotion of local economic development and advising local and national governments (Bunel 1995, 34–35). There are also agricultural chambers, to which French farmers belong, but they are not an important player in the politics of French training and I do not discuss them further here.

the apprenticeship tax—which was itself collected by the CCIs (Huré et al. 1995, 62). Until the reforms following the Five-Year Law in 1993, the CCIs were also able to collect the payroll tax for youth *alternance* training while at the same time managing over four-hundred continuing training centers (ACFCI n.d.).

France is not Germany. It is not surprising that the organizations of workers and employers developed differently in the two countries or that the political conflicts that orient vocational training were different on each side of the Rhine. However, in reforming the system of vocational education and training, France tried to empower employers' associations to serve as private-interest interlocutors for governments, just as their counterparts in western Germany had done throughout the history of the Federal Republic. The reforms of 1982 and 1993 attempted to empower regional governments to coordinate training policies, with the input of employers and unions. And the historically evolved organizational plan of these groups—in which the regional organizations were either weak or nonexistent—was less than ideal for developing a regional policy. There are two analytically distinct questions that need to be addressed here. First, did French employers in the best-organized national sector, metalworking, have coordinating capacity equivalent to that of their western German counterparts at their constituent organizing level? Only after we have answered this question can we then take up the second question: Why have regional governments and employers failed to work together to develop public policy informed by private information?

THE ASSOCIATIONAL CAPACITY OF FRENCH EMPLOYERS

The UIMM is the richest, most powerful member of the CNPF, and its subnational network of territorial associations is the best-organized of any sector in France (Bunel 1995, 69); in this section I examine the capacity of these subnational associations and evaluate their coordinating capacity. Although the existing literature on the French political economy has clearly documented that national employers' associations do not have the same functional capacities as German employers, there is less work on the constitutive units of French employers' associations: the territorial associations. If collective capacity is demonstrable in any group of associations, it is most likely to be found in these units of the employers in the metalworking sector.

The analysis of company interests in chapter 2 has clear implications for the preferences of French companies about the collective capacities of their associations. In contrast to eastern Germany, French large firms were indifferent to the collective capacities of employers' associations. They did need an effective instrument for information circulation because they had no interest in coordinating their training investments. Given their dominant product market strategies of flexible Fordism, French large companies did not prefer to adopt apprenticeship-style training which involved significant firm-level investment in general skills. Their preferred strategy did not require any associational coordination, and they had no incentive to seek it. This was true in the area of professional training, but it was also true more broadly of their position in the French political economy. Given the organizational weakness of French unions, particularly at the shop-floor level, French large firms did not need to develop a countervailing collective capacity to negotiate with them (Hancké 2001, 309). Thus, we do not expect to see French large companies exerting any effort to reinforce the capacities of employers' associations.

The same cannot be said of SMEs in France. Recall from chapter 2 that French SMEs did have a potential interest in using firm-based training contracts to attract qualified workers, who otherwise preferred to work in larger firms. However, SMEs were also tempted by the prospect of free riding on the general skills investments of other SMEs and poaching workers from them. They therefore had a collective action problem and would have benefited from having collective capacity to help them solve it.[11] Voluntary associations had an incentive to prove their worth to members by providing them with selective incentives (Olson 1965). However, employers' associations were typically most responsive to their largest members, which were also the ones that contributed most to the association. Given this interest configuration among companies, we anticipate that the collective capacities of employers' associations in France should have been inversely correlated with the size of their preponderant constituency. Those dominated by large firms would have little interest in developing a capacity to fulfill collective functions such as information circulation, whereas those catering primarily to small firms would have more of an incentive to develop such collective capacity.

To assess the capacities of French associations, I use case studies of five employment zones located in three French regions: Greater Strasbourg in Alsace, Amiens and the Vimeu in Picardy, and Lyon and the Valley of the Arve in Rhône-Alpes. Two of these areas—Greater Strasbourg and the Arve—have been identified by Aniello and Le Galès (2001, 129) as areas of dynamic economies with locally constructed

[11] As Bates (1988) has shown, however, the fact that a collective capacity would be helpful does not automatically give an individual actor the incentive to provide it. The provision of this capacity creates a second-order collective action problem (cf. Ostrom 1990).

identities.[12] Constructivists would expect associational capacity and decentralized cooperation to be highest in these regions and lower elsewhere. In addition to the information gathered from the interviews in industrial firms in these areas, I draw on information from forty-one interviews with actors in French governmental and secondary associations that were active in the area of youth training. These include employers' associations and unions, education officials, and regional government officials.

As I discuss in chapter 3, the group of twenty-nine industrial firms that constitute my sample is not a random cross section of the French metalworking industries in these five employment zones. I solicited the assistance of the employers' associations in constructing my sample, and only one of these firms was not a member of the association.[13] Although the representatives of some of these firms were quite critical of the association, it is nevertheless likely that the firms in my sample were on average more satisfied with the employers' associations than firms would be in a truly random sample. Thus, this sample constitutes a crucial case with respect to French employers' coordinating capacity—if it shows up in any sample, it should show up in this one (cf. Eckstein and Gurr 1975). Conversely, a finding of very limited coordinating capacity in a sample of firms handpicked by the employers' association as interlocutors must be considered a very reliable finding for the sector and for French employers generally.[14]

---

[12] "These include localities far from Paris which have kept some cultural identity, which is likely to be reinterpreted and mobilized in favour of economic development, and regions that have not been transformed by the forces of the old industrialization" (Aniello and Le Galès 2001, 129).

[13] Contrast this with the eastern German sample, which I assembled independently of the association. In that sample, more than one-third of the firms were not members of the association, which is roughly the same proportion of firms (by total employment) in the total population of eastern German companies that do not belong to the association. I adopted this sampling strategy in light of the extreme difficulty of soliciting French firm participation without having a port of entry into the firm. Whereas in eastern Germany in 1995, an American researcher was still considered exotic, in France this was certainly not the case. I made it clear to all firms that I had no connection to the employers' association, and that no results from their individual firm would be made available in recognizable form to the association. Although the potential for bias in the sample as a result of enlisting the help of the employers' association is a drawback, it is doubtful that I could ever have assembled a sample this size in France without such aid.

[14] King, Keohane, and Verba (1994, chap. 5) make the valid point that, given the possibilities for random and measurement error, a single case can never represent a truly "clean knock-out over a theory," as Eckstein argues. Yet their argument about overestimating causal effects through selection bias support exactly the point I am making here: my results may overestimate employer coordinating capacity in France, but they are exceedingly unlikely to underestimate it.

French metal employers have both territorial and subsectoral associational memberships. For example, a firm in Lyon might belong to both the Lyon territorial association directly and also to the national federation of mechanical industries (Fédération des industries mécaniques, FIM), which itself belongs to the UIMM. In many of the firms I studied, the companies had this dual membership. Typically, firms had closer ties to the territorial associations, and issues of training, such as the designation of qualification contents for the CQPMs, fell under the responsibility of the territorial associations. In the Valley of the Arve, all the metal firms I studied produced for the bar-turning industry, to which association they belonged, as well as belonging to the territorial metal association of Upper Savoy. Representatives of these firms viewed their local subsectoral association as their primary membership, and they responded to all questions about the collective actions of employers by referring to this association rather than to the (faraway) territorial association in Annecy. This was unique behavior in my firm sample, and these responses had their origins in the functions provided by the association for member companies.[15]

Amiens, Strasbourg, Lyon, and the Vimeu
Recall the four functions of coordination that employers' associations can provide: information circulation, dialogic capacity, monitoring, and sanctioning. The western German model depends only on the associations' being able to provide members with the first two functions. Among the five French employment zones whose associations I studied in-depth, collective capacity varied dramatically. In Alsace and Amiens, the role of the association in providing collective goods was minimal, limited only to the provision of legal advice related to labor law and wage bargaining. Two further zones, Lyon and the Vimeu, had associations that were able effectively to circulate information among member companies. Only in the Valley of the Arve was there an association capable of providing dialogic capacity in addition to the capacity to circulate information.

These results appear to be due more to the size of the firms to which associations tried to appeal than to the existence of a common identity, as constructivists would expect. The Valley of the Arve was composed

---

[15] The organization of metal employers in Alsace was also slightly different from the French norm. Instead of firms' belonging directly to the metalworking employers' affiliate, these firms in Alsace paid dues directly to the Chambre Patronale des Industries du Bas-Rhin, whose membership included all industrial firms in the department. In practice, this association shared personnel extensively with the metalworking employers' group, and many local industrial elites are officials of both groups (Int FRE15).

almost entirely of small and very small firms. The Vimeu had a similar industrial structure to the Arve, overwhelmingly dominated by SMEs. Lyon had a large stratum of SMEs, but also a substantial number of large companies. Associations in Strasbourg and Amiens, however, were dominated by large companies. Of the five employment zones, the Arve, the Vimeu, and Strasbourg all appear to have had the most pronounced regional identities, yet these three had very different levels of collective capacity. It is worth underlining that Alsace was also culturally and geographically closer to Germany than any other French region, and yet this cultural inheritance had no impact on the results of interfirm cooperation documented in chapter 3.[16]

Across all five French employment zones, there was an almost universal agreement on the two basic functions played by the territorial employers' association: to update firms on the collective bargaining agreement and to inform them of legislative changes in the labor code. Most firms in my sample were quite satisfied with the expertise of legal specialists at the local affiliates or at the national office of the UIMM. Yet this focus on expertise could hamper the development of wider collective capacities. One personnel manager from a large firm in Alsace (FL6) complained that the focus on legal expertise diminished the effectiveness of the organization for members: "At the association, there is not yet enough ability to stand back and reflect. I want to go there to meet colleagues from other companies so that we can have a discussion. When I have a problem, I call the local association and I get a very limited, factual response. They are not there to provide advice, they prefer to recite the law to me." This emphasis on legal expertise and the association as a simple service provider was common to firms in all the regions I studied. This expertise was not in the realm of training but in the realm of general labor law.

Regarding the effectiveness of the associations in either diffusing information specific to training or in facilitating contacts with other

---

[16] There is a methodological warning here for those who find that the development of a constructed shared history is an important determinant of current cooperation. Self-reported identities may not correlate with self-reported behavior. A representative of a large firm in Alsace (FL3) told me sincerely of the influence of shared regional identity on the behavior of her firm: "Apprenticeship is an old practice in this company, as we are close to the Germans here." She must have meant *geographically* close to the Germans. In 1995, the company hired 117 people directly from the labor market and only one apprentice. The training practice of this firm, with a training ratio of 0.7 and a retention rate of zero, was in fact nothing like the investment practices of large German firms in the high-skill equilibrium. By using interview evidence in combination with evidence about individual company actions with respect to cooperation, I am at least able to verify whether a firm's practice was consistent with its statements.

training firms, responses differed by employment zone. In Amiens and Strasbourg, interviews with firm representatives yielded no evidence of regular information circulation related to training. Firm FSME5 in Strasbourg noted, "the association does not do much for training. We talk with other enterprises, but only on general subjects." At another firm in Strasbourg (FL9), I was told the association did "nothing at all for training. They tried to take up training issues again two years ago [i.e., just after passage of the 1993 law], but they have achieved nothing; they have not become very operational." A large firm in Amiens (FL7) observed that the association was not necessarily where a large firm would go for information exchange: "we're big, we have a lot of contacts already, the association is more important for the small companies. . . . It is important to have exchanges with my colleagues, but it does not necessarily happen through the employers' associations." A second representative of a large firm in Amiens (FL5) was more concise about the power of large companies in the association: "when one is big, rich, and powerful, one has nothing to complain about in the association." In Amiens and Strasbourg, where associations catered primarily to large companies, firm representatives did not enunciate any role for the association in serving as a locus for information sharing on training issues.

In the Vimeu and in Lyon, by way of contrast, companies were persuaded that the association played a role of information exchange. A large company in Lyon (FL4), summarizing the role of the association, drew attention to the fact that there was information circulation, but it primarily served small firms: "The association can be useful, it permits exchanges of information, and if we did not do that, we would see other companies relatively little. The only problem is that among metalworking firms in Lyon, there is a bit of a different problem for us and for the other firms. They are smaller than we are . . . there are a lot of SMEs in [this area]." The manager of a small company near Lyon (FSME13) confirmed the role of SMEs in associational life in the area: "It is true that we depend more or less on the CNPF, which doesn't give a damn about SMEs. I know the people in the UIMM well, but it is dominated by bureaucrats, almost like the government. But at the interstices of the big firms, people [from small firms] can become important." In the Vimeu, too, small firms used the association for its ability to circulate information. The summary of one firm in the Vimeu (FSME11) typifies the perception of companies there: "for training, the association has more precise information [than companies] on all that is going on in this domain, and we have access to their training center. In general, it is a place for sharing information among local companies, where we can deal with common concerns." Another firm there (FSME10) added, "if I did not go to the meetings of the employers' association, I would never meet people from other firms around here."

In both the Vimeu and Lyon, the local associations facilitated information circulation among companies, but their capacity to provoke extended discussion and develop collective strategies was limited. The secretary general of the employers' association in the Vimeu, for example, noted that associational training policies were handed down from Paris rather than emerging from discussions among local employers: "Our training centers are the actors in the politics of training, and these strategies come down from the UIMM [in Paris]; the procedure is more top-down." Although these organizations provided circuits through which information circulated, they did not develop the capacity to use that information themselves to promote interfirm discussion and problem-solving. At the regional level, where much of this discussion took place in the German context, the territorial affiliates of the UIMM readily admitted that there was no regional coordinating mechanism to promote discussion among employers (Int FRE13). In most places in France, employers possessed no collective problem-solving capacity at either the local or the regional level.

The Valley of the Arve: Dialogic Capacity and Distrust

The only employment zone in my French sample in which employers manifested the capacity to develop common strategies through joint discussions was in the bar-turning sector in the Valley of the Arve. Nestled in the mountains between Annecy and the border with Switzerland, the companies in the Arve Valley accounted for 60 percent of the total production of the French bar-turning industry, a metalworking sector consisting almost entirely of suppliers and dominated by small companies.[17] The firms in my sample from the Arve reported having a distant relationship with the territorial metalworking employers' association, located in Annecy, while maintaining much closer contacts with the professional association located in the valley. "The territorial association supplies juridical support, in case of problems: on legislation, the labor code, the collective bargaining agreements. The association has a very wide membership—the mechanical industries and everybody else is represented there. The SNDEC [Syndicat National du Décolletage, the bar-turning association] is here to defend the interests of the profession" (Int FSME20). Some interlocutors were more blunt: "we belong to the

---

[17] Bar-turning (*décolletage*) refers to the production of cylindrical components, in small or large production runs, through the use of automated lathes that perform precision operations on the revolving components. These parts are used in a wide array of industrial goods, particularly in the production of automobiles, trains, and airplanes.

SNDEC, which itself belongs to the territorial association. The territorial association does nothing for us, but the SNDEC does great things for the profession—like the content of training for the profession. . . . The SNDEC designed [new qualification] contents for bar-turning, and it pushes to update these contents" (Int FSME19). These CQs, negotiated through the SNDEC with the support of its technical center, were seen by all of the firms in my sample in the Arve as being responsive to the needs of the industry.[18] In light of the collective weaknesses of employers in other parts of France, how was the SNDEC able to achieve the information flows and dialogic capacity necessary to promote these universally acclaimed skill certificates?

The three strengths of the association were its primary orientation toward SMEs, its high level of technical competence, and its proximity to member firms. Small companies were preponderant in the Arve and in the membership of the SNDEC. In order to move closer to its members, two-thirds of which were located in the valley in the Arve, the SNDEC in 1989 moved its main office from Paris to Cluses, the center of the valley (Poleyn 1996). There it joined the technical center of the bar-turning industry, the Centre Technique de l'Industrie du Décolletage (CTDEC), which provides expertise on issues of training and research for the bar-turning industry. Representatives of these two organizations spoke of their close cooperation in very similar terms: the CTDEC provided research and training expertise, whereas the SNDEC facilitated discussion about the interests of the profession. The director of the SNDEC summarized the cooperation thus: "the CTDEC and we work hand in hand together, without stepping on each others' toes. The CTDEC never speaks in the name of the profession, and I never present myself as the technical representative. In other mechanical sectors [in France], this cooperation works perhaps less smoothly. . . . Our proximity [the two are located within a mile of one another] helps us to keep this cooperation running very smoothly. We are very close, and not just geographically" (Int FRE9). The close working relations between the association and its technical center gave it access to extremely good local information. A study of the bar-turning association by scholars from the University of Grenoble in the early 1990s found that

> the principal strength of the CTDEC is its active knowledge of the bar-
> turning milieu and especially, thanks to its research function, its
> capacity to anticipate some of the future technological orientations of
> the companies. This competence is duty bound to be put at the disposal

[18] This was true even of the one area firm in my sample that had no youth trainees at the time of interview.

of the training service [of the CTDEC], and it should be noted that of the center's 75 employees, there are 33 operational specialists involved in training, with eight full-time monitors and seven professionals who come directly from the industry. [There are] all the pedagogical elements sufficient to assure excellent training at all the necessary levels. (De Bernardy 1991, 55)

The information circulation capacity of the CTDEC, which was tied to the dialogic capacity of the SNDEC, was remarkable in the Arve, especially in light of contemporary discussions about generalized trust and cooperation and its potential links to economic development (Putnam 1993; Helliwell and Putnam 1995; Fukuyama 1995). By all accounts, the concentration of bar-turners in the valley had led to extreme interfirm suspicion (Poleyn 1996, 4). One firm interlocutor expressed the situation in the valley in these terms:

The structuring facts [of the economic life of the valley] are this competition and the similarity of the training that we all received. We are all more or less cousins in the valley. For example, I have five cousins who have their own bar-turning factories. I have visited the factories of two of these cousins, and vice versa, but I was never alone in their factories, to see whatever I wanted to see, and they were never alone in mine. The other cousins have never even entered the doors of this factory. We all have our secrets of production, and we do not let others in to see our toolmakers. . . . The exchanges at the SNDEC are very general, and always anonymous. The people at the CTDEC work under the obligation of confidentiality. The CTDEC does not pass on the secrets of the *savoir-faire* involved in specific products; they bring general knowledge to our aid. . . . Between firm managers, training is not a subject that one broaches easily with others. (Int FSME18)[19]

This description of collective wariness is more reminiscent of Banfield and Putnam discussing southern Italy than of Tocqueville in America.[20]

Given this level of distrust, the SNDEC and the CTDEC acknowledged the absolute need for confidentiality in their dealings with companies, but they worked to facilitate the necessary sharing of information:

---

[19] Upon receiving this answer, I asked the firm representative why he had agreed to talk with me—a rank outsider—about the firm's training practices. He answered, "we think that a study like yours could be useful for the profession, because of the comparison with Germany, and [anyway] we are discussing rather general themes."

[20] Indeed, using density of secondary associations as a proxy for the strength of the social capital within an employment zone, as in Putnam (1993), the Valley of the Arve was no haven of trusting choral societies. The density of secondary associations in the Arve fell in the bottom one-third of all French employment zones (INSEE 1998).

there are enterprises that do not trust us, but we try here to have a
certain code of ethics: it is the general interest of the bar-turning
industry that we are trying to defend, so we do not do things that would
privilege only a single company. If someone shares confidential
information with us, which does happen, we do not make it public. This
problem is even worse for the CTDEC than for us, because they are
involved with technology, which is central to [interfirm] competition.
But the CTDEC also shares this same code of ethics based on the
general interest of the companies. (Int FRE9)

Representatives of companies in the Arve did not, as a rule, trust one
another; but the combination of the capacity for collective discussion
(through the SNDEC) and for information circulation and diffusion
(through the CTDEC) gave them an organizational means both to circulate general information and to take positions on that basis. In the
Arve, the SNDEC indeed achieved coordinating capacity equivalent to
that of employers' organizations in western Germany.

Compared to the SNDEC, it would seem that the organizational
model of the UIMM retarded the pursuit of collective capacity by the
territorial associations. This is ironic because the UIMM prides itself on
being a federated organization that accords total autonomy to its constituent units: "UIMM has no power of coercion on the territorial associations; this principle is fundamental for the organization" (Int FNE4).
However, the organizational strategy was to rely on the national development of a coherent policy for vocational training rather than to
promote the development of diverse policies suited to local circum-
stances. Thus, the organization strongly opposed the empowerment
of the regions in vocational training policy. "For us, having different
regional policies for vocational training is not reasonable. This must be
managed at the national, sectoral level. Sectoral organizations have
information based on a wider perspective, because they have companies
with plants in several different regions" (Int FNE4). As the employer's
representative in the Vimeu noted earlier, this led to a top-down training policy rather than one defined by individual associations at the local
level.

So it was that the sectoral employers' organization in France that was
best organized at the local level espoused a nationally defined policy
rather than one based on the idiosyncratic features of local employment
zones. By way of contrast, the SNDEC moved its headquarters away from
Paris in 1989, establishing itself in close proximity to the actual companies located in the Valley of the Arve and to its technical center established there. Instead of trying to establish a top-down policy, the
organization established as its priority the development of a policy

informed by the problems of individual firms. It was able to develop a dialogic capacity because its organizational strategy made clear to companies that policy would be articulated on the basis of local problems rather than coming from the center.

The prerequisite of being able to develop this capacity was the ability to circulate information among firms, and the organization in the Arve had that capacity; but so did the associations in Lyon and in the Vimeu. Because the organization in the Arve was not committed to a top-down strategy, it was able to use its access to information to promote collective problem-solving. And that enabled its firms, almost uniquely in France, to overcome the problem of creating cooperation inherent in human capital provision.

THE EVOLUTION OF FRENCH POLICY
The regional policies spawned by the French training reforms were built on the fragile foundations of a weak private-sector coordinating capacity. The evolution of French training policy since the original decentralization reforms of 1982 was marked by progressive attempts to facilitate the development of coordinating capacity among private-sector actors at the regional level. This was a Sisyphean task. The failure of French training reforms stemmed largely from the inability of national and regional governments to find associational interlocutors with access to private information and dialogic capacity. Embedded policy-making requires not only that states cede authority to private associations, but also that those private associations possess these collective capacities. And these capacities were hard to find in France.

The principal training reforms of the 1980s and 1990s were intertwined with the goal of strengthening the political role of the regions. Yet the two policy objectives were in direct tension with one another until 1993: the two important reforms of the training system in 1984 (*alternance* contracts) and 1987 (extension of apprenticeship) undercut the ability of the regions to develop a coherent policy because these instruments lay outside the ambit of regional authority. This was the first obstacle to the regional exercise of policy-making competence in vocational training. This obstacle, however, obscured a more fundamental flaw in the reforms, which I illustrate in this section using the example of Rhône-Alpes.

Rhône-Alpes was one of the few regions to develop a serious training policy agenda during the 1980s, but the initiatives of the regional government to make policy were frustrated by the incapacity of employers' associations to provide the government with reliable information about the needs of its members. The most recent of the three major French training reforms, adopted in 1993, was designed to overcome the limitations on the regions revealed by the earlier reforms. The law explicitly ceded competence over the coordination of all youth training measures to the regional governments, and it foresaw a set of institutions whose goal was to allow regional councils to be able to involve private-sector associations in the making of policy. But that reform, like those that had preceded it, was unable to overcome the weaknesses of employers' organizations in developing policies that could convince companies to increase their uncovered investment in the general skills of their workers.

The Defferre decentralization laws of 1982–83 gave the regional governments jurisdiction over apprenticeship and professional training. They did not, however, specify the instruments that would allow the regions to exercise their control, leaving that question to the regions themselves to resolve. Although some financial resources were transferred along with this responsibility, the national government retained its control over the funding of training institutes with capacities in multiple regions, as well as the responsibility for sectoral and for targeted populations (e.g., youth) (Lichtenberger 1993, 11).[21] During the 1980s, the latter sorts of training became the most important ones for subsequent human resource development in France. Thus, regional governments watched their proportion of the total spending on training decline slightly between 1983 and 1989, even as the total public expenditure on training almost doubled during that time (Pascaud 1991, 3). French regions after 1983 did not assume any significant power over training, because the exception of state competence for targeted groups provided a large loophole through which the creation of the *alternance* contracts would be made possible.

The revolution in French training policy began under the guise of the 1984 law creating the *alternance* contracts.[22] The most important of these new measures was the CQ, because, like apprenticeship, it established a youth training contract in the workplace that also required the trainee to spend significant time in a training center. The CQ was not financed directly by the state but was instead financed through the training funds created in the wake of the 1971 continuing training law, into which

---

[21] The phrase "targeted populations" referred to specific groups that were present in all regions, which constituted an issue for legitimate state intervention under the rubric of national solidarity.

[22] Like every other piece of legislation on French continuing training since the law of 1971, the law amplified earlier contractual agreements between employers' associations and unions; in this case, the law built on the accords of September 1982 and October 1983 (D'Iribarne and Lemaître 1987, 16).

employers had to pay by law (Dubar 1995, 24).[23] The state later inter-vened with tax incentives for employers to use the CQ, and the law allowed employers to pay the youth recipients at wages below the minimum wage. But the state did not underwrite the CQ directly, as it had past employ-ment policies. The creation of the CQ quickly set up a significant rival to the apprenticeship contract that was entirely under the control of the social partners.[24] In other words, this contract was beyond the control of the national education ministry and of regional governments.

The next legislative pillar of the new structure of French in-firm train-ing was the 1987 law that enabled apprenticeship to be used in con-junction with educational diplomas up to the level bac + 2, not just the lowest level degrees (such as the CAP). The 1987 law effectively severed the link between apprenticeship and only the lowest level diplomas, giving companies the chance to use the apprenticeship formula for those entering the workforce at high levels, with up to two years of post–high school education.[25] Like the introduction of the CQ, this measure gave employers a new vehicle to invest in youth training at high skill levels. But, also like the CQ, the new measure did nothing to empower the regional governments to develop a policy for persuading employers to use these contracts.

One of the very few regions to develop an ambitious youth training policy in the wake of these reforms in the 1980s was Rhône-Alpes.[26] Following the passage of the 1987 law reforming apprenticeship, the regional council adopted a policy whose goal was to increase the overall use of in-firm training contracts, in order to provide workers with edu-cational certifications at the bac level particularly demanded by indus-try.[27] Their plan, which was adopted by the regional council in 1988,

[23] The Delors law mandated that employers contribute a fixed percentage of their payroll for the continuing training of employees; the initial payroll percentage, 0.8 percent, was raised several times, arriving in 1993 at the level of 1.5 percent. Companies with fewer than ten employees had to contribute 0.25 percent of their payroll for train-ing costs. Following the 1984 reform, part of this money was designated specifically for financing *alternance* contracts (Dubar 1995).

[24] Recall from chapter 3, that the number of new apprentices was essentially unchanged between the mid-1980s and the early 1990s, whereas during the same time the CQ grew from zero to almost as many young people per year as apprenticeship (Möbus 1996, 20).

[25] In 1990, the government passed a law extending the eligibility of apprenticeship contracts to the university engineering level (bac + 5).

[26] This discussion draws on the CEREQ's extensive study of the Rhône-Alpes policy and the four publications from collaborators in the project: Brochier et al. (1994, 1995), Margirier and Richard (1995), and Verdier (1995). I have supplemented this material with interviews in the region and documents from the regional council.

[27] "Bac level" refers to qualifications of level IV in the French system, which includes the professional degree known as the Brevet professionnel.

stated a quantitative goal (to increase the number and level of professional trainees); a general means (cooperation between sectoral employers' associations and the education authorities); and a new institutional creation to embody this cooperation, the Unités de Formation par Alternance (UFAs) (Brochier et al. 1995, 13). The idea behind the UFAs was to create centers for training apprentices in high schools, which were under the pedagogical control of the education ministry, but to delegate control of the programs to employers (Int FRG3; FRG4). The architects of the UFA program pointed explicitly to the German dual model as their inspiration, and such a model obviously required the employers to develop specific programs to meet the future skill needs of their member firms.

Unfortunately for the regional government, employers' associations could not agree on a strategy for implementing the UFA program, nor did they possess the information necessary for the government to be able to design incentives to attract new firms to apprenticeship training. The region very clearly prioritized the input of employers over that of the education authorities; the UFA program "presupposed on the part of the employers a strong capacity to be the prime mover in the building up of the regulation of alternating contracts, and it called therefore for the creation of intermediate institutions that would be sufficiently active to negotiate the recognized competencies with the education authorities and their inspection corps" (Brochier et al. 1995, 55). The industrial employers in Rhône-Alpes—which had unquestionably the best organized regional employers' organization in France (Bunel 1995, 60)—lacked the capacity to propose qualifications and negotiate them with the educational authorities. The region responded to the growing need for consultation between employers and education authorities by creating a concertation committee in 1991, but this committee only succeeded in agreeing on the mechanisms for negotiation between sectoral organizations and the educational authorities at the end of 1993, more than five years after the beginning of the UFA program (Brochier et al. 1995, 84).

In its report diagnosing the weaknesses of the UFA policy, scholars from the CEREQ blame both the region and the employers' associations for failing to spread information about the program that would have increased the involvement of private actors, underscoring "the fatal gap between the UFA program's central protagonists and the microeconomic agents whose decisions underpin the effectiveness of the policy: especially the youth and the companies tied by a labor contract, but also the decentralized actors of the educational system" (Brochier et al. 1995, 115). The internal divisions among employers meant that the central actor on which the UFA program depended was capable neither of advising the region on how best to incite more firms to participate nor of using grassroots sectoral employers' organizations to spread information about and mobilize support for the program among companies.

The problems of the UFA policy in Rhône-Alpes influenced the means by which the national government tried again in the early 1990s to strengthen the role of the regional governments in organizing youth training policy. The election of a conservative RPR/UDF coalition government in 1993 brought to national power a number of prominent advocates of reform of the system of professional training. Above all, this was true of the president of the UDF group in the national assembly, Charles Millon. Millon was also president of the regional council of Rhône-Alpes, and he had taken a leading role in the development of regional policy for professional training. The goal of Millon and the UDF in advocating a reform of the training system was to strengthen the role of the regions in managing the different training programs by clarifying and extending the initial decentralization of powers for training from 1983 (as reported in *Le Monde* 17 June 1993; Int CRRA1).[28] The reforms of 1984 and 1987 had expanded the options of firms wanting in-firm training contracts, but French employers had not been persuaded to invest large sums of money in youth training contracts. The government diagnosed this failure as one based on the uncoordinated nature of the system, and the 1993 law tried to bring coherence to the various measures that had been created, setting up the regions as the locus of coordination.

Can an Autonomous State Legislate Embedded Policy-Making?

In order to assist the regional councils in coordinating a new system of private interest governance of vocational training, the new reform law established deliberative forums in which the social partners could discuss issues of common interest in the area of youth training.[29] The

---

[28] The weakness of the regions in the area of vocational training was clearly perceived by the voting public. Nationally representative surveys of 13,500 people in France in 1990, 1992, and 1993 found that more than 80 percent of respondents said that the power of the regions over apprenticeship and professional training should be developed, a higher proportion than for any other named policy area (OIP 1990, 1992, 1993).

[29] In this section, I am fortunate to be able to draw on the French government's analyses of regional policy and the Five-Year Law. Undertaken by an independent assessment committee attached directly to the prime minister's office with the help of the CEREQ, these studies are an invaluable source of information about the capacity of employers' groups and regional policy-making in France. I use the studies by the Comité de Coordination des Programmes Régionaux d'Apprentissage et de Formation Professionnelle Continue (1996a, 1996b, 1996c, 1999), as well as the technical reports for the 1999 report prepared by Bel, Gérard-Varet, and Verdier (1999) and Casella and Freyssinet (1999).

COREF was to be the new equivalent of the German LAB, a source of private information to advise state governments on the best ways to achieve their policy goals.[30] One reason for the failure of the 1982–83 reforms that had ceded competence over youth training to the regions was the fact that the *alternance* contracts had been managed by the social partners at the national level, through the sectoral training funds they controlled. To overcome this problem, regional training-fund collectors (OPCAREGs) were established, which were to be controlled by the social partners but capable of negotiating regional training priorities with the regional government. The goal of national policy-makers was to compensate for the lack of coordinating capacity among private employers' associations by creating legally recognized institutions in which employers could negotiate with other concerned actors.

Given the weak coordinating capacities of French employers and unions, it was highly unlikely that the COREFs and the OPCAREGs could have functioned as the core of a system of private-interest governance at the regional level, even if the social partners had agreed with this goal. But, in fact, neither the COREFs nor the OPCAREGs were successful even in establishing themselves as capable interlocutors for regional governments because the private-interest organizations that were supposed to work through them instead marginalized them. Where French regional governments were successful in creating regional expertise in the 1990s, they did it by means of empowering public offices (Observatoires Régionaux de l'Emploi et de la Formation, OREFs) that collected statistics at the regional level (Comité de Coordination 1999; Bel, Gérard-Varet, and Verdier 1999). In other words, some regions succeeded in setting up regionally proficient sources for gathering public information, although they all lacked the means to get good private information. These policies were not, therefore, able to target the firms seen as the most likely to invest in high-skill training over the long term.

The law's most important intended change was the transfer of competence over the entirety of professional training for those under age twenty-six to the regions. The goal of the reform was to designate the regional government as the priority-setting center of policy-making, with much of the detailed knowledge about the direction of training to come from the private actors on the ground: employers' associations, unions,

[30] The French regions already possessed the regional social and economic council (Conseil Économique et Social Régional, CESR), which included representatives of employers, employees, and private associations and whose task was to advise regional councils on all issues of consequence to the social partners, including those related to training. But given this broader brief, the CESR was not composed of training specialists, and so it could not be the site of regional expertise that lawmakers hoped to create in the COREF.

and educational representatives. This being France, the preferred method of the law for writing down the joint objectives of concerned actors was a plan: an overall regional plan (Plan régional de développement des formations professionnelles, PRDF) supplemented by sectoral contracts (contrat d'orientation, CO). The reform designated the PRDF as the plan of the regional councils for coordinating the various training programs (apprenticeship, alternating training, and in-school vocational education) in the region, "while taking into account regional economic realities and the needs of the young people, in such a manner as to ensure their best possible chances of employment [afterward]" (Five-Year Law §52). The PRDF was to be developed by the regional council in consultation with the relevant actors, including unions, employers' associations, and the CCIs. The COs were agreements on the future skill requirements of individual sectors; the sectoral COs were to serve as the building blocks for the intersectoral PRDF, being negotiated with sectoral employers and unions (Five-Year Law §52). Through the national reform law, the government tried to establish a model of private-interest governance of in-firm training, but a private-interest governance that would function under the newly expanded umbrella of regional supervision.

The intent of the law was that the COREF would become the regional center for the discussion of projects by the representatives of employers' associations, labor unions, chambers, teachers' unions, and parents (Five-Year Law §77). In practice, the COREFs carved out no significant role in most regions: "the COREF exercises neither a real, serious function of consultation for the economic and social actors nor a role of coordinating actions between the region and the national state" (Casella and Freyssinet 1999, 26). The employers' associations and unions instead built up a previously inactive body, in which only they were represented, the Comité Paritaire Interprofessionnelle Régionale de l'Emploi (COPIRE). Although the COPIREs had existed on paper since 1969, it was only in the wake of the Five-Year Law that the CNPF and the CFDT union confederation agreed to make them active regional players (Int FNE3; FNU1; FNU2). Both organizations had an interest in strengthening the role of social partners at the regional level, and both agreed that there were too many other organizations (such as teachers' unions) represented in the COREF.[31] Regional councils apparently encouraged the move from the expansive COREFs to the COPIREs, with

---

[31] For the CNPF, the COPIRE was another way to strengthen its weak regional organizations; for the CFDT, the best organized of the unions at the regional level, using the COPIREs to make the region a more important level for social partner negotiation gave it an advantage over the FO and the CGT because neither of the other major union confederations had a strong regional organization.

their more restricted membership. A comment by the administrative director of training in Rhône-Alpes exemplifies this attitude: "for consultations with the social partners, for the PRDF and in general, I have made an effort to consult the COPIRE, which seems more legitimate than the COREF; there are only unions and employers there, and they are involved in CQs, in in-firm training, etc. The COREF is less legitimate than the COPIRE, even if it is, legally, the more appropriate interlocutor" (Int FRG3).

Did the COPIRE succeed in becoming an interlocutor capable of providing the state with private information to shape regional policy? No. In neither Picardy nor Alsace had employers' associations and unions manifested the ability to gather private information and make concrete recommendations based on their access to this information. Neither regional council went out of its way to involve the intersectoral employers' association, and in neither region did the association have sufficient capacity to force its views to be taken into account. A difficulty noted in the report by the Comité de Coordination and confirmed by regional representatives with whom I spoke in the regions was the inability of employers' organizations to deliver good information about what was going on inside their member firms. The evaluative report authored by the prime minister's Comité de Coordination makes clear the need for regional information on predicted change in overall employment needs, in light of "the weakness of sophisticated knowledge on the part of the sectoral employers' organizations. . . . A second type of knowledge needed has to do with the evolution of the crafts and the professions, and particularly on the perception of new, emerging crafts and professions. . . . From this point of view, the methods [of information acquisition] are rarely provided and poorly mastered [by employers' associations]. An additional difficulty comes from the structure of the employers' organizations and their analytical and forecasting capability" (1996b: 69). The COREFs were relegated to the sidelines as forums of regional negotiation because unions and employers' associations wanted to minimize the input of other regional interest groups on training policy. Yet the COPIREs, which the social partners had elevated as alternative forums of negotiation, foundered on the incapacity of the social partners represented there to gather information about firm preferences and use it to inform regional policy.

Because of the existence of the French training tax, employers' associations focused much of their organizational energy on controlling the proceeds of this levy through their financing organizations. One task mandated by the Five-Year Law was to reform these financing organizations so as to make them more transparent to firms, individuals, and policy-makers. Because the regions were to function as the coordinators of all youth training policies, it would have been logical to construct a regional interlocutor with some control over the funds used for *alternance* training. The CNPF and the union confederations tried to establish such a fund alongside the reformed sectoral training funds; according to the terms of their joint agreement, sectoral organizations such as the UIMM would have been required to contribute 35 percent of the funds they collected for training to the new regional funding bodies, the OPCAREGs (*Accord national interprofessionnel relatif aux modalités d' articulation entre les OPCA nationaux professionels et les OPCA interprofessionnels*, 26 July 1995). This accord was an attempted compromise between the sectoral associations, which insisted on their preeminence in apportioning training funds, and the intersectoral CNPF, which wanted to strengthen the regional organizations and thereby its own role vis-à-vis the national sectoral employers' organizations (Int FNE3; Mériaux 1999, 412). Even though the sectoral groups were still dominant in this scheme, the UIMM was not prepared to surrender a single sou of its financial resources to the regional intersectoral groups. When the accords of the social partners went to the national assembly to be put into law, the UIMM successfully lobbied lawmakers directly for an exclusion of this 35 percent contribution for itself and fifteen other sectors. As the single largest sector, the exclusion of funds collected from the metal employers greatly weakened the power of the regional fund collectors (Int FNE3; Mériaux 1999, 414).[32]

Because the financing organizations made decisions about how to allocate money for in-firm training contracts, the fact that the OPCAREGs controlled very little of the funding available to companies deprived the regional councils of a local interlocutor with which they could coordinate regional priorities for these contracts. This disparity between the regional coordination of training and centralized sectoral management of training funds rendered virtually impossible any regional coordination of the CQ (Bel, Gérard-Varet, and Verdier 1999). Furthermore, for sectors that lacked a dense network of support institutions for companies—which was the case for every sector in France except metalworking and construction—the fact that their funding was controlled by organizations in Paris increased the opacity of the system,

---

[32] According to a representative of the union confederation FO, the exclusion of the metal sector from funding converted the regional organizations into "empty shells, [that] only get the crumbs [left over from the training funds]." The money collected by the regional funds was roughly 700 million FFr, compared with a total enterprise contribution to the training funds of 5.4 billion FFr; this means that the regional funds controlled only approximately 13 percent of the total funds for in-firm training for the young (Bertrand 1996, 11; Int FNU1; FNU4).

and presumably the difficulty with which they began in-firm training (Int FRU5; FRE11).[33]

Despite the statutory changes wrought by the Five-Year Law, French regional councils still had no reliable access to private information about companies. They were unable, therefore, to target aid to those companies most likely to begin investing in general skills through youth training. As shown earlier, regional employers' groups in France did not have the capacity to bring together information from their own member companies in order to formulate independent negotiating positions for regional policy-making discussions. The sectoral plans, the COs, that were to be drawn up by regional governments and employers' organizations were recognized by the Comité de Coordination as "a relative defeat as instruments for making coherent [regional policy]," given the weakness of the employers' groups with which they were to be negotiated (1999, 21). Moreover, as in the case of the COREFs and the OPCAREGs, employers' organizations frequently spent much of their time trying to undercut one another and to minimize the role of unions in the supposedly bipartite bodies in which they both sit. The Comité de Coordination nicely summarized the problem for regional governments: "the dispersal of representative professional organizations, the internal conflicts that cut across them, and their unequal expertise at the regional level are . . . a great difficulty" (1996b, 117).

In short, every major institutional innovation born of the Five-Year Law failed to enable regional councils to coordinate training policy effectively. These shortcomings all resulted from the weak capacity of employers' associations at the regional level.

POLICY-MAKING AND INFORMATION IN THE FRENCH REGIONS
Embedded policy-making requires capable societal interlocutors. The regional governments whose training policies I explore in this section, Rhône-Alpes, Picardy, and Alsace, were differently interested in incorporating private actors into the policy-making process, but all confronted the inability of the employers' associations to deliver private information about what firms would need in the future and how to convince them to invest in youth training. Rhône-Alpes, Picardy, and Alsace all had gov-

---

[33] The government's evaluation of the Five-Year Law come to the same conclusion: "The centralization of the system of collecting funds by the [sectoral organizations] at the national level, the 'indecision' in the implementation of the OPCAREGs, and the opacities that remain about the percentage of money returned from the centralized collection to the regions are all factors that create obstacles to the control of the means of a global regional training policy by the regional councils and by the actors in the regions. Thus [the CQ] escapes the attempts to organize coherently the regional supply of training" (Comité de Coordination 1996b, 123).

ernments of the right (UDF/RPR) after the passage of the Five-Year Law,[34] yet they responded in different ways to the national political project (of the UDF) of decentralization and the expansion of in-firm training. Still, the policies they eventually adopted depended exclusively on public, rather than private, information. The information they assembled came through regional bureaucracies, from the new training observatories, or from the regional representatives of the Ministry of Education, which were responsible for the school-based vocational training track.[35] But the information was unlikely to come from employers' associations. In all three regions, policy-makers complained about the inability of employers to speak with a coherent voice about the needs of the private economy. Without access to private information, governmental scope for action was limited to domains of policy-making in which regional councils could articulate policies that did not depend on the cooperation of private-interest groups. They therefore were stymied in developing policies that could incite companies to begin investing in high-level training.

Rhône-Alpes

Of all regions in France, Rhône-Alpes was the one in which we might most expect to have found embedded policy-making. The regional president in 1993, Charles Millon, had a long-standing interest in decentralization in general and training policy in particular; the region had the most well-organized regional employers' association in France; and the government had already established a special working group for bringing together private-interest groups to deliberate over regional problems in the area of vocational training.[36] And indeed, once the Five-Year Law was passed at the national level, Rhône-Alpes was one of only two regions to assume the entire range of regional responsibilities over youth training on the first date legally possible, July 1, 1994.[37]

---

[34] Between 1992 and 1998, all three regional governments were UDF/RPR coalitions, and all three regions had a president from the UDF: Charles Millon in Rhône-Alpes, Charles Baur in Picardy, and Adrien Zeller in Alsace.

[35] Subnational education authorities in France (*rectorats*) were coextensive with the regions, although independent of the regional councils, in all but three regions (Rhône-Alpes, Provence-Alpes-Côte d'Azur, and Ile-de-France) in France.

[36] Recall from the previous section that the concertation committee was established in 1991 as part of the UFA program in Rhône-Alpes.

[37] The only other region to move as quickly to assume all legal competencies was Languedoc-Roussillon. All regions acquired the competence to organize qualifying professional training measures for those under age twenty-six (including apprenticeship and the CQ) on July 1, 1994. Regional governments then had the choice of assuming the remainder of the functions previously performed by the national government—orientation and advising of youth, prequalifying actions, and measures for the integration into working life (*insertion*)—any time before the end of 1998 (Five-Year Law §49–50).

The regional council moved swiftly to design a regional plan, the PRDF, as the governing document for its reforms of local training practices. The PRDF enacted by the large majority of the regional council in October 1995 was not even an indicative plan. Instead, it was an agenda laying out the principles that would provide coherence among the different elements of youth training in Rhône-Alpes and the means that would be used to achieve those ends (Comité de Coordination 1996c, 128–32). In recognizing the goal of coherence, the PRDF prioritized reflection about specialties of cross-sectoral relevance (e.g., salesperson and secretary) over those relevant mainly for a single sector (e.g., automobile mechanic). The principal tool foreseen by the region for "managing [the link between] employment and training in a manner oriented toward future requirements" was the elaboration of sectoral COs in consultation with the individual sectoral associations (Comité de Coordination 1996c, 129–30). In other words, the PRDF was a detailed exhortation for an integrated reflection about training at the regional level, with the details to be sorted out by the orientation contracts with sectoral employers' associations. Yet the regional bureaucracy found it was very difficult to get from employers' associations of either type the sort of prospective, regionally focused information necessary to negotiate such detailed contracts. Eventually, because the regional government could not get good information about the CQs from the employers' organizations, it had to commission the regional observatory, the OREF, to undertake a detailed study of the contracts (Bel, Gérard-Varet, and Verdier 1999, 27). Because private information was not available, the region had to use this public institution to get the best public statistics possible.

The regional council in Rhône-Alpes seized its prerogatives of training very early and encouraged a broad reflection on the goals that the newly empowered region should pursue. In the context of the French reforms, this creation of public reflection at the regional level was a significant achievement. But the region was not able to translate those goals into sectoral targets, let alone begin shaping firm-level incentives to make greater use of alternating training. This was because the regional council ultimately had to rely on its own expertise and that of the educational authorities located in the region to try to achieve its goals of increasing the use of apprenticeship contracts at levels III and IV. Between 1992 and 1997, the region indeed saw an increase of more than two-thirds in the number of apprentices in education, and most of those were at these higher educational levels, but it achieved this goal more by creating places in publicly funded schools than by convincing firms to invest heavily in firm-based apprenticeship (Bel, Gérard-Varet, and Verdier 1999, 28).[38] Given the aggregate information available to the region, this was the most logical way to proceed, but it did not persuade firms to invest in general skills. The region did not put forward any such policies, and no company in my firm sample mentioned any role for regional incentives in inciting it to train. The region's approach to stimulating apprenticeship depended on tinkering with the supply of degree programs through apprenticeship centers and, because there was no effective coordinating capacity among regional employers, the regional council lacked any mechanism for linking the growth in apprenticeship places to the supply and demand for apprenticeships in specific industries.

Picardy
As in Rhône-Alpes, the regional council in Picardy attempted to increase the number of apprenticeship contracts in the region. Faced with a dearth of private information, however, its policy shifted from an attempt to focus on measures directly targeting firms to a policy that made the market of training suppliers more transparent. It made this transition in part because the social partners were not capable of providing the private information about companies that was necessary to target firms. In 1993, the region established a policy aimed at inciting firms to hire apprentices. For companies that had not previously trained apprentices, the region offered to subsidize the wages of apprentices and in-firm tutors—those workers whose job it was to supervise the practice of apprenticeship in industrial French firms. But, as the regional director of training told me, "that policy only lasted one year, it was very taxing for the region—you really have to be committed to do something like that, it takes people on the ground [to make it work successfully]" (Int FRG2).[39] The region did not have "people on the ground" who could operate the policy because it did not work closely with employers' associations.

Confronted by the incapacity of the employers' associations, the response of the regional administration was to develop a policy that did not depend on private associations for its implementation. The primary focus of regional policy-making did not lie in the economic demands for skills (at either a company or a sectoral level) but instead on a project

---

[38] The dual system was a model for the French because, unlike the school-based system, it convinced employers to invest in general skills. This ensured that the skills were relevant to the workplace and that companies believed there would be future jobs for those with such skill sets. Increasing the population in the purely school-based vocational track had neither of these advantages.

[39] No company in my samples of metalworking firms in the Picard employment zones of Amiens and the Vimeu reported having been persuaded by this policy to train.

in which the informational resources of a bureaucracy could be effective: creating a transparent, competitive market for youth training in the region, such that youth could compare among different training providers in their given training area. The main training program in Picardy was ABC Picardy,[40] a policy put in place by the regional council for continuing training for adults. ABC Picardy, jointly funded by the region and by the state, established twelve centers across the region to serve as "one-stop shops" for all those seeking employment through training. The centers brought together representatives from public and private training providers, the unemployment office, and the chambers. With the assumption of competence for regional policy for the young, the region simply extended this model to young people, through the establishment of the Espaces Jeunes, which provided exactly the same sort of functions as the ABC Picardy centers. The orienting idea behind the approach, according to the regional director of training policy, was "to give individuals the choice, as [informed] consumers, among several training centers" (Int FRG2).

The program in Picardy unified the diverse organizations involved in counseling young people about the training choices they were making. However, this program had no link to the needs expressed by companies in the economy. If every individual who went to the ABC center wanted to be an auto mechanic, then every individual received an assessment of the skills he or she needed to acquire and a list of the training centers that offered these qualifications. There was no mention of how many jobs there were for auto mechanics or of connections to companies that might hire them in training contracts. The reason that dual-system-style training proved so politically attractive in France was its presumed downward effect on youth unemployment, closing the gap between the skills provided by the purely school-based track and those demanded by the companies that actually used the system. Rather than attacking the problem of youth training and its relation to employment, the approach of the regional government in Picardy was to try to rein in financial abuse by the training organizations (Int FRG2).

Employers and unions shared a lukewarm response to the policy, which they had not helped craft. A regional employers' representative argued that "in Picardy we have an approach centered on the individual and what he wants, and not what the firms need. . . . Where is the economic need [in this scheme]? Where are the firms?" (Int FRE11). The regional chamber similarly criticized the absence of a link between training and employment and shared with the representative of the CNPF the

---

[40] The ABC stood for "*accueil, bilan, conseil*" (welcome, assessment, advice), which is what these centers were supposed to provide.

fear that the system increasingly concentrated regional resources in the costs of administering the program rather than in training itself. "This is very unwieldy and very slow for the firms; if they want someone to do a qualification contract it takes four months to go through the [ABC consultation], by which time the firm has lost interest. . . . The new system in Picardy is not necessarily a success." On the union side, the CFDT also voiced concern about the excessive bureaucratic structure created at the regional level for the ABC Picardy program, without training being connected to a place in the working world (Int FRU3). In response to a question about how a government of the right could produce a policy opposed by every major employer group, a CNPF representative responded, "I do not understand how a Soviet-style system of training comes from a liberal majority. . . . [Because] the regional plan was conceived by technocrats but voted on by our political allies, we do not want to attack our political allies too strongly. We talk to them in the corridors, but here in Picardy, employers are insufficiently organized, so we are not always taken seriously" (Int FRE12).

Alsace
Alsace occupied a special place in the French training landscape because it maintained the legal traditions handed down from its time under German rule. The chambers were more heavily involved in vocational training in Alsace and Moselle than elsewhere in France, and even the training tax functioned differently. But this institutional heritage did not lead to a miniature dual system operating in the border region. In fact, one result of the region's special position was the dominance of craft apprenticeship. Alsace has long maintained the highest proportion of apprentices of any French region, but the traditional apprenticeships in Alsace are artisanal not industrial.[41] Thus, the relatively high proportion of youth on the apprenticeship track in Alsace (14 percent of youth vs. 9 percent nationally) should not be construed as being analogous to the state of industrial apprenticeship in Germany—relatively low-skilled, low-investment occupations such as bakers and masons swelled the ranks of apprentices in Alsace, not industrial mechanics.[42]

---

[41] The first center for industrial apprenticeship in Alsace was not built until 1988, twenty-seven years after the first industrial apprenticeship center for metalworking in Rhône-Alpes opened (Int FRE14; FRG4).

[42] This is certainly not to denigrate the quality of French bakers, whose products are very much admired by the author. It is, rather, a reference to the distinction made throughout this book between occupations in which apprenticeship training involves heavy company investment in general skills (which attract candidates of higher educational achievement) and those involving little or no net investment (which attract candidates of lower educational achievement and create few collective dilemmas).

Where the region most lagged was in the creation of apprentices at the higher levels of qualification, which was loudly demanded by local industrial employers (Int FRE15). The regional administration in charge of youth training was also responsible for education in Alsace, and it was dominated by the educational authorities, to the detriment of the social partners (Casella and Freyssinet 1999). The regional administration, for its part, admitted that employers and unions should have a role to play in sectoral planning, but "they need to demonstrate their capacities if they want to be involved; on the question of the qualification contract, for example, they need to play a much more important role than they have so far" (Int FRG1). Lacking such capacities, neither employers nor unions were included in regional policy-making for youth training, and the regional government pursued policies diametrically opposed to the goals of the social partners.[43] Rather than trying to incite firms to engage in high-skill training, they focused on creating apprenticeship places at the lowest educational level.

The experiences of these three regions were typical of regions across France in the wake of the Five-Year Law. Regional councils that attempted to take over authority for the coordination of a regional youth training policy found that the tools they had been given by the Five-Year Law did not work and that the organizations with which they were supposed to collaborate could not deliver good private information. The most important sectoral organizations, led by the UIMM, ensured that the new regional financing bodies, the OPCAREGs, would not gain access to any of the funds managed by sectoral representatives; this in turn meant that the OPCAREGs had little financial wherewithal to orchestrate regional continuing training priorities. Employers' associations successfully used the COPIREs to undercut the COREFs, but the COPIREs (which brought together unions and employers) were useless interlocutors for regional governments. Each of the mechanisms given to the regions by the Five-Year Law was premised on the functioning of effective private-sector associations, and that feature was absent at the regional level and very rare at the subregional level. As a result, even the regional councils committed to developing innovative policy in the domain of youth training were only able to develop policies that did not depend on private information.

---

[43] Two union representatives dissented from the regional plan recommending this goal, noting acerbically that the region was emphasizing "training of the CAP type. That is to say, the training that had been denounced several months previously as the track of failure and exclusion" (CRA 1993).

Table 5.2 Training in the French Employment Zones

Employment Zone	High-Skill Training Index (%)[a]	Proportion with retention > 0.67 (%)[b]	N
Arve	40	75	5
Lyon	25	25	4
Vimeu	14	50	7
Strasbourg	11	25	9
Amiens	0	0	4

[a] Refers to the proportion of companies adjudged to be training according to western German standards, as determined by the training ratio and the retention rate.

[b] Proportion of firms with at least one trainee whose retention rate was equal to or exceeded the western German average (0.68). The numbers are calculated on the basis of those firms that actually had trainees finish their training program in the previous two years; firms that do not train have no retention rate (See appendix A).

THE STRANGE CASE OF THE VALLEY OF THE ARVE

French regional policies failed to secure decentralized cooperation. Not a single company in my sample of French metalworking companies ever pointed to a regional policy as having a bearing on their decision to train. There was no regional aid program available that convinced wavering firms to risk investment in the new training system. Yet the firms in Valley of the Arve somehow succeeded in generating a widespread pattern of high-level investment in apprenticeship training, without the aid of regional policy. Table 5.2 documents this success, using the metrics for the training behavior of companies (in chap. 3) for the five French employment zones. The first column shows the proportion of companies within an employment zone that trained at quantitative levels that fall within the French target range (2.5–6.5 percent of employment) and with retention greater than or equal to the western German average. The second column compares retention rates only. By both measures, the companies in the Arve far outperformed those in the other employment zones. How was this possible?

The triumph of the Valley of the Arve depended on the ability of the local employers' association to use national subsidies to create a program targeted at waverers. Recall that the employers' association in the Arve was unique in having developed information circulation and dialogic capacities. With these capacities, the association was able to devise a program that appealed disproportionately to the waverers in the population of firms in the Arve. The 1,000 Technicians program enabled individual firms to use national subsidies to offset the risks they perceived from investing in general skills. The association targeted the analytic uncertainty of the waverers by investing in the improvement of the training center of the CTDEC, which could then serve the same function played by the large firms in the *Verbund* in Saxony of assuring SMEs that their investment in training would result in high-level skills for their workers. By convincing these companies to work together through the training center, it allowed them to exchange information with one another and with center personnel, who were more persuaded of the benefits of youth training than the general population of companies. Thus, the subsidies served to underwrite a transitional apprenticeship in cooperation for the wavering SMEs in the Arve.

In the mid-1980s the industry had faced a problem of acute labor shortage that led the CTDEC to take over the problem of training for the industry. The CTDEC undertook an extensive survey and set of discussions with firm managers to canvass their needs for youth training (Int FRE7). On the basis of this information the SNDEC and the CTDEC worked together to devise a plan that would create useful skill certifications and convince companies to use them (Int FRE7; FRE8). In 1988, after settling on the CQ as the means best suited for developing these skills, the SNDEC and CTDEC promoted an extended discussion among local companies about how exactly to design the certifications and the best way to get local companies, who were unfamiliar with the CQ, to invest in general skills through this measure (Guichonnet 1998, 244–48; Int FRE8). The association secured approval for four new CQPMs by the national commission in 1989. A further three CQPMs were approved over the course of the next three years (UIMM 1997).[44] Having created the tools for skill development, the bar-turning association announced its goal to train 1,000 technicians between 1989 and 1999, and the CTDEC became an aggressive lobbyist for more training from individual companies to meet this goal.

The adoption of these qualifications and the announced goal of producing 1,000 new technicians before the end of the century were only the first steps on the road to cooperation. Yet by the target date of June 1999, the CTDEC had surpassed its goal, training 1,022 technicians. The evidence from my sample of bar-turning companies in the Arve Valley confirms this trend toward high-level firm training practices, with firms

---

[44] In 1989, the four bar-turning CQPMs accounted for almost 10 percent of the CQPMs approved in France overall (UIMM 1997). In contrast to the top-down style of training governance noted by associations in other French regions, the detailed information about firm preferences available to the SNDEC allowed the association to dictate the number of new qualifications created for the industry, against the declared preference of the UIMM for fewer bar-turning certifications (Int FNE5).

training at high quantitative levels and afterward hiring roughly 90 percent of their trainees—both levels that far outstrip the training results achieved in the other employment zones in the French sample. The department of Upper Savoy benefited from this program by showing a substantial increase in the total number of highly skilled workers in the 1990s, whereas this proportion remained unchanged in France as a whole (Poleyn 1996).

The shortage of skilled technical workers afflicted all the French mechanical industries, not just the bar-turning sector. So how did the companies in the Arve succeed where so many other French experiments in cooperation failed? They succeeded because their association developed a strategy to target wavering firms and then used national subsidies to offset the risk perceived by these waverers in beginning to invest in youth training.[45] The prerequisite for adopting this strategy was the ability of the association and its training center (the CTDEC) to collect sensitive information about companies' training needs while assuring companies that this information would not be used in ways contrary to their interests. The capacity to design such a program was unusual for employers' groups in France, as we have seen in this chapter. Asked why there was such a success rate in the Valley of the Arve, the director of the CTDEC noted that the program had been specifically targeted at firms planning to retain their trainees, that is, at those companies most interested in using the training contracts to make serious investments in human capital: "other places in France, the big firms hire 20 young people [in a training contract], and only want to hire one [at the end of the contract]. Our firms hire one young person, and want to keep [him or her]. [And] the young people stay in the firms [that trained them]."[46]

The major source of analytic uncertainty for the waverers in the Arve was the intrinsic value of the new training contracts, particularly given their past experience with the national education system, whose vocational training they universally deplored. Having surveyed firm requirements for training, the personnel at the CTDEC knew that the level of training needed to be clearly superior to past alternatives to attract waverers. As one firm manager noted, "if we had been satisfied by the national education system, we would not have needed this 1,000

---

[45] Firms in the Arve still had to invest in training costs. According to the director of the CTDEC, they received 40,000 FFr in subsidies and they had to pay 80,000 FFr for the cost of training a single young person in a CQ. The subsidies thus halved the potential loss of having a trainee poached by another firm (Int FRE8).

[46] The association also considered alternative means to respond to waverers. It unsuccessfully lobbied the national government in the 1990s to support a measure that would allow companies to bind apprentices to the firms after their training as a way to overcome the worry of waverers that their trainees would be poached by other, nontraining firms.

Technicians program. The education ministry does not sufficiently prioritize technical education, and so it does not invest enough" (Int FSME19). However, in contrast to the employers' association in Saxony, the association of bar-turners lacked a set of committed cooperators—such as the German large firms—whose state-of-the-art training facilities could be used as the basis for building cooperative alliances among the wavering small firms of the Arve valley. Thus, the association drew up a proposal under which it would share the costs of upgrading the training equipment of the CTDEC with various governmental agencies, allowing for a total new investment of more than 13 million FFr ($1.9 million). This investment enabled the CTDEC to boost both the quality and quantity of training machinery available to it, to increase its training personnel, and to do all this in a training center that was physically close to most of the firms demanding the training (Guichonnet 1998). Having made this investment, the technical training center could then more credibly mobilize companies to begin using training contracts. It could take existing government subsidy programs and propose a clear risk reduction to companies: "you get some money to cover training, and you know our center has the capacity to produce highly skilled workers." In other words, the potential losses to cooperation were decreased (because the reputation of the association for training expertise was well established), and the potential gains were increased.

If the program in the Arve successfully convinced some waverers of the long-term benefits of training investment, we would expect to observe a decreased dependence on subsidies for later training decisions. As their trainees went through the training program, firm managers and personnel directors would have observed firsthand whether the investment in cooperation was indeed a good one. If it delivered the benefits promised, we would expect them to have increased the expected value they assigned to training and to be willing to train in the future without the transitional subsidies. Moreover, if the group polarization effect kicked in, their extended conversation with other waverers and training personnel of the CTDEC should have had an independent effect in persuading them that the investment in general skills was worthwhile.

In my sample of companies, all of the companies training in the Arve said that they would now continue training without subsidies. By contrast, in the Vimeu (the district most economically similar to the Valley of the Arve in my sample), four of the five companies training said they would train fewer trainees in the absence of subsidies.[47] One firm

[47] Subsidy dependence is measured by the response of individual companies to the question, "In the absence of subsidies, would you still train?" All French companies that trained received subsidies, so this question is the best available way of measuring subsidy

manager from the Arve, who had in the past poached from other firms rather than train himself, was surprised, once he took on trainees, to discover advantages of youth training: "Without a doubt, youth training costs more than hiring someone already trained, but it changes the atmosphere in the company, which is better than before. Previously, I would hire people from other firms, and it was difficult to change them: they had their habits, their manner of working, and change was difficult. But young people, they are brand new, you can train them the right way [from the beginning]" (Int FSME20). As in this case, subsidies helped companies in the Arve to make the decision to begin training, and their experience in cooperative training had already led them to revise upward their estimates of the returns on that investment in human capital development.

ALTERNATIVE EXPLANATIONS

The associational capacity and cooperative achievements of employers in the Valley of the Arve were exceptional in the context of the French political economy. The major claim of this chapter is that this capacity and these achievements were causally linked: employers in the Arve were able to secure decentralized cooperation because their association had the dialogic capacity necessary to design a strategy that it could use to attract waverers and then persuade them of the intrinsic merits of an investment in youth training. This strategy was only able to succeed, I argue, because the association could use generally available national subsidies to reduce the costs of the initial experiment with cooperation by wavering companies. Nowhere else in France did I observe this level of associational capacity among employers, and nowhere else in France was decentralized cooperation successfully secured. These observations, too, are causally linked. Even those regional governments that tried to develop a practice of embedded policy-making discovered that French employers' associations were not capable of using private information to promote collective discussions among their members about effective strategies to promote private investment in human capital. Embedded policy-making requires not merely that the state collaborate with social actors, but that those social actors have their own collective capacities. The failure of regional policy to secure decentralized cooperation in

---

dependence. It is possible to claim that the companies in the Arve were lying about their true dependence, but if that were so, then it would have to be proved that companies in the Arve were systematically more likely to lie than companies in other regions. In the absence of better indicators, there is absolutely no reason to assume that the Arve was populated by more liars per capita than the other regions studied.

Rhône-Alpes, where all the conditions favored the emergence of a negotiated model of policy-making, bears eloquent witness to the serious
shortcomings of the French strategy premised on using employers'
associations as relays between public policies and private societal
information.

Before discussing the wider implications of these findings, let us
consider some reasonable objections to this account of why the Arve
succeeded when no other group of companies in my sample did. One
potential alternative explanation is a straight sectoral account. According to this story, the collective capacity and strategy of employers in the
Arve were epiphenomenal. The real reason that companies in the Arve
succeeded when others failed was that companies in the bar-turning
sector simply had a more pressing need for skilled labor than anybody
else. They were willing to take the risk of investing in the general skills
of young workers because their need for them was so desperate. There
are two problems with this story. The first is that it lacks microfoundations: even if companies in the bar-turning industry did rely more heavily
on skilled workers than companies in other sectors, there was still a
problem of collective action in convincing them not to poach from each
other. Second, firms in mechanical industries throughout France noted
a pressing shortage of skilled workers. This is why employers' associations were active supporters of the general idea of policies to develop
human capital in France, even if they disagreed with the government
on some important details. There is no good reason that a shortage of
skilled workers enabled employers in the Arve to overcome their collective action problems but was unsuccessful in doing so elsewhere in
France.[48]

An explanatory alternative that takes seriously the problems of cooperation created by a reform premised on company investment in general
skills (unlike the straight sectoral account) comes from the literature on
the industrial districts. The concentration of small supplier companies
in the Arve makes it an industrial district, and many industrial districts
are better able to solve cooperative problems than were economic areas
lacking this distinctive industrial structure (cf. Benko and Lipietz 1992;
Piore and Sabel 1984). According to this alternative explanation, the
collective capacities of employers were indeed important; what was
unnecessary in my account was the strategy targeted at wavering com-

---

[48] There is nothing specific to bar-turning that explains the success of the Arve. What
may have helped employers in the area in developing the collective capacity of the SNDEC
was the homogeneity of the district (cf. Ostrom 1990). However, homogeneity cuts both
ways: the sectoral uniformity of the Arve actually exacerbated the problem of building
trust because firms were so competitive with one another.

panies. In this view, the strategy of the 1,000 Technicians program was not causally important.

This objection cannot be dismissed on the basis of faulty microfoundations, but only by an appeal to the evidence. To consider the merits of the industrial district story, we need another employment zone in France that looks like an industrial district, preferably with a concentration of companies in the bar-turning sector. Fortunately, I included such a case in my study, the Vimeu. The Vimeu is an industrial district comprising companies from several different supplier industries in Picardy. Roughly equidistant from Paris, London, and Brussels, the Vimeu had the second-largest concentration of firms in the French bar-turning industry (behind the Valley of the Arve) and an extremely high concentration of metalworking SMEs.[49] There is no better terrain in which to test the sectoral and industrial districts counterclaims than in the Vimeu. Yet, as table 5.2 shows firms in the Vimeu had a mediocre record of investing in the general skills of their workers. From my sample of seven companies in the area, only one invested in training at the levels associated with the high-skill equilibrium; these firms maintained a far lower proportion of trainees to workforce and retained a lower proportion of those trained than the companies located in the Arve Valley. One firm manager I interviewed in the Vimeu said the training center created for the skills initiative was unable to use most of its capacity due to the lack of firms in the area willing to train; as of 1998, the director of the center said it trained only about fifteen young people per year in the bar-turning certifications (Cuminal 1998, 254).

This is because, in fact, associational strategies did matter. The association in the Vimeu lacked the dialogic capacity of the SNDEC in the Arve, and so its strategy failed to target the most likely cooperators in the population. In contrast to the SNDEC and the CTDEC in the Arve Valley, the association in the Vimeu and its technical center, the Centre de Transfert de Technologie du Vimeu (C2T), took no measures to identify waverers and encourage them to begin training for the first time. Indeed, one manager in my Vimeu sample said his most recent trainee had been hired with explicit awareness of both the trainee and the C2T that the work was temporary and would not result in a work contract, which subverted the whole point of the youth training contracts (which were intended to be a bridge from education to work) (Int FSME8). This abuse was far from unique among the firms I studied in France, but the C2T's acknowledgement of the temporary nature of this firm's contract ran directly against the retention strategy pursued by the

---

[49] Roughly three-quarters of the workers in the Vimeu are employed in the metalworking industry (Lefebvre 1992).

CTDEC in the Arve. Companies seeking to use the contracts for cheap, temporary labor were very unlikely to be on the cusp of cooperation (i.e., to be waverers); they were most likely to be the firms who trained only when subsidies make it remunerative for them to do so.

This indiscriminate approach of the association in the Vimeu, trying to attract any firm to take on trainees, demonstrated its inability to target the most likely cooperators in the local population. This strategy, as we would expect, led to dissatisfaction from waverers, such as firm FSME9. "The training at the C2T is not optimal: it does not have the resources, the young people they recruit are not good ones, and perhaps the [other] firms are not ready to invest enough money to move forward [with the training initiative]." Because the association had not devised a mechanism to target waverers, many of the firms training through the C2T were clearly not convinced of the value of cooperative training— and recall that most firms in my sample from the Vimeu would have reduced their training if it had not been subsidized. Thus, one of the conduits for revising expectations that we observed in the Arve was inoperative in the Vimeu: the strategy of the local association did not ensure that wavering participants came into contact with other firm managers who were themselves waverers. The logic of group polarization was unlikely to kick in when the group of training companies included committed defectors.

We can easily dismiss any argument that the amount of subsidy support available to firms was the real cause of the divergent outcomes between the Arve and the Vimeu. The associations had access to the same firm subsidies for taking on young trainees—exactly the same amount per firm because these were national subsidies. Both associations joined public authorities to invest serious money in their refurbished training and technology transfer centers; although the overall investments in the Arve were very slightly larger ($1.9 million vs. $1.7 million), the investment per worker employed was actually substantially larger in the Vimeu than in the Arve. The association in the Vimeu certainly spent sufficient money to have succeeded, but its strategy of mobilizing firms indiscriminately undermined its objective of convincing firms to begin investing seriously in training for the first time.

Implications for the French Political Economy

What does the juxtaposition of the failed general training reforms with the success of the Arve tell us more broadly about the organization of the French political economy? First, it certainly calls into question the analysis of Bob Hancké, who claims that "the modernization of the French economy over the last two decades was not a state- or market-led process, but a firm-led one, whereby large firms used public resources and institutions on their own terms and for their own adjustment, and then induced other actors, through power, competition, and cooperation, to act in a manner which supported their trajectory" (2001, 312). The vision of the French political economy that emerges from Hancké's audacious argument is one in which large companies used regional policies to provide collective goods for their supplier firms as well as to underwrite the costs of their own modernization. The problem with this interpretation is empirical. In the most important decentralization policy—vocational training—large firms played no role in promoting the emergence of cooperation among SMEs. Indeed, success was only achieved in the Valley of the Arve because of the *absence* of large companies in the local employer milieu. French large companies are assuredly major players in the French political economy, but their primacy had negative consequences for state attempts to create cooperation. We can predict with confidence, *pace* Hancké, that the greater the involvement of large French firms in a given geographical or policy area, the less likely that firms there could overcome their own collective action problems.

Evidence from the French training reforms supports the finding of Jonah Levy (1999) that the failure of regional institutions in France was a product of weak private associations in civil society. However, Levy's analysis ultimately attributes the weakness of private associations not to the interests of employers, as I have, but to policy mistakes of the state. "France's problem is not just that the state is doing too much ... but that for primarily political reasons, the French state is doing the wrong sort of things" (Levy 1999, 292). The large firms that dominate associational politics have little or no interest in cooperating with one another or with SMEs. It is, therefore, incorrect to attribute the failures of public policy to strengthen private associations to the political mistakes of French governments. These initiatives failed primarily because large firms in France do not have an interest in developing a stronger collective capacity.

The dominance of large companies in associational politics posses a formidable barrier to the success of future reforms premised on decentralized cooperation. Merely providing regulatory support or more resources to French institutions of private-interest governance would not be sufficient to allow them to create cooperation (cf. Levy 1999, 304). One premise of the French reforms was that giving private associations a legal role similar to that they enjoy in Germany would enable them to assume the functions of private interest governance. This was a false premise: even the richest of French employers' associations had great difficulty matching the coordinating capacity of their German counterparts. If the French government is to encourage the strengthening of private associations, my analysis suggests it will either have to make it more difficult for the largest French employers to live without the fruits of employer coordination or convince small companies, who do have a potential interest in having collective goods, to develop associational capacity that can enable them to pursue their joint goals effectively.

THE LESSONS OF THE VALLEY OF THE ARVE

The evidence in this chapter has demonstrated that the dysfunctions of the French training reforms had their roots in a common cause: the organizational incapacity of employers. I have focused on the territorial affiliates of the single best organized sector in France, metalworking, and shown that most of them were incapable of enabling information circulation and problem-solving discussion, unlike their counterparts in eastern Germany.

When compared to eastern Germany, the French government faced a second weakness that also militated against the success of convincing private actors to cooperate with one another: the lack of a population of convinced cooperators (analogous to the large private firms in eastern Germany), around which alliances in cooperation could be constructed. There was no natural set of cooperators on whom the national and regional governments and the associations could depend to help pay some of the start-up costs for new cooperators. French large firms continued to view the attractions of flexible Fordism and the multiple alternatives available to them through the French educational system as adequate compensation for a workforce lacking the combination of general and firm-specific technical skills conferred by in-firm training systems. Employers' associations in France did have a compensating virtue, relative to their German counterparts—they had technical training centers that could provide the state-of-the-art machinery that would allay the uncertainty of wavering firms about the quality of training. But the training centers were at best an imperfect substitute for large companies because they were not themselves firms, making heavy investments in training to recoup the benefits in increased productivity later on. The demonstration effects they provided were those of bringing together other waverers, who could help convince one another of the benefits of training in a subsidized environment.

This strategy was used extremely successfully by the association of bar-turning companies in the Valley of the Arve. Instead of joining the fracas of groups trying to elevate themselves as the privileged interlocutor of the regional council, the group developed a policy that used existing national policy tools to support local investment in high-level training. And once member firms had adopted the 1,000 Technicians program, the CTDEC became an energetic voice to mobilize wavering firms to invest in high-level training. Contrasting this process with the results obtained in the Vimeu demonstrates that the success of the Valley of the Arve was a product of the strategy of targeting waverers. As in the Arve, the association in the Vimeu mobilized public money to underwrite investment in new machinery. But unlike the SNDEC, the association in the Vimeu used a scattershot approach that did not target waverers, so company managers were not able to persuade one another that a training investment could indeed generate a positive payoff. Whereas in the Arve, waverers training through the technical center were likely to engage in repeated discussion with other waverers, the program of the Vimeu offered no such concentration of potential cooperators. Thus, the average firm participating in the training center was as likely to interact with companies that were exploiting their trainees as cheap labor as to interact with those trying to develop a high-skill training regimen.

Given their interests, French large firms were not likely to invest heavily in general skills training through apprenticeship. Many French SMEs, however, faced increasing pressure to improve their supply of skilled labor in order to stay competitive in international markets; some of them could be persuaded to invest in high-skill training. These firms, on the cusp of cooperation, were those most likely to respond favorably to the French government's plea to increase the importance of in-firm technical training. To begin cooperating, however, these companies sought reassurances that this uncertain new method of skill provision could indeed deliver high returns. Although national and regional governments in France had designed a variety of subsidy programs to lure firms into training, the famously interventionist French state found itself without access to the private information about companies that would allow it to tailor subsidies closely to the concerns of the companies that were indeed most likely to train. Companies would only exchange this information with a reliable interlocutor, and few employers' associations in France fit that description. Moreover, without the coordinating capacity necessary to assemble information about firm needs and set negotiating priorities on this basis, even the SMEs in France that might have been interested in training initiatives had no reliable associational mechanism through which to develop broad qualifications in which companies could invest.

For French policy-makers, the success of the Arve does not yield lessons that will be easy to extend other areas. They could infer from these findings that firms need more that just enticements (subsidies and tax relief) to invest in the provision of general skills; these enticements have been the primary element of French policy thus far. The problem is not one of merely getting the incentive structure right for firms to invest, but one of convincing them to make a coordinated move toward a high-skill equilibrium. Recycling past legislative attempts to develop associational coordinating capacity would not likely succeed in facilitating this coordinated move. Instead, the most promising route to the creation of cooperation may instead be to encourage a diversity of experimental alliances among SMEs, which do perceive potential gains from cooperation with each other. Promoting experimental efforts like the 1000 Technicians program, rather than trying to reinforce the power of existing associational actors, is the most likely way for the French state to acquire the information it requires about how best to elicit decentralized cooperation among companies.

CHAPTER SIX

Private Puzzling and Public Policy

Governments in France and Germany took on a challenge for which the tools of past policy-making proved inadequate. The goal of creating cooperation among companies did not prove amenable to solution through either the raw exercise of state punitive power or the lavish but indiscriminate use of state spending. Financial sanctions were adopted in France and periodically threatened in Germany, but neither the existence nor the threat of a training tax compelled companies to coordinate around a high-skill equilibrium. Likewise, the numerous subsidies to which French and eastern German companies had easy access led largely to the development of low-cost training schemes that were profitable for those companies in the short term, but that failed to convince them to invest in the general skills of their workers. And that, after all, was the whole point of the training reforms.

What these governments discovered is that the policies premised on securing decentralized cooperation posed problems that they were ill-equipped to solve. These policy problems shared three core characteristics: strategic interaction, multiple equilibria, and analytic uncertainty. First, the policies aimed to influence the strategic interaction of actors with potentially competing interests. In itself, this characteristic is not overly restrictive—many types of traditional regulation, such as antitrust or competition policies, explicitly target private interaction and limit the negative consequences generated by such interaction. But what the strategic element underlines is that individuals make choices dependent on the choices of other individuals, whereas a traditional policy for improving skills requires no strategic interaction. Consider, for example, one of the most successful educational policies in U.S. history, the GI Bill. This initiative dramatically lowered the costs for members of the armed services of attending institutions of higher education, and it consequently resulted in a massive increase in the levels of educational certification. But the GI Bill, as a public policy, acted purely at the individual level—the decision of one GI to take advantage of the program to attend college was completely independent of the choice of any other soldier to attend school. Not so in a problem of decentralized cooperation. The French and German training reforms depended not on the choice of any one company to invest in apprenticeship, but on convincing a number of firms to invest more or less simultaneously in such training.

The element of strategic interaction underlines the second, related characteristic of problems of decentralized cooperation, coordinating behavior around one of several competing plausible alternatives. The problem of coordination arises when there are what game theorists call multiple equilibria; in other words, in situations in which there are several jointly preferred possible outcomes around which actors can coordinate their behavior. A large and a small company may both prefer the adoption of some standard for skill certification, so that they can better assess the skill set of potential employees when hiring them. Yet the large company prefers the standards defined by an association for large companies, whereas the small company prefers the standards set by a consortium of small employers. Each kind of company prefers the standards set by the other association over having no standard at all, but each would rather have its own standards than those of the other guys. Depending on the strategies used, such a situation can result in the adoption of no standard, with the result that every company is then worse off. This sort of situation is widespread in strategic situations. "To achieve cooperation in a moderately complicated repeated game . . . it is necessary to make sure that all players arrive at the same expectations about which of many available equilibria they will adhere to. Nearly any interesting problem with multiple equilibria is a coordination problem" (Calvert 1995, 243). One problem frequently posed by having a number of outcomes that are mutually preferable to other outcomes, as in the standard-setting example, is that they introduce distributive conflict (Scharpf 1997).

Such problems of coordination are further exacerbated by a third characteristic, the uncertainty generated by reforms premised on securing coordinated behavior. In the case of standard setting, companies are at least able to predict with a high level of confidence what they gain from adopting each sort of certification system. As we have seen in the experiences of managers in eastern Germany and France, it is often very difficult for actors to estimate with any certainty what they stand to gain if a cooperative move is in fact met by cooperation. The gains to apprenticeship training were not clearly apparent to some of the firms in my sample until, with the help of subsidies, they began investing in such training and retaining their young trainees as employees. When cognitive unfamiliarity with an issue area is high, bounded rationality is likely to limit the predictive power of individual actors. When, in contrast, results are easily predictable, there is no issue of analytic uncertainty. Redistributive tax policies, for example, involve neither strategic interaction nor analytic uncertainty: we have a pretty good idea what we will gain or lose from a change in the marginal tax rate, and our gain or loss is independent of what others do. Nuclear politics is clearly strategic, but there is not much analytic uncertainty. If an opponent launches its entire nuclear arsenal as a result of a perceived defection, the results will be predictably catastrophic. Decentralized cooperation combines a strategic element with a degree of analytic uncertainty about the nature of the new payoffs to cooperation.

THE ADVANTAGES OF EMBEDDED POLICY-MAKING

Analytic uncertainty constitutes a core characteristic of the politics of decentralized cooperation, and it is in situations characterized by such uncertainty that the framework I have developed should be applicable to reforms other than those of French and German human capital policies. As I argue in chapter 1, the elegant theoretical solution of sanctions lacks credibility when the sanctioning regime is part of the new institution that a government is attempting to establish. And the clear empirical prediction that emerges from this framework, in a case of decentralized cooperation, is that sanctions are unsuccessful in extracting cooperation from private actors because they are not credible. This creates the need for some other mechanism to persuade actors of the benefits of cooperation, and it increases the value of reliable information circulation (Calvert 1995; Ostrom, Gardner, and Walker 1994). In the realm of the political economy, we can expect that the best candidate capable of playing this intermediary role is an employers' association or a union.[1]

The information to which a private association must have access is of two sorts: technical and relational. The advantage of private-interest groups in gathering technical information is not new. Studies of the U.S. policy process have long underlined the informational strengths of interest groups, which can be the routine patrollers of agency implementation that Congress cannot (McCubbins and Schwartz 1984). Likewise, those who have written about the advantages of corporatist governance have underlined the importance of the ability of groups to exercise such competence in assuming a role in policy implementation (Schmitter and Lehmbruch 1979; Visser and Hemerijck 1997). This technical expertise is indeed a prerequisite to successful group action in promoting decentralized cooperation, but it is subordinate in importance to relational information.

---

[1] In human capital policies, the problems of employer coordination are paramount, and for this reason this book focuses on the coordinating capacity of employers' associations. Unions play a less central role in this policy area, although this varies somewhat depending on national contexts; the strength of unions was quite important in imposing constraints on employer strategies in Germany, but was much less so in France.

Relational information concerns the cooperative propensities of actors: Where do actors stand in relation to other potential cooperators in the population on the question of whether to cooperate? Associations need to have access to this information in order to target the most likely cooperators in the population in their efforts to mobilize and persuade them. The combination of technical and relational expertise allows these organizations to assist governments in designing aid that appeals disproportionately to the most likely cooperators in the population, the waverers. And convincing the waverers is the heart of the problem of decentralized cooperation.

This argument pivots on the claim that private associations are much more likely to have access to relational information than are state policy-makers. This is a claim made frequently by those who study economic policy-making in all sorts of states—advanced industrial, developing, and postsocialist (Evans 1995; Sabel 1995; Stark and Bruszt 1998). For these scholars, it is evident that companies are continually responding to rapid changes in the world economy and that states simply lack the ability to stay abreast of this constant evolution unless they are somehow embedded in private informational networks. For those brought up on a diet rich in Weberian logic, however, this claim might seem question-able.[2] They could perhaps point to Herbert Kaufman's (1960) classic study of the forest ranger as a demonstration of the ability of govern-ments to draw information up from society through an extremely decentralized network of agents in the field.[3] Kaufman shows how, against the odds, the U.S. Forest Service seemed able to use a set of pro-cedural, monitoring, and selection devices to keep rangers in the field as loyal agents of the policies developed in faraway Washington. The rangers had to negotiate timber contracts with private interests and maintain the physical integrity of forests from fire threats, all the while managing a recreational resource visited annually by thousands of people. And yet, according to Kaufman, these agents managed to combine the sort of private information necessary to negotiate compe-tently while developing the local information necessary to identify the threats of fire or disease to their forests. Kaufman might well ask why a Decentralized Cooperation Service analogous to the Forest Service could not discharge these functions as well as, or better than, private associations.

---

[2] Yet even the most ardent advocates of "bringing the state back in" to social science have acknowledged, quite correctly, that "states are likely to have only partial or incom-plete knowledge at their disposal" and that the access of states to social information is therefore a question of central analytical interest (Evans et al. 1985, 358).

[3] I am indebted to Robert Putnam for suggesting this example.

The answer is simple—relational information is harder for state agents to acquire than is information about appropriate timber prices. State agents are inextricably tied to an apparatus that can supply private actors with bountiful rents, but which can also use its coercive power against them in ways that are extremely costly. These private actors will preface their answers to questions about cooperative thresholds with another question: Who wants to know? If it is the resource-rich state, which will use information to determine the allocation of subsidies, then everyone has an incentive to act like a waverer. However, if the question is posed by a representative association trying to develop a collective strategy to respond to the interests of its members, then the answer is more likely to fall close to the truth. But even this way of stating the difference between the state and associations obscures the fact that this is not a one-time question but is one asked as part of a sustained pattern of interaction. Private associations in the economy are engaged in frequent interaction with their members, and they have better information about their members simply due to the frequency of exchanging information with them. The state's agents are always external to this process because they possess a different resource base and a different potential threat to the private actors. The state is always in a hierarchical relationship to society, and this creates a distance that limits its access to private information of all sorts.

There is a second role for associations in this process, one that goes beyond (but presupposes) information circulation: dialogic capacity. Dialogic capacity is the ability of an association to use the exchange of private information among its members to design commonly agreed-on strategies to promote cooperation. This is a process of discussion, understood as collective problem-solving. The iterated exchange of ideas, brainstorming, convinces actors to think of solutions that had not previously occurred to them. The possibility of such a powerful tool for problem-solving is acknowledged both by rational-choice theorists and theorists of deliberative politics (Fearon 1998, 52; Mansbridge 1992, 42). This function is useful to associations because it allows them to adopt collective strategies aimed at overcoming the analytic uncertainty that prevents their members from engaging in Pareto-improving cooperation. Associations that possess this capacity can develop the best strategies for overcoming uncertainty among waverers. Only they know who the waverers are, and only they have the capacity to design a strategy that will disproportionately attract waverers and entice them to interact with one another and with existing cooperators.

Associations, or their functional equivalent, seem to be a necessary condition for securing decentralized cooperation. Yet the cost of creating cooperation de novo means that private organizations will have difficulty financing cooperative experiments on their own. The literature on private-interest governance is motivated by the twin claims of greater efficiency and greater democratic legitimacy when groups self-regulate (Streeck and Schmitter 1985; Ayres and Braithwaite 1992). I share with this literature a strong claim about the informational advantages of groups vis-à-vis state regulators for detailed policy-making. Where I diverge from it, however, is in drawing attention to features of policy design that specifically target waverers in the population and in the implicit assumption that the resources necessary to get cooperation started, where it has not previously existed, require that the state not disengage entirely from the process.

Government is in fact indispensable to the process of securing decentralized cooperation: it sets broad goals, limits organizational rent-seeking, and subsidizes experimental programs for convincing waverers. In almost all such cases, the most effective way for the state to intervene is to pay some of the start-up costs of waverers (cf. Marwell and Oliver 1993, 86–88). Through policy-making that is embedded in private networks, the state can gain the information necessary to design a policy to attract waverers, not those actors who are unlikely to be convinced of the long-term merits of cooperation. Only if the state can design policies that attract a large enough proportion of waverers and allow them to convince one another of the benefits to cooperation, will the behavior eventually spread through the population; otherwise it will fizzle. And only states that design policy using insights available through private information—whether gleaned through collaboration with private associations or through some functional equivalent thereof—will be able to target policies to attract waverers. Policy-making must be embedded, therefore, in networks of private information (Stark and Bruszt 1998). State policy uninformed by private information will target only the characteristics the state can easily measure, and these efforts will not be effective at attracting waverers disproportionately. They are overwhelmingly likely to fail in securing decentralized cooperation.

LEARNING AND UNCERTAINTY IN RATIONALIST ANALYSIS
The prediction of failure in cooperative endeavors is a common one in rationalist analyses of politics.[4] Faced with a situation in which they have no existing institutions to establish credible commitments, actors will find it difficult to cooperate with one another. Elinor Ostrom's research on common-pool resource (CPR) dilemmas has shown that actors can succeed in creating institutions to limit free-riding, under some condi-

----

[4] See Olson (1965), Hardin (1968), and North (1990) for classic statements of collective problems.

tions. However, the conditions that facilitate solutions to these CPR dilemmas differ from those characteristic of the politics of decentralized cooperation. Most notably, Ostrom argues that actors in a CPR dilemma are more likely to succeed when they share the view that they will be harmed if they do not develop a mechanism to promote cooperation (Ostrom 1990, 211). Ostrom's actors generate their own solutions, especially when not doing so would lead to a catastrophic outcome. This is the catalyst that gets them over the status quo bias. The prospect of irretrievably losing a precious resource, like the prospect of a hanging, concentrates the mind wonderfully. In situations of decentralized cooperation, however, failure usually *is* an option. It is possible to imagine muddling through with current conditions, even though general welfare would improve if decentralized cooperation could be secured.

The difference in this strategic situation alters the credibility of a sanctioning mechanism, which is the preferred rationalist tool for ensuring the credibility of commitments. Ostrom's actors, faced with the possible exhaustion of a CPR, develop institutional solutions that depend for their success on the existence of graduated sanctioning mechanisms (Ostrom 1998, 8). If they have commonly acknowledged the problem and been involved in the design of these sanctions, they are likely to find the sanctions more credible than those developed in the wake of a state reform exhorting them to cooperate with one another, even though they have never done that before. In reforms premised on securing decentralized cooperation, by contrast, private actors are uncertain about how others will act, uncertain about the payoffs to cooperation even if it is requited, and they are skeptical that either the state or private associations will be able to develop enforcement mechanisms in this climate of uncertainty. Paradoxically, even though the state is usually the enforcer of last resort, the fact that the new societal equilibrium is a goal set by the state renders the possibility of effective sanctioning even more implausible because the capacity to sanction requires a detailed understanding of the policy area in question (which, we have seen, the state does not generally have). In the fisheries and forests studied by Ostrom, actors who themselves had local knowledge and exploited the CPR set the rules, and these rules might consequently have more credibility. But in the situations studied in this book, sanctions did not work because they were neither credible nor ipso facto effective.

The blanket rationalist prediction, given these preconditions, is that such a reform will fail to promote cooperation. And indeed, as demonstrated in chapter 3, the majority of companies that were subsidized to train apprentices in both economies did not appear to be making the heavy investment in general skills that is the most enviable quality of the western German apprenticeship system. These states were pouring millions of dollars per year into subsidies that were, in the main, failing to elicit cooperation among firms. This was particularly true in France, where very large firms were eligible for training subsidies despite the fact that their preference orderings made it extremely unlikely that they would ever be convinced of the merits of investing in transferable skills. They were content to let the state provide transferable skills through the system of general education and then to provide firm-specific training to employees as necessary.

And yet, despite the pessimistic expectations of the orthodox rationalist, cooperation can be catalyzed even under these unpropitious conditions. In the one area where we observed success in France—the Valley of the Arve—an employers' organization used state subsidies to promote company investment in the general skills of workers. This was an area (see chap. 5), where intercompany distrust was endemic, and stocks of social capital should have been low (cf. Putnam 1993; Fukuyama 1995). In the Valley of the Arve, employers first did exactly what Ostrom would expect them to do: they asked the state to provide some sort of sanctioning capacity because the association was unable to play this function on its own. The state was unable to create an effective sanctioning mechanism to prevent poaching among companies in the Arve, yet the association managed to frustrate the grim predictions of game theorists by convincing wavering companies to experiment with high-skill training. These companies, brought together in repeated interaction through the courses of their trainees, persuaded one another of the wisdom of the training system even as they gained confidence in the ability of the system to deliver workers of high qualification levels.

How was this possible? One answer offered by constructivist critics of rational choice is that interests are far more changeable than rationalists believe. Charles Sabel has argued compellingly in this vein, asserting that the very process of talking to one another can "transform the actors' understanding of one another in relation to the commonly defined world in which their interests are rooted" (Sabel 1994, 155). The very process of talking about how to solve the problem of skill provision may, in this view, lead company managers to establish the fragile foundations of trust necessary to make such a seemingly irrational investment. If this is correct, its implications are radical: "cooperation can arise from situations where interests were not aligned, and alignment [of interests] by itself does not secure continuing cooperation" (Sabel 1994, 159). This view of deliberation as transformative of interests asserts that cooperation can emerge anywhere, anytime, if the process of deliberation can be provoked.

This is a tempting view for policy-makers facing a Palermo-like vicious circle of mutual defection. Yet it is probably wrong. The evidence in this book suggests that no amount of processual discussion, or "learning by monitoring," could have convinced large firms in France that their interest lay in cooperating with one another. French large firms were able to turn public policies aimed at the collective good into subsidies benefiting them only. They acted this way—eminently rationally—in response to human capital policies, but also in response to industrial policies promoting the development of research and development or clusters for promoting innovation (Hancké 2001; Aniello and LeGalès 2001). It is certainly possible that large firms acted this way because the French state failed to create discussions among large firms in a given area. However, it seems more likely that French large firms had few stakes in cooperating with one another and that French policy was relatively unsuccessful in changing their minds.

Yet those views grounded in communicative discourse are asking the right question, even if they may have the wrong answer. What is going on cognitively with actors facing the problem of cooperation when the institutions that normally stabilize commitments are either not yet established or are changing? Rationalist scholars of institutional change are well aware that game theory is stumped by this challenge. "The really big puzzle in the social sciences is the development of a consistent theory to explain why cooperation levels vary so much. . . . A coherent theory of institutional change is not within reach, however, with a theory of individual choice that predicts no innovation will occur. We need a second-generation theory of boundedly rational, innovative, and normative behavior" (Ostrom 1998, 9; cf. Bicchieri 1993). In other words, to understand why some actors cooperate and some do not, "the analytic framework we must build must originate in an understanding of how human learning takes place" (North 1995, 347). Recent rationalist analysis has attempted to be particularly attentive to the way that individuals learn norms, particularly norms of reciprocity (Ostrom 1998, 10–12; Bicchieri 1993, 221–55).

Although the focus on how norms emerge is an important part of explaining the creation of cooperation, there are other sorts of cognitive problems that merit attention from political scientists. In this book I suggest that the problem of analytic uncertainty, in which actors are uncertain of the value of a requited cooperative move, is a significant barrier to the creation of cooperation. In Chapters 3–5, we saw that uncertainty about the payoffs of an investment in general skills prevented wavering SMEs from engaging in cooperation. Although the strategic uncertainty presented by poaching was perceived by firms in both countries, there was a simultaneous problem of uncertainty that an investment in general skills could be worth its certain costs. Employers' associations were powerless to prevent poaching, but they were able to design policies aimed at reducing the analytic uncertainty of small companies.

Employers in some areas used public policy to overcome these difficulties, whereas others did not. In eastern Germany, for example, the two states of Saxony and Saxony-Anhalt adopted very different models of policy-making. The Saxon state government attempted to incorporate associational actors deeply into its process of policy-making and therefore had access to associational proposals about the best ways to attract wavering small firms. The government in Saxony-Anhalt largely excluded private interests from the policy-making process and developed policies through its own administrative apparatus. As a result of this difference, the Saxon state government adopted a policy program that was more effective than any other eastern German subsidy policy in convincing companies to mimic the training behavior of western German companies. In Saxony-Anhalt, where policies were designed only in light of the government's informational resources, state policies were unsuccessful in securing decentralized cooperation among companies.

The Saxon *Verbund* policy concentrated groups of wavering firms together in a training alliance, often using a large firm committed to high-skill training as the central node of the alliance. The *Verbund* targeted the particular concerns of waverers: the high costs of training in the first year and the quality of the general training received during this year. And, in the process of doing so, it brought waverers together with one another and with one or more committed cooperators, the model firms hosting the *Verbund*. Over the three-year life of an apprenticeship contract, these actors talked about the practice of training and, in the process, often persuaded one another of the value of the training investment that each had made. In this small group, the choice to cooperate came to seem not an implausibly high risk but a reasonable investment in the long-term skill prospects of the company. Interfirm discussion and experience with the infrastructural institutions of the training system allowed these companies to overcome their status quo bias and their analytic uncertainty about the value of cooperation.

Part of the process may have involved learning norms, but, in fact, much of it involved learning about the world. It is well established that credible information is of crucial importance in resolving problems of social cooperation and coordination because this information allows actors better to understand the costs of not coming to an agreement.[5]

---

[5] One of the ingredients of success in the California groundwater basins studied by Ostrom was the dissemination of technical information about the consequences of different patterns of exploitation of the common resource. "The practice of obtaining the best information available and diffusing it widely increased the degree of understanding and level of cooperation among participants" (1990, 116).

In situations characterized by analytic uncertainty, benefits, too, can be uncertain to individual actors. I have argued that states can best catalyze cooperation when they establish groups in which actors are temporarily insured against the possibilities of loss.[6] Participation in a group such as the Saxon *Verbund* appears to affect the way individual actors understand causal processes at work in the world. During this interval of state-supported interaction, groups deliberately constituted from those most likely to be persuaded in the value of cooperation (the waverers) have time to convince one another of the individual benefits to a cooperative move. This is the process of group polarization (Isenberg 1986; Sunstein et al. 1998). At the same time that they are persuading one another, these actors are gaining real empirical experience of how cooperation can be worthwhile. The balance between empirical updating and the persuasive effects of group polarization are difficult to disentangle empirically, but both appear to be important.

That actors learn about causal relationships in the world conforms to our real-world experiences. Yet many rationalists will be unhappy with the sacrifice of parsimony entailed in the assumption that sometimes the payoffs to requited cooperation are not clear to actors themselves. This approach has shown some promise in explaining how, during a chaotic process of institutional change, states try to influence private interaction by promoting the learning of actors about cooperative payoffs. These propositions need to be refined and tested beyond the natural experiment of human capital reform in France and Germany. Game theorists have acknowledged that, in fact, cheap talk unenforced by sanctions can promote the emergence of social cooperation (Calvert 1995; Ostrom 1998). There may be an analogy here to the ability to change individual beliefs about causal processes in the world as another way in which cooperation can be promoted in the absence of credible sanctions. If these findings about the problem of analytic uncertainty are confirmed in other studies, this opens up a further avenue for exploration of how strategic and cognitive considerations interact in different sorts of cooperative dilemmas.

THE SHIFTING BALANCE OF STATE-SOCIETY RELATIONS

These theoretical questions have important implications for state policy-makers. In order to convince actors to break out of noncooperative

---

[6] There is an interesting parallel in these findings to evolutionary accounts that predict that cooperation begins in small groups and then spreads to the larger population (Axelrod 1984; Bicchieri 1993). However, both the character of learning and the mechanism of diffusion are quite different. Rather than learning norms, the explanatory framework of chapter 2 concentrates on learning about the world; and rather than diffusing through evolutionary mechanisms, cooperation diffuses through threshold effects (Granovetter 1978; Lohmann 1994).

social traps, states may want to underwrite the learning of waverers about the world. Yet their ability to identify waverers and their resultant capacity to design strategies likely to appeal disproportionately to them are limited. States need to develop access to social information that they are poorly equipped to find out on their own. Policy-making, in other words, needs to be embedded in social networks.

The two most influential conceptions of policy-making in political science—command-and-control regulation and neocorporatist exchange—are both wrong-footed by the challenges of decentralized cooperation. Traditional command-and-control regulation involves setting up the incentives and deterrents to push firms or individuals toward choosing behavior more consistent with the public interest or away from the production of negative externalities (Stokey and Zeckhauser 1978; Glazer and Rothenberg 2001). This view assumes that the consequences of a given choice are known to actors, that they regard the new incentives as credible (or that they can probabilistically determine the likelihood of being sanctioned), and that their calculus vis-à-vis these consequences is independent of what other private actors decide to do. These conditions do not hold in a reform such as that of vocational training, in which the calculus of individual returns depends on the decisions of other firms.

In a reform in which a government changes incentives and encourages private actors to follow new patterns of behavior, neither the government nor any individual actor knows how other actors will respond collectively. For instance, a core feature of the third-way policies proposed by governments of the left across Europe during the 1990s was their desire to create an active labor market policy. Rather than using incentives such as early retirement to subsidize individuals who withdrew from the labor market, these policies delegated the power for local implementation to tripartite bodies (rather than state agencies), which could tailor policies that responded to the conditions that applied specifically to local employers (Auer 2000). But how local employers respond will depend on the perceived effectiveness of the new local institutions, the success of the measures in attracting motivated individuals, and how they see other employers using the system.[7] It is not merely the level of the incentives set, but also the interaction of the different participants, that influences how individual actors respond to this sort of policy change.

---

[7] Given these problems of coordination, it is not surprising that large-N studies consistently find that the level of spending on active labor market policies is associated with the organizational capacities of employers (Hicks and Kenworthy 1998; Swank and Martin 2001).

Neocorporatist analysis underlines the necessity for the state to work together with social actors in order to implement policy. Even before the explosive growth of this literature in the 1970s, scholars of European politics had observed that "the increased range and subtlety of the public and private sectors have made it less feasible to govern by decree. The system will not function unless private organizations give their willing collaboration to the pursuit of public purposes" (Shonfield 1965, 389). Formalizing these terms through grants of power to monopolistic, functionally represented groups was the base of the neocorporatist compromise and still resonates today in the coordinated market economies that depend on social actors to achieve meaningful reforms of their welfare states (Visser and Hemerijck 1997). Yet reforms in many policy areas in both liberal and coordinated market economies require that social actors not merely to accept a role in implementing the goals of the government, but coordinate their actions with one another.

In essence, the logic of neocorporatism is one of exchange, whereas the logic of embedded policy-making is one of problem-solving. The neocorporatist compromise assumes that the problem of achieving policy goals is primarily to get collective actors to acquiesce to them, in exchange for some sort of benefits. This is essentially an elite-based model in which the leadership of unions demobilizes their members in exchange for benefits that insulate their peak organization from competition with other organizations (Baccaro 2002). In sectors undergoing restructuring, such as agriculture, a state engages in sectoral corporatist trade-offs with a dominant union to limit the scale of socially destabilizing protests (Keeler 1987). Thus, although the state trades some of its exclusive decision-making authority to private organizations in the neocorporatist compromise, it does so on the presumption that the organizations deliver the acquiescence of their members to a policy crafted by the state.

The capacity to demobilize opposition is a different order of problem than the capacity to secure decentralized cooperation. In embedded policy-making, governments rely on the private information of associations to devise a solution to a collective problem, not to trade the acquiescence of their members for collective benefits. This trade follows a logic of problem-solving. As Hugh Heclo argues in comparing the social policies of Britain and Sweden, "Politics finds its sources not only in power, but also in uncertainty—men collectively wondering what to do. . . . Governments not only 'power' (or whatever the verb form for that approach might be); they also puzzle" (Heclo 1974, 305). A central claim of this book is that governments faced with the problem of decentralized cooperation are not likely to succeed if they puzzle on their own. This difference has important implications both for the making of economic policy and the way in which political scientists think about it. The implications of the increased importance of social puzzling depend on the existing associational structure of a given political economy.

VARIETIES OF CAPITALISM, INSTITUTIONAL CHANGE, AND THE FRENCH ECONOMY

How do we expect the organization of political economies to affect the incidence and success of policies premised on securing decentralized cooperation? The approach adopted in this book is strongly informed by the literature on the varieties of capitalism, and its findings reinforce the importance of viewing coordination as an issue of central importance in understanding how actors in the political economy respond to public policy (Kitschelt et al. 1999; Hall and Soskice 2001). The distinction between LMEs and CMEs turns on the mechanisms by which actors within the political economy—preeminently, business firms—coordinate their actions with one another. Information circulation and dialogic capacity are especially important components of stabilizing behavior around a given equilibrium because how firms react to any given market signal depends on how they think other firms will react to that same signal. By focusing on the ways in which institutions work in concert, the varieties of capitalism approach specifies plausible micro-foundations to support its main theoretical claims. The core argument is that two groups of institutionally self-reinforcing equilibria exist in the advanced capitalist countries, each with its preferred mode of coordination: primarily free markets in the LMEs and primarily nonmarket coordination in the CMEs. Thus we understand why market rigidities such as wage bargaining have largely been suppressed in one set of economies, but only modified slightly in others (Soskice 1999; Iversen 1999). In both its theoretical focus on coordination and its empirical concentration on companies, this book embraces many of the principal tenets of the varieties of capitalism approach.

There is, however, an important distinction to be made with that approach having to do with the principal flaw in the framework of comparative institutional advantage—namely, its difficulty in dealing with political change. Given the strongly self-reinforcing nature of the two equilibria among market economies, it is very difficult to see how governments can ever hope to create nonmarket coordination when they do not already possess it. LMEs rely on the market, and CMEs rely on employers' associations and unions, and the sorts of coordination achieved allow for different institutional advantages. This theoretical approach leads to an ideal-typical arrangement in which there are two existing equilibria toward which political economies tend, and movement away from these equilibria is posited to be extremely difficult (Hall and Soskice 2001; Wood 2001). Holding other things equal, it is true that the preexisting organizational structures of an economy make some political economies (the CMEs) more conducive than others (the LMEs) to meeting the challenges posed by the politics of decentralized cooperation. This is a proposition supported by the evidence from eastern Germany, where the assistance of western German associations was crucial in developing the organizational capacity of employers. In spite of all the problems created by the transition to capitalism in eastern Germany, the successful establishment of strong employer organizations provided governments there with a large advantage in securing decentralized cooperation among companies.

Yet change is not impossible, even in economies that have not been absorbed into the framework of a CME, as was eastern Germany; the varieties of capitalism approach is ultimately too static. The success achieved in the Valley of the Arve undercuts any deterministic theory that claims that France is doomed to fail in creating nonmarket coordination because it does not already possess the mechanisms of a CME. In terms of the private organizations that could facilitate coordination, it is true that France finds itself in a uniquely bad situation: it lacks the organizational capacities of a CME, but it nevertheless has a set of entrenched private-sector organizations engaged in bitter competition with one another. This is not a new situation in France, nor is it one peculiar to vocational training (Howell 1992; Levy 1999). But my focus on the determinants of company interests and group capacity suggests some positive lessons for the French state.

On the one hand, the relatively weak coordinating capacity of employers' organizations in France implies that policies that do not depend on decentralized cooperation have a better chance of succeeding than do those that depend on solving the cooperative problems inherent in apprenticeship training. For instance, the increase in the number of students receiving two-year college degrees is suggestive of the sort of policies that are more likely to succeed in France. These degrees use the general education system to provide transferable skills that are perceived by companies to be useful in the production process. Such degrees are still subject to the problems of general education, in that the skills they signal are likely to be further removed than those of in-firm certificates from the companies that actually use them (cf. Lynch 1994). But they can be used to increase the skill levels of the workforce without having to overcome the cooperative problems encountered in firm-based youth training.

On the other hand, there are some strategies that may enable the French government actually to improve the chances of success of future reforms that require decentralized cooperation. The findings of this study suggest that national and regional governments should shift the emphasis of French subsidy policies. Indiscriminate subsidies to companies for hiring trainees do not promote investment in general skills. This effort can be redirected to underwrite local and regional programs—such as the 1,000 Technicians program in the Arve—and then to diffuse information about these programs to other associational actors in the economy. We have seen already that the state, because of its informational weaknesses, has difficulty identifying the most successful programs a priori. However, by setting common performance criteria, it can assess over time which programs are working, and it can help circulate this information among other associations.[8]

The approach of embedded policy-making suggests that the French national and regional governments need to encourage experimentation among private groups rather than trying to be more directive in setting policies. Such an empirical approach to policy-making runs directly against the grain of conventional French thinking on the role of the state. In his comparison of French and German industrial policies, Nicholas Ziegler observes that "since French officials were expected to know the procedures and formulae that would lead to successful outcomes, their own deductive approach made it difficult for them to acknowledge unsuccessful policies or learn from their experiences" (1997, 205). Learning from empirical experiments is both costly and slow, but we have seen already that the expensive indiscriminate subsidies of the national government failed to change firm training practices. As private associations gain information about how other programs are working, they may initiate discussion among their members to strengthen the capacity of the association to deliver collective goods. This solution lacks Cartesian elegance, but given the informational limits of the state this sort of approach offers the best way—an experimental, resolutely empirical way—to allow organizations to learn from one another and the state to learn from them.

NEGOTIATED REFORMS AND COORDINATED MARKET ECONOMIES

CMEs such as Germany seem well placed to cope with policies premised on securing decentralized cooperation. Compared to LMEs, they are. Yet the strong capacity of employers and unions is a double-edged sword for the CMEs. Although those organizations may possess the information-circulation and dialogic capacities necessary to succeed in targeting waverers, they may choose not to do so if it threatens their established

---

[8] Although our analytical premises differ, these policy prescriptions are close to those of Charles Sabel and Archon Fung, and my thinking has been influenced by their work (see Sabel, Fung, and Karkkainen 1999).

bases of power within the political economy. In other words, the power and autonomy of interest groups in CMEs also allows them to insulate themselves from pressures for reform (Hassel and Ebbinghaus 2000). Once entrenched in power, they may find little reason to deviate from their established position, which means the state is without a viable partner for implementing the reforms. The problems facing CMEs therefore result more from the strength of their organizations of private-interest governance than from their weakness. As Jelle Visser and Anton Hemerijck (1997) and Peter Katzenstein (1987), along with many others, have noted the ubiquity of corporatist decision-making structures in many CMEs facilitates stalemate if there is an unhappy social partner that wants to block social change.

What is the best way for CMEs to introduce reforms that can improve the competitiveness of companies in the international economy? Recent research on this question stresses the ability of states to pressure private-interest groups to negotiate social pacts as the basis of institutional reforms (Rhodes 1998; Ebbinghaus and Hassel 2000). The danger in this approach is to read into contemporary national bargains the renewal of the corporatist concertation of the 1970s. As Marino Regini has underlined, the deals that resulted from the negotiated reforms of the 1990s were motivated by different policy goals than those of the 1970s: "What the recent [Italian] negotiations over collective bargaining procedures, incomes policies and pension reform have involved is the devolution of policy-making functions to organized interests (especially to trade unions) in a framework of regulative rather than redistributive policies" (Regini 1997b, 268).

There was no real secret to exercising wage restraint in the heyday of corporatist exchange: unions traded off exclusive representational rights—thus insulating them from membership discontent—for wage moderation and few strikes (Schmitter 1974; Goldthorpe 1984). By contrast, developing and implementing solutions to contemporary problems of policy-making requires that policy-makers be able to draw on the information of private associations. These associations have the potential to develop problem-solving strategies that states are unable to develop on their own. In the neocorporatist bargain, unions delivered their members. Now, they (or employers' associations) deliver private information and a capacity to solve problems facing public policy-makers.

The difference in micrologics between the traditional neocorporatist wage bargain and the reforms of human capital provision reveals a problem with analyses that stress the importance of the "shadow of the state" in convincing the social partners to compromise in reforms of the political economy (Ebbinghaus and Hassel 2000). Where unions are too strongly embedded in the workplace, as in Germany or Sweden, they can insulate themselves from the pressures for reform and refuse to come to the bargaining table. Weak unions, such as those in France, are simply unable to negotiate reliably with the state. Where states can credibly threaten to intervene—as was the case in Italy and Netherlands —this potential intervention is said to be enough to compel social partners to engage in negotiation over reforms to the welfare state or the wage-bargaining system. Yet if the dialogic capacity of private associations is as crucial as I have argued it is for the successful development and implementation of reforms aimed at securing decentralized cooperation, the strength of unions and employers' associations is more a resource for reform than a barrier. The unstated assumption in this work is that government, either through bureaucrats or through politicians, carries reforming ideas, and that interest groups block them. This assumption is often wrong.

States only have access to certain kinds of information, and the information to which they have access is not always the sort necessary to enable reforms to succeed. They can define the broad ends of policy, but the move away from redistributive toward regulatory policy-making asks states to do what they are worst at doing—to problem-solve. Governments are great standardizers, and they can collect an impressive amount of easily measurable and observable data about the polities they govern (Scott 1998). But they are not good at dealing with the idiosyncrasies of local knowledge, nor do they have access to reliable information about the cooperative propensities of individuals. These are the sorts of information that appear to be of paramount importance in securing decentralized cooperation: local knowledge because of the importance of responding to locally salient problems and relational information for using that local knowledge to attract the most likely cooperators in the population. To develop solutions based on this sort of information, states need to work with private groups because states themselves have trouble getting this information.

The idea of a coercive state imposing solutions on recalcitrant social partners loses some of its appeal when the social partners are the only ones that have the information the state needs to problem-solve effectively. The coercive state accomplished many things in the twentieth century—many of them not altogether desirable—but states cannot effectively coerce cooperation. To the extent that states need to rely on private information to develop solutions, then, the "shadow of the state" is a relatively empty threat in forcing bargaining partners to capitulate in reforms of economic, social, or environmental policy. Given that the ability of these organizations to overcome collective action problems is one of the institutional comparative advantages of the CMEs, such a strategy amounts to closing off the most promising avenue of reform. If I am right in underlining the rising importance of information for designing context-appropriate policy solutions, then reform in CMEs will be difficult with the social partners, but it will be almost impossible without them.

IMPLICATIONS FOR LIBERAL MARKET ECONOMIES

The advantage of CMEs lies in their organizational capacity; the great strength of LMEs is their reliance on free markets to coordinate expectations. And, make no mistake, the free market is the best mechanism for the decentralized coordination of action in human history. Yet markets sometimes fail to produce socially optimal outcomes; this is the vexing, but all too common, problem of market failure. One of the prime cases of market failure is that of suboptimal investment in the skills of the workforce, on which this book has focused (see Booth and Snower 1996). Markets similarly fail to build the cost of negative externalities, such as pollution, into the system of prices. The problems of environmentally threatened areas frequently remind us that markets do not solve all ills.

There is a move underway to reinvent government in the United States, exemplar par excellence of the LME (Osborne and Gaebler 1992; Donahue and Nye 2001). Does the option of mimicking market mechanisms provide a way for LMEs to overcome their informational deficits in solving problems of decentralized cooperation? Probably not. The problems of government in gaining access to information that is either local or relational are not in any way eased by the adoption of market mechanisms. One clear example of the informational limits of markets was the marketization of training provision adopted in the French region of Picardy (see chap. 5). The regional council first attempted to adopt a policy to stimulate firm investment in training, but quickly realized it lacked the informational resources from private associations necessary to enable the policy to succeed. The region then moved to adopt measures to clarify the market for training provision, establishing measures for allowing individuals to compare training providers directly before choosing one. This policy did nothing to elicit employer coordination because it was unable to target aid directly at the most likely cooperators in the population. In promoting efficiency in the existing market of training providers, the policy was likely to succeed; but in convincing actors to change their patterns of human capital investment, it was a failure.

LMEs also have to develop organizational interlocutors for states if they want to succeed in securing decentralized cooperation. Other things equal, the organizational weakness of LMEs means that policies premised on decentralized cooperation are more likely to fail than in CMEs. And the weakness of organizations in the American case extends beyond employers' associations and unions. Skocpol (1999) has amassed an impressive array of data showing that organizations with strong federalist structures—that is, with a central leadership but with organizational and mobilizing capacity across the states of the union—are in decline (cf. Putnam 2000). They are being replaced in the U.S. organizational landscape by groups that maintain offices and a presence in Washington, with little local organizational structure to support those central offices (Berry 1999). Such organizations are no more likely than the government itself to have access to local or relational knowledge when their organizations do not exist at the local level. Countries lacking the solid mechanisms for nonmarket coordination characteristic of CMEs are disadvantaged in this respect, and they have an incentive to develop either associational capacity or some sort of functional equivalent to be able to benefit from the insights of private information.

How might either private actors or the state develop such associational capacity, where powerful associations have not already established a history of common knowledge embedded in legal regulation? Although there is no unequivocal recipe for success, there are two necessary conditions that must be met for experiments in the development of associational capacity to take root in the barren organizational landscape of LMEs. The first such prerequisite is a shared assessment, by actors with divergent interests, that there are potential gains from cooperation. If actors cannot be convinced that there might be gains from trade, there really is nothing for them to talk about.[9] The second prerequisite is that, once actors agree that they might have grounds for cooperating with one another, they must institutionalize a forum for discussion through which they may be able to establish regular information exchange. These are relatively forgiving prerequisites; in no sense do they constitute sufficient conditions for the emergence of dialogic capacity. But they are likely to be necessary, for any group attempting to develop collective capacity. Whether or not actors use these conditions to construct a stronger collective capacity depends entirely on the actors themselves.

Decentralized Cooperation in Industrial and Environmental Policies

In what sorts of policy areas are we most likely to observe problems of decentralized cooperation in LMEs? Where, in other words, are cooper-

---

[9] Note, however, that this assumes neither that they will suffer serious losses if they do not cooperate nor that their discussion will result in the redefinition of their own interests.

ative dilemmas especially likely to be combined with issues of cognitive complexity in a way that leaves actors facing strategic and analytic uncertainty simultaneously? In addition to policies of human capital development,[10] two fields seem especially plagued by these sorts of challenges. The first is industrial policy, including the problems of technology transfer (Ziegler 1997) and the promotion of clusters of innovative companies (Porter 1998, 197–287). Such policies often ask firms to interact in ways that leave them strategically vulnerable and causally uncertain, even when there is a welfare-improving strategy to be followed. The second such area is environmental policy. Diffuse environmental problems involve the coordination of multiple actors to improve a collective resource. These problems depend on the mutual exercise of restraint by different types of actors; there are often a bewildering number of potential solutions that improve the environment, each of which has different distributive consequences; and the effects of any of these choices on a given actor is often highly uncertain (Mazmanian and Kraft, 1999). Let us briefly consider examples from each of these policy areas where governments have encountered problems of decentralized cooperation.

Wales is a nationally distinct region within the LME of the United Kingdom, and an economically disadvantaged region at that. In its efforts to promote innovation among regional companies, the Welsh Development Agency (WDA) was selected in 1994 as a pilot region for the European Union's exercise in developing Regional Technology Plans (RTP).[11] The goal of the RTP program was to enable regional agencies to more effectively promote innovation among companies. But to achieve this goal, the preferred means for regional agencies was the initiation of a discussion among companies and governmental authorities over "the disposition to collaborate to achieve mutually beneficial ends. In short, the RTP exercise is about building social capital in regions where these assets are thin on the ground" (Morgan 1997, 497). In practice, this meant that representatives and companies had to talk with one another. "Because the process (collaboration) was widely perceived to be integral to the success of the product (raising innovative capacity), the RTP consultation exercise lasted eighteen months and over 600

---

[10] For studies of how problems of decentralized cooperation arise in the area of human capital development in the United States, see Parker and Rogers (1999) and Dresser, Rogers, and Zdrazil (2001).

[11] The original RTP program, launched in four less favored regions, was later adopted by the European Union as a generalized instrument of regional policy. The name of the program was then changed to the Regional Innovation Strategies (RIS) program (Thomas 2000).

organizations were actively involved in what turned out to be the most comprehensive iteration process ever undertaken in Wales in the field of economic development" (Cooke and Morgan 1998, 153). This effort thus attempted to promote the development of innovative capacity by engaging firms and policy-makers in iterated discussions about how they could better collaborate to achieve jointly desired ends (Henderson 2000, 351).

The proof is in the pudding, and it is too early to say whether in fact the Welsh experiment has secured decentralized cooperation among actors in the economy. It does appear, at a minimum, that the WDA has provoked sustained information exchange among local actors, "stimulating processes of talk as the basis for precedent setting and confidence building among regional institutions" (Henderson 2000, 355).[12] Talk is cheap, but not without value for LMEs that do not have well-established associations for promoting information exchange and collective problem-solving. In so doing, state policy-makers have come to understand the limits of their own ability to intervene in the economy. "[The RTP process] confirmed the WDA in its belief that firms learn best from other firms—whether they be suppliers, customers, or competitors— because they see their corporate peers as being more credible interlocutors than public agencies. These findings resonated with the agency because it was already coming to the conclusion that the most effective business-support initiatives were those that were designed *with* rather than *for* firms . . ." (Cooke and Morgan 1998, 154). Although it is certainly premature to pass final judgment on the Welsh RTP project, it seems that the regional government has demonstrated that it is at least possible to promote information exchange and discussion in a LME.

Environmental regulation in the industrialized states has in the past been a policy area in which governments adopt laws and then establish an agency to enforce the rules. The birth of the Chesapeake Bay Program (CBP) in 1983 represented implicit governmental acknowledgment that such an approach would not succeed in repairing the degradation inflicted by pollution on the largest estuary in the United States. What separated the Chesapeake from other cases of environmental regulation was the nature of the strategic situation created by pollution from many small sources rather than from a few large industrial plants (Stranahan 1993, 298).

---

[12] Observe, however, that Sabel's optimistic view of the ever-present possibility of interest redefinition does not find support from those who have studied the Welsh case, who note the difficulty of convincing actors to change their minds "in policy environments characterized by more entrenched interests and responsibilities" (Henderson 2000, 355).

Point sources of pollution are pipes that discharge nutrients directly into the bay, such as sewage plants. States can regulate point pollution easily enough because they merely have to know where the pipes are, monitor their discharge, and impose sanctions for excessive pollution. Nonpoint pollution refers to run-off from storms: rain washes nutrients (e.g., nitrogen and phosphorous) off farmland, which then seeps into streams or the water table.[13] This makes nonpoint pollution difficult to measure and ipso facto difficult to regulate because the efforts to enlist farmers to reduce such pollution are voluntary. In Maryland, for example, they generally involve state subsidies for farmers to install best management practices, including the elaboration of a nutrient management plan. However, the state does not verify whether farmers are actually implementing the nutrient plans (Davison et al. 1997; CBP 1994). In order for the goals of the CBP to be reached, the state governments had to convince farmers and property developers to agree to cooperate with the goals of the program, even though the states possessed no feasible way to measure individual compliance and no means to compel it.

What was the character of the strategic interaction here? The farmers living on bay tributaries viewed their land as their principal asset, one whose long-term value was strongly determined by the local environment (Paolisso and Maloney 2000). The action of any one farmer to limit his or her runoff would only have an aggregate effect if most farmers agreed to limit their runoff; but limiting runoff was costly, and no one was sure what the others would do. If one farmer invested in a nutrient management plan while no other farmer did so, then he or she received the worst possible outcome: he or she paid but received no benefit to the environment. But each farmer would prefer that the majority of farms invest in nutrient management plans. Although farmers were not the only actors in this dilemma, their position was central, and it was among them that the waverers were likely to be found.[14] Analytic uncertainty compounded the cooperative dilemma facing farmers and other actors in the Chesapeake Bay because they were not certain how to estimate the costs or the benefits of a nutrient management plan: "the cost picture is very confused: a farmer may actually save money from reduced fertilizer and pesticide purchases ..."

---

[13] In 1996, 66 percent of the phosphorous and 57 percent of the pollution in the Chesapeake Bay came from nonpoint sources (CBP 1999, 24).

[14] There were environmentalists, government officials, and fishermen on one side; developers and industries stood on the other. The first group of actors was highly concerned with decreasing the pollution in the bay, whereas the second group stood to gain from the minimal regulation of pollution in the bay, at least in the short term.

(Matuszeski 1995, 54). Given the complexity of the strategic interaction among the various stakeholders in the bay, it is hardly surprising that farmers were not at all clear what they would gain and what they would lose if they restrained pollution from agricultural runoff, even if other farmers also cooperated.

The bay is a complex ecosystem, and governments tried to combine their technical expertise with the local information of residents to monitor water quality throughout the system (Hudson 1995). The availability of these data led the CBP participants to shift in 1992 to a tributary strategy: rather than attacking the central stem of the bay, the CBP encouraged the development of local solutions focused on the specific problems of individual tributaries (Matuszeski 1995; Sabel, Fung, and Karkkainen 1999). There were no obvious interest-group interlocutors that possessed the necessary organizational capacities to promote information circulation and discussion, so the CBP assembled Tributary Teams, comprising local citizens, farmers, business representatives, and government officials (Macdonald 1997). Lacking associational conduits to the private information that was required to enable the CBP to encourage the development of local cooperation, the state put together forums in which its technical expertise could be informed by the local and relational knowledge of private citizens. The Tributary Teams not only collected information that the state was unable to collect; they also used this information to foster the development of strategies to convince wavering cooperators in the population, most notably farmers. The Chesapeake Bay Trust established grants to facilitate the local projects of the teams, giving priority to "education projects that promote a behavior change toward the bay" ("*Trib Team Monitor*" 1997)[15]. There is certainly a continued role for the traditional regulation of environmental pollution, yet the need to develop regulations that cross jurisdictions and require cooperation among many small polluters portends a growing role for problems of decentralized cooperation in the future of environmental policy (Stranahan 1993).

The attempts by governments to secure decentralized cooperation in Wales, in the United Kingdom, and in the states of the Chesapeake Bay, in the United States, may well fail. I have not asserted that they will succeed in their ultimate goals, and in neither case is there enough evidence to make a definitive judgment. These disparate cases do already show two things about LMEs. First, states in these economies face problems of decentralized cooperation, and they are problems that rein-

[15] In other words, to target waverers.

venting government on market principles cannot solve. Second, in spite of their weak associational infrastructure, governments in LMEs are capable of establishing forums for private information exchange and discussion. Their problem is the mirror image of that facing governments in CMEs. For example, in the case of the Chesapeake Bay, once the need to clean up the bay was widely acknowledged, the lack of groups with established negotiating routines was advantageous in that it did not set off a competitive dynamic among organizations defending their organizational turf. Thus, the advantage for governments in LMEs is their ability to construct ad hoc cooperative institutions without the threat that existing organizations will actively undermine them. Yet their disadvantage, in comparison to CMEs, is the difficulty of sustaining and institutionalizing these forums for information exchange and discussion.

The challenges of decentralized cooperation seem to taunt state policy-makers. There are a set of potential, cooperative, welfare-improving solutions out there to be adopted, if only they can persuade private actors to coordinate their actions on such an outcome. But, to the great exasperation of the policy-makers trying to secure decentralized cooperation across the industrialized world, these private actors are already locked in a stable pattern of interaction. If a single actor chooses to deviate from its standard pattern of behavior while almost all other actors do not, then it gets an outcome worse than that achieved by those who do not pursue the cooperative path and who instead take advantage of the solitary cooperator. Because reforms aimed at generating decentralized cooperation create tremendous uncertainty among actors about what the potential payoffs to different courses of action are, success depends on identifying and changing the minds of the most likely cooperators in the population, the waverers. And states, for all their information-gathering prowess, are not well-adapted to identify and know how to persuade the waverers.

I have argued throughout this book that private-sector associations are uniquely well placed to gain access to private information about the waverers and to develop policies to target them disproportionately. Strategies premised on using sanctions to convince actors to move to the desired equilibrium are ineffectual because they lack credibility; sanctioning only works once a certain number of actors have moved to the new societal equilibrium and defection from this equilibrium is widely acknowledged as being sanctionable. Because states are very good at levying sanctions but very bad at procuring private information from actors that want to conceal it from them, they need to be able to work with private-sector organizations to develop policies that can most effectively target the waverers and convince them of the benefits to requited cooperation.

Of course, the organizational infrastructure of a polity influences the odds of success in such a reform project. In problems of decentralized cooperation, CMEs enjoy an advantage over LMEs. But this disadvantage is not insurmountable—public policy, anywhere, can enable states to overcome stable, societally deleterious patterns of behavior. Despite the tremendous insights generated by societal equilibrium scholars such as Robert Putnam (1993) and David Soskice (1999), their work is grim reading for policy-makers who want to improve the lives of their citizens. These scholars are right that stable patterns of interaction are very hard to break out of, and my study confirms this. Creating decentralized cooperation is difficult, and we have seen that there were many more cases of failure than of success. States must learn that information is a precious commodity in their attempt to create decentralized cooperation, whereas sanctioning is a relatively weak capacity. Governments must build and use links to private information because they will not be able to get the information they need without such conduits. In this narrow sense, Max Weber now has little to teach them—their information is no longer especially pertinent, and their monopoly on legitimate coercion is no longer particularly effective. Yet once they recognize the value of private and local information and of private dialogic capacity built on this information, states can succeed in eliciting new forms of cooperation, even in societies marked by past patterns of distrust. Politics is the art of the possible, and policy-makers may draw some comfort from the fact that the politics of decentralized cooperation is still a question of using state capabilities, in combination with private information, to contribute to the common good.

Issues of Measurement

We can only explain the causes of successful decentralized cooperation once we know what success looks like, both at the level of the individual firm and at the level of the employment zone. There is little disagreement about the importance of firm-level behavior as an explanandum, at least in theory (Hall 1999). But actually measuring firm behavior to assess who are the defectors and who are the cooperators in the game of vocational training is extremely difficult. It is therefore rarely attempted. Such an area of theorizing, which has been central to debates about the nature of political economy in the advanced capitalist countries, is simply too important to ignore because of the difficulty involved in making inferences about individual and collective outcomes. In this appendix I present the criteria I have used to make these inferences.

I take as central to the success of reform of both the French and eastern German systems the key characteristic of the dual system in western Germany: that firms themselves are willing to bear a significant share of the investment in the development of general skills. This criterion poses two important methodological issues: How much investment in human capital through apprenticeship training constitutes high-skill training in an individual firm, and how can we classify a group of firms in a sector, an employment zone, or a country as having moved successfully to a high-skill equilibrium, at least with respect to its training practices? Just as the stylized fact of the high-skill equilibrium is based on abstraction from the practice of in-firm training in western Germany, so too must the answers to these questions be found in the training practices characteristic of western Germany.

It is difficult to assess the net investment that western German employers make in training, because neither the costs incurred nor the benefits procured are easily measurable (for a more complete discussion see von Bardeleben, Beicht, and Fehér 1995; Wagner 1999). On the cost side, apprenticeship wages are straightforward, and the wages of their trainers as well as the costs of the equipment used to train apprentices seem easy enough to calculate. On the benefit side, the immediate productive output of the apprentice is not as easy to determine, but rough estimates have certainly been made.[1] However, these figures obscure many of the opportunity-cost savings that companies achieve through their apprenticeship training. In the training workshops of large industrial firms, there may be a trainer whose only job is to supervise the apprentices in the workshop; this trainer's job consists almost entirely of the instruction of apprentices, using machines that are exclusively dedicated to apprenticeship training. This contrasts sharply with the case of a skilled worker in a smaller firm who has an apprentice under his wing in the work process, but who is concurrently doing his own job. If trainers have other tasks in the company, and the machines are necessary anyway for production, then the real costs of apprenticeship are only the amount of money that would not otherwise have been spent. Many companies, especially smaller ones, train their apprentices in periods of slack demand, when machines and trainers (who are themselves productive skilled workers) would otherwise be idle (Soskice 1994). Thus, companies with dedicated training workshops spend far more per apprentice than do companies whose apprentices train mainly on the job (Wagner 1999; von Bardeleben, Beicht, and Fehér 1995). Further savings accrue through avoiding the costs of training newly hired skilled workers (with their high wages) in firm-specific skills, savings in recruitment costs, and being able to screen apprentices for affinity with the prevailing culture of the company (Cramer and Müller 1994; Wagner 1999; von Bardeleben, Beicht, and Fehér 1995). Taking into account these different sorts of considerations suggests that apprenticeship training costs vary widely among different types of companies.

Breaking costs down by company size and type in western Germany, two results are striking: the net costs to the company of training in the craft sector are negligible, whereas the net costs of training in industry are substantial; and small companies on average invest a much lower amount per trainee than do large firms (von Bardeleben, Beicht, and Fehér 1995). Based on data from 1,370 training firms, a study by the German Federal Institute of Vocational Training (BiBB) on the cost of training to firms controlled both for the benefit to the firm of work performed by the apprentice and for the fact that many trainers are actually skilled workers who would work for the firm whether or not it were training (See Table A.1.). Thus calculated, the variable net cost of training (per apprentice per year) for the smallest German firms in 1991 was

---

[1] In the firms in which I conducted interviews, personnel managers and training supervisors were often reluctant to estimate this figure, and only one or two had actually made an estimate of the productive contribution of trainees.

Table A.1 Annual Costs of Training per Apprentice by Company Size, 1991[a]

	Average	≤9	10–49	50–499	≥500
Gross costs	18,051	13,868	15,075	20,283	28,197
Net costs	6,340	1,647	3,610	8,184	17,886

[a] In deutschmarks.

Source: Von Bardeleben, Beicht, and Fehér (1995).

Table A.2 Annual Costs per Apprentice, Industry and Crafts Sectors, 1991[a]

	Industry and Trade	Crafts
Gross costs	20,509	12,936
Net costs	9,193	400

[a] In deutschmarks.

Source: Von Bardeleben, Beicht, and Fehér (1995).

1,647 DM, or 12 percent of the total (gross) cost of training for firms of this size (13,868 DM). In contrast, the total cost of training was over twice as high for firms having over 500 employees (28,197 DM), and the net cost of training (17,886 DM) for these larger firms made up over 60 percent of this (higher) total cost (Von Bardeleben, Beicht, and Fehér 1995, 16).

Similarly, as a result of lower average training wages in the craft sector and the fact that craft apprentices are integrated more quickly into the workforce and bring a higher level of productivity at an earlier stage than do their counterparts in industry, the net cost of training for craft firms was significantly lower than for industrial firms (See Table A.2.). Thus, the same BiBB figures for 1991 reveal that, of an adjusted total training cost to industrial firms of 20,509 DM, the net cost to the firm was 9,193 DM (just under one-half the total); yet of a lower adjusted total cost to craft firms of 12,936 DM, the net cost to firms was only 400 DM (3 percent of total cost) (von Bardeleben, Beicht, and Fehér 1995, 15).

Because craft firms are on average smaller than industrial firms, there is a great deal of multicollinearity between the effects of firm size and the effects of being an industry or crafts firm. Although the exact contributions of the two factors remain unclear, both seem to make a significant difference to the net costs of training to firms. But, in effect, as argued in Soskice (1994), there are two sectors in the German training system: one comprising craft firms and one comprising industrial firms.[2] For many craft firms, there is no reason to worry about losing money by investing in the training of workers who then abscond with their newly acquired skills to a competing firm; the net investment of the firm in apprenticeship training is often very close to zero. Industrial firms pay a lot more per apprentice than do craft firms, and it is logical that they therefore maintain a lower proportion of apprentices to their workforce. Industrial firms are also likely to retain a much higher percentage of those they train. They want to hire almost all the trainees in whom they have invested, and they do not want to make this substantial investment in someone whom they are not planning to hire. Craft firms, on the other hand, lose little if anything in hiring apprentices; they therefore maintain higher ratios of apprentices in relation to their total employment and have lower rates of postapprenticeship retention. For them, apprenticeship is predominantly cheap labor.

It is relatively unproblematic for a government to implement a new system of in-firm youth training when that system costs firms very little. The problems of decentralized cooperation associated with the wholesale reform of a training system are most severe for industrial firms that have to invest heavily in the development of their workforce. It is only in the training patterns of industrial firms that we can observe the ideal-typical game in which the firm has to be willing to make the uncovered investment in the training of a skilled worker in order for both to reap the payoff of the high-skill equilibrium.[3]

THE METAL AND ELECTRONICS INDUSTRY

Two measures are used to assess the degree to which eastern German and French training practices approximate the stylized model of western German training: the ratio of apprentices to the total workforce (training ratio) and the rate of retention of apprentices after their training (retention rate). In western Germany, the training ratio considered by

[2] David Soskice has influenced my thinking on this point, and this paragraph relies largely on the account developed in Soskice (1994). The industry versus crafts distinction refers to the sorts of occupations in which companies train and the correspondingly responsible chamber: of industry and commerce (IHK) and of crafts (HWK). In the real world, there is obviously a much less clean bifurcation of types of firm training.

[3] Because industrial company data are those most important for trying to establish that firms are investing in in-firm initial training, I concentrate on firms in this sector in structuring the comparison between France and eastern Germany. However, my firm sample from the metal sector in Germany, eastern and western, does include several craft-sector companies, whose training practices were very much in line with the predictions that follow from the two-sector model (i.e., they maintained higher average training ratios and lower retention rates than the industrial firms).

Table A.3 Apprenticeship Training Patterns in Western Germany, 1990 and 1995[a]

Number of employees	Training ratio (%)		Companies training (%)	
	1990	1995	1990	1995
1–9	10.9	8.0	21	17
10–49	8.3	6.6	52	47
50–499	5.9	4.5	74	68
500+	5.2	4.3	94	94
Average	7.0	5.5	28	24

[a] Source: Wagner (1999), based on data from the Bundesanstalt für Arbeit and the BiBB.

firms and by training experts in the metal and electronics industry as necessary to maintain the level of skilled workers is approximately 6 percent. That is, on average these firms need to train six apprentices per one hundred workers to fill the gaps left by skilled workers moving on (to other firms), moving up (to management positions), or moving out (to retirement). This figure was cited to the author in 1995 by several people familiar with training in the German metal and electronics industry (in the employer's associations, in the chambers of industry and trade, and in the firms themselves). Evidence from western German industrial companies confirms the validity of this benchmark. As indicated in table A.3, the average training ratio for western German companies of all types fell from 7.0 percent in 1990 to 5.5 percent in 1995, the year in which I conducted my study of eastern German firms.[4]

Given that eastern German companies function with exactly the same educational institutions from which to draw skilled workers as do their western compatriots, this range must be considered the goal for bringing the eastern German training system into line with the western one. The 6 percent figure is obviously approximate, so I use a margin of error of ± 2 percent in defining the target range (4–8 percent) in which I

[4] These data also confirm that larger firms maintain lower training ratios than smaller firms, as expected from the two-sector model. Note in table A.3 that the difference in the training ratio by category would be even starker if considered in combination with the proportion of companies, in any given size category, that trained. Only 17 percent of companies having 1–9 employees actually trained apprentices in 1995, which means that the ratio for companies in this size range is on average much higher on average than 10.9 percent for the few companies (one in five) that actually have apprentices. Similarly, fewer than one-half the companies with 10–49 employees trained apprentices, whereas 94 percent of companies with more than 500 employees did train apprentices.

classify training in the metal industries of eastern Germany as conforming to western German training patterns. Firms training above this level, unless they are growing at a very rapid rate, are training more workers than they need to replace their workforce and, other things being equal, are likely to be investing less per apprentice than are companies with ratios in the target range. Companies training below this level are likely to be shrinking or are not investing at a sufficiently high level to be able to replace the skilled workers lost to natural attrition. Average training ratios outside this range suggest different training patterns than those that maintain the dual system in western Germany. Because it is available and easy to calculate, this ratio represents the best single measure of training practices in companies in the metal and electronics industries.

Does France aspire to having its firms in the metal and electronics industry perform in the same range? Certainly the French government has encouraged its companies to mimic the use of in-company training contracts in western Germany. Yet French companies are also able to rely on general educational institutions and a further training system that has advantages over the German institutions (Regini 1995, 1997a). French companies continue to rely on this comparative advantage by hiring relatively more highly skilled graduates of the general technical education system than do German companies, even as they increase the use of in-firm training contracts—or, in many cases, they try to combine the two (e.g., by developing higher level apprenticeship contracts). In an interview, the former head of training for the French metal employers said the association would like to see a ratio of apprentices/workforce of 4–5%, slightly below that enunciated in western Germany (Int FNE5). If that is so, then the equivalent target range for French metal companies should be ± 2 percent around 4.5 percent. The target range I use for French companies in this study is therefore 2.5–6.5%.

Do these two different target ranges capture the same, or analogous, phenomena? If the baseline is the idealized western German practice of high investment per trainee, it is helpful to adduce an additional criterion for the French companies, which should not vary from the western German standard. This criterion—the retention rate—also has its basis in the presumed investment of companies in the training of their apprentices. Companies that invest a lot in apprenticeship training want to secure the return on their investment by hiring their apprentice after training. As suggested by the differential training costs of large and small companies, the retention rate of western German small firms is much lower than that of larger firms, in which the firm invests significantly more in training per worker (Pfeiffer 1997; BMBW 1999). Data on

Table A.4 Criteria for Assessing Training Investment, Industrial Firms

	Training Ratio, Target Range	Retention Rate, Minimum
Eastern Germany	Minimum: 4.0% Maximum: 8.0%	Not applicable
France	Minimum: 2.5% Maximum: 6.5%	68.0%

western German companies from an IAB panel show an average retention rate across all western German industrial firms of 0.68 in 1995 (Pfeiffer 1997, 15).[5] The rates of postapprenticeship retention offer a second good measure of firm investment in youth training, and I take the 0.68 figure as a benchmark retention rate characteristic of western Germany and I use this retention rate as a second indicator of firm investment in trainees in the French case. French training ratios may be lower than in Germany because of the greater relative role of the two-year technical college track (bac + 2), but there is no reason that French companies should retain fewer of those trainees they do train through in-firm contracts if they have incorporated in-firm training contracts as an enduring part of their strategies of human capital development (see Table A.4).

The problem with using retention as a measure for eastern Germany is that if no apprentices finished in the previous year, there is no retention rate. A large number of eastern German companies, which had only very recently started training again when I conducted my interviews in 1995–96, had no data on retention. Moreover, many of the eastern German companies that did train during the early 1990s allowed their current apprentices to finish their training, in spite of large reductions in other parts of their workforce that reduced the availability of jobs for the apprentices after their training. Thus, some of the retention data that are available for 1995 reflect the decimation of employment several years earlier. I have data on retention rates from only a few eastern German companies, which I discuss for particular cases in this book. Yet, given the paucity of data points, I do not rely on retention rates for the eastern German metal industry to classify either companies or employment zones.

[5] The retention rate is the percentage of apprentices hired into a contract after the successful (passing) completion of their apprenticeship exams.

EMPLOYMENT ZONES

This study tests various hypotheses about the prerequisites for creating decentralized cooperation in the area of vocational training, which requires comparing the performance of the nine employment zones in which I constructed industrial firm samples.[6] Interviews in these industrial firms as well as with local political and associational actors have provided a wealth of insight into the process of deciding whether to engage in cooperation. But, to use this information to understand the politics of decentralized cooperation, the data about individual firm training practices must be aggregated in order to assess the success or failure of the nine employment zones studied.

Success depends on the proportion of firms investing substantially in training contracts because the nature of the training ratio as a measure means that averages per zone are not a good indicator, since training either below or above the range is problematic.[7] So, the issue is how to determine the proportion of firms in an employment zone that must be exhibiting high-skill training practices in order to qualify the zone as a case of success. For each zone, I calculated a score that I call the high-skill training index, which is simply the proportion of companies in a zone that fulfills the criteria just delineated.[8] What does a successful high-skill training index look like? The benchmark I have chosen, consistent with the other indicators used in this study, is the proportion of firms in the western German metalworking industry that were training apprentices in 1995, 34 percent (Wagner 1999, 64). Employment zones where more than one-third of metalworking firms in my sample met the

---

[6] As I note in chapter 3, the sample consists of four zones from eastern Germany and five from France, as well as one control zone from western Germany (Mayen). The four from eastern Germany are Leipzig, Plauen, Halle, and Sangerhausen; the five from France are the Valley of the Arve, Lyon, the Vimeu, Amiens, and Strasbourg.

[7] Thus, within a given employment zone, an average training ratio of 6.0 might mean there are three firms, two of which have no apprentices and the third of which maintains a ratio of eighteen apprentices per one hundred workers, indicating that the third firm is only using apprentices as cheap labor. This is not a high-skill equilibrium. By contrast, average retention rates are meaningful because the higher the retention rates, the more likely (other things equal) firms are making substantial investments in general skill provision through youth training contracts. But, because I do not have good retention data for eastern Germany (because the firms were just beginning to train at the time of my study), I cannot use the average retention rate for the German zones. For the French employment zones, I do use average retention rates to compare across regions the extent to which high-skill training practices have taken root.

[8] For eastern Germany, this is measured by the training ratio; in France, this is measured by companies having both a training ratio in the French target range (between 2.5 and 6.5) and having a retention rate greater than or equal to the western German average of 0.68.

high-skill training criteria were counted as successes; those where fewer than one-third did were counted as failures.[9] The control zone from western Germany (Mayen) has a high-skill index of 42 percent, which suggests that the threshold I have set is in accordance with what we might expect from western German employers in the metal and electronics sector. The median size of my sample zones is only five firms, so the results are not beyond empirical challenge. Yet given the paucity of work in measuring high-skill training as a regional attribute, these results seem to me the best way to proceed. The next step for future research is, of course, to test these findings further and to refine the measures used.

[9] Critics may object that this marker is either too low or too high. Those arguing for the too low position may point to the fact that this measure understates the proportion of training firms in Germany because there are many very small firms, that do not have any apprentices, which bring this number down. That is doubtless correct, and my sample almost certainly includes a lower proportion of very small firms than does the overall population (see the discussion of sample construction in chap. 3). However, as the proponents of the too high position may hasten to add, not all firms that train in western Germany, even in the metal industry, fall within my target range. Admittedly, however, my sample overrepresents larger firms, where it is not a stretch to believe that at least one-third train according to high-skill criteria. Given the two possible sources of bias in my sample—the overrepresentation of larger firms and the greater likelihood of including firms unusually persuaded of the value of apprenticeship training—using the average for the metal industry seems the most appropriate index. Yet the index probably is imperfect. However, the lowest scoring success zone in my sample has a proportion of 40 percent and the highest scoring failure zone has only a proportion of 25 percent, so a slight error in either direction is not likely to throw off the validity of these assessments.

Training Results from the Firm Sample

Table B.1 Eastern German Firms with at Least 500 Employees[a]

Firm	Training Ratio (%)[b]	Ownership[c]
EGL1	7.0	TH
EGL2	4.6	C
EGL3	5.4	C
EGL4	8.0	C
EGL5	12.0	C

[a] Source: Interviews conducted in 1995 in eastern Germany. All companies are members of the chambers of industry and commerce.

[b] Equals apprentices as a proportion of total employment.

[c] TH, owned by the Treuhand's successor organization; C, owned by a corporation. All of the corporately owned firms in this table were owned by western German corporations at the time of interview.

Table B.2 French Firms with at Least 500 Employees[a]

Firm	Training Ratio (%)	1996 Retention Rate (%)[b]	Ownership[c]
FL1	3.2	0	I
FL2	0.4	96	C
FL3	0.7	0	C
FL4	1.0	0	C
FL5	3.0	60	C
FL6	3.0	57	C
FL7	6.4	0	C
FL8	0.2	na[d]	C
FL9	1.7	67	C

[a] Source: Interviews conducted in 1996 in France. All companies are members of the chambers of commerce and industry.

[b] Equals apprentices plus qualification contracts as a proportion of total employment.

[c] I, independently or family-owned firm; C, owned by a corporation.

[d] Firm FL8 had no youth finish a contract in either 1995 or 1996 and so has no retention rate.

Table B.3 Eastern German Firms with Fewer than 500 Employees[a]

Firm	Training Ratio (%)[b]	Ownership[c]
EGSME1	15.1	H
EGSME2	46.5	I
EGSME3	0.0	I
EGSME4	0.0	I
EGSME5	0.0	I
EGSME6	0.0	TH
EGSME7	2.3	TH
EGSME8	14.0	TH
EGSME9	14.0	TH
EGSME10	0.0	C
EGSME11	0.0	C
EGSME12	1.5	C
EGSME13	1.6	C
EGSME14	1.6	C
EGSME15	2.2	C
EGSME16	2.2	C
EGSME17	2.9	C
EGSME18	6.2	C

[a] Source: Interviews conducted in 1995 in eastern Germany. All companies are members of the chambers of industry and commerce.

[b] Equals apprentices as a proportion of total employment.

[c] H, a former Handwerk cooperative, with cooperative private ownership; I, independently or family-owned eastern German firm; TH, owned by the Treuhand's successor organization; C, owned by a corporation, either western German or foreign.

Table B.4 French Firms with Fewer than 500 Employees[a]

Firm	Training Ratio (%)[b]	1996 Retention Rate (%)	Ownership[c]
FSME1	1.0	0	C
FSME2	2.7	64	C
FSME3	3.8	18	C
FSME4	6.5	25	C
FSME5	7.0	67	C
FSME6	0.0	na	I
FSME7	0.0	na	I
FSME8	0.9	50	I
FSME9	1.1	100	I
FSME10	1.9	na	I
FSME11	2.9	80	I
FSME12	3.4	100	I
FSME13	4.0	100	I
FSME14	5.0	67	I
FSME15	9.1	50	I
FSME16	0.0	na	I
FSME17	2.9	100	I
FSME18	3.0	100	I
FSME19	8.7	50	I
FSME20	13.3	100	I

[a] Source: Interviews conducted in 1996 in France. All companies are members of the chambers of commerce and industry. Not applicable, na.

[b] Equals apprentices plus qualification contracts as a proportion of total employment.

[c] I, independently or family-owned firm; C, owned by a corporation.

Interview Sources

Interviews are cited parenthetically in the chapters in the format (Int ••) and refer to interviews with representatives of the following secondary associations or governmental actors. The interviews with firms are not included here for reasons of confidentiality. Separate interviews with the same office are given separate identifying codes.

FRANCE

FNE1　ACFCI, Peak Association of Chambers of Commerce and Industry, Paris

FNE2　CNPF, Peak Association of French Employers, Paris

FNE3　CNPF, Peak Association of French Employers, Paris

FNE4　UIMM, Peak Association of Metal Employers, Paris

FNE5　UIMM, Peak Association of Metal Employers, Paris

FNG1　AFPA, Paris, Association pour la Formation Professionnelle pour Adultes, Paris

FNG2　CdC, Comité de Coordination des Programmes Régionaux d'Apprentissage et de Formation Professionnelle Continue, Paris

FNG3　CdC, Comité de Coordination des Programmes Régionaux d'Apprentissage et de Formation Professionnelle Continue, Paris

FNG4　CdC, Comité de Coordination des Programmes Régionaux d'Apprentissage et de Formation Professionnelle Continue, Paris

FNG5　CdC, Comité de Coordination des Programmes Régionaux d'Apprentissage et de Formation Professionnelle Continue, Paris

FNG6　EN, National Education Ministry, Paris

FNU1　CFDT, Union Peak Confederation, Paris

FNU2　CGT, Union Peak Confederation, Paris

FNU3　FEN, Peak Federation of Education Workers' Unions, Paris

FNU4　FO, CGT-Force Ouvrière Peak Confederation, Paris

FRE1　CCA, Regional Chamber of Commerce and Industry of Alsace, Strasbourg

FRE2   CCA, Regional Chamber of Commerce and Industry of Alsace, Strasbourg

FRE3   CCP, Regional Chamber of Commerce and Industry of Picardy, Amiens

FRE4   CRCI, Regional Chamber of Commerce and Industry of Rhône-Alpes, Lyon

FRE5   CSMA, Departmental Association of Metal Employers of Haut-Rhin, Alsace, Mulhouse

FRE6   CTDEC, Centre Technique de l'Industrie du Décolletage, Cluses

FRE7   CTDEC, Centre Technique de l'Industrie du Décolletage, Cluses

FRE8   CTDEC, Centre Technique de l'Industrie du Décolletage, Cluses

FRE9   SNDEC, Syndicat National du Décolletage, Cluses

FRE10   UDIMERA, Regional Federation of Employers in the Metal Sector for Rhône-Alpes, Lyon

FRE11   CNPFP, Delegation of Inter-Sectoral Employers' Association of Picardy, Amiens

FRE12   CNPFP, Delegation of Inter-Sectoral Employers' Association of Picardy, Amiens

FRE13   CSIMV, Territorial Metal Employers' Association of the Vimeu, Woincourt

FRE14   UPA, Regional Intersectoral Employers' Association of Alsace, Strasbourg

FRE15   UPA, Regional Intersectoral Employers' Association of Alsace, Strasbourg

FRE16   UDIMEC, Territorial Association of Employers in the Metal Sector of the Isère, Grenoble

FRG1   CRA, Regional Council of Alsace, Directorate of Education and Professional Training, Strasbourg

FRG2   CRP, Regional Council of Picardy, Directorate of Professional Training, Amiens

FRG3   CRRA, Regional Council of Rhône-Alpes, Directorate of Professional Training, Charbonnières-les-Bains

FRG4   CRRA, Regional Council of Rhône-Alpes, Directorate of Professional Training, Charbonnières-les-Bains

FRG5   RRA, Rectorat of Lyon, Lyon

FRU1   CFDTA, Regional Union Confederation of Alsace, Strasbourg

FRU2   CFDTC, Local Union Association, Cluses

FRU3   CFDTP, Regional Union Confederation of Picardy, Amiens

FRU4   CFDTRA, Regional Union Confederation of Rhône-Alpes, Lyon

FRU5   FORA, Departmental CGT-FO, Union Confederation of the Isère, Valence

EASTERN GERMANY

ERE1   IHKB, German Chambers of Industry and Commerce, Berlin

ERE2   IHKH, German Chambers of Industry and Commerce, Halle

ERE3   IHKL, German Chambers of Industry and Commerce, Leipzig

ERE4   IHKL, German Chambers of Industry and Commerce, Leipzig

ERE5   IHKSWS, German Chambers of Industry and Commerce, Plauen

ERE6   LVSA/VMESA, Federation of Employers' Associations in Saxony-Anhalt/Metal Working Employers' Association of Saxony-Anhalt, Magdeburg

ERE7   LVSA/VMESA, Federation of Employers' Associations in Saxony-Anhalt/Metal Working Employers' Association of Saxony-Anhalt, Magdeburg

ERE8   UVB, Berlin, Federation of Employers' Associations for Berlin and Brandenburg

ERE9   UVB, Berlin, Federation of Employers' Associations for Berlin and Brandenburg

ERE10   VAS/VSME, Saxon Federation of Employers' Associations/ Saxon Metal Working Employers' Association, Dresden

ERG1   AAL, District Employment Office, Leipzig

ERG2   AAP, District Employment Office, Plauen

ERG3   KMSA, Culture Ministry, Saxony-Anhalt, Magdeburg

ERG4   KMSA, Culture Ministry, Saxony-Anhalt, Magdeburg

ERG5   LAASA, State Employment Office, Saxony-Anhalt, Magdeburg

ERU1   DGBB, Peak Union Federation, Berlin

ERU2   DGBS, Saxon Trade Union Federation, Dresden

ERU3   DGBS, Saxon Trade Union Federation, Dresden

ERU4   DGBSA, Saxony-Anhalt Trade Union Federation, Magdeburg

ERG6   LAAST, State Employment Office, Sachsen-Anhalt-Thüringen, Halle

ERG7   MWSA, Saxon-Anhalt Ministry for Economy, Magdeburg

ERG8   SSWA, Saxon State Ministry for Economy and Labor, Dresden

WESTERN GERMANY

WNE1   BDA, Confederation of German Employers' Associations, Bonn

WNE2   DIHT, Peak Association of German Chambers of Industry and Commerce, Bonn

WNE3   Gesamtmetall, Peak Association of Employers in the Metal Sector, Berlin

WNE4   Gesamtmetall, Peak Association of Employers in the Metal Sector, Cologne

WRE1   VEMRP, Metal Employers' Association of Rhineland-Palatinate, Koblenz

WRU1   DGBRP, State Union Federation of Rhineland-Palatinate, Mainz

References

Acemoglu, D., and J.-S. Pischke. 1998. "Why Do Firms Train? Theory and Evidence." *Quarterly Journal of Economics* 113(1): 79–119.

ACFCI (Assemblée des Chambres françaises de commerce et de l'industrie). N.d. "La Direction de la Politique de Formation." Internal Document. Paris.

Aniello, V., and P. Le Galès 2001. "Between Large Firms and Marginal Local Economies: The Making of Systems of Local Governance in France." In *Local Production Systems in Europe: Rise or Demise?* edited by C. Crouch, P. Le Galès, C. Trigilia, and H. Voelzkow, 117–53. New York, Oxford University Press.

Argyris, C., and D. Schon. 1978. *Organizational Learning: A Theory of Action Perspective.* Reading, Addison-Wesley.

Auer, P. 2000. *Employment Revival in Europe.* Geneva, International Labour Office.

Axelrod, R. 1984. *The Evolution of Cooperation.* New York, Basic Books.

Ayres, I., and J. Braithwaite. 1992. *Responsive Regulation: Transcending the Deregulation Debate.* New York, Oxford University Press.

Baccaro, L. 2002. "Negotiating the Italian Pension Reform with the Unions: Lessons for Corporatist Theory." *Industrial and Labor Relations Review* 55(3): 413–31.

Bates, R. 1988. "Contra Contractarianism: Some Reflections on the New Institutionalism." *Politics and Society* 16(2–3): 387–401.

Baylis, T. 1993. "Transforming the East German Economy: Shock without Therapy." In *From Bundesrepublik to Deutschland: German Politics after Unification.* edited by M. Huelshoff, A. Markovits, and S. Reich. Ann Arbor, University of Michigan Press.

Becker, G. S. 1964. *Human Capital: A Theoretical and Empirical Analysis, with Special Reference to Education.* National Bureau of Economic Research (NBER). New York, Columbia University Press.

Bel, M., L.-A. Gérard-Varet, and E. Verdier. 1999. "L'évolution des modes de construction de l'offre régionale de formation." Report produced for the Comité de coordination by the GREQAM and LEST research centers, Marseille and Aix-en-Provence, February 1999.

Bendor, J. 1993. "Uncertainty and the Evolution of Cooperation." *Journal of Conflict Resolution* 37(4): 709–34.

Benko, G., and A. Lipietz, eds. 1992. *Les régions qui gagnent: Districts et réseaux; les nouveaux paradigmes de la géographie économique.* Paris, Presses Universitaires de France.

Berry, J. 1999. "The Rise of Citizen Groups." In *Civic Engagement in American Democracy,* edited by T. Skocpol and D. Fiorina, 367–94. Washington, D.C., Brookings Institution.

Bertrand, O. 1996. "Financial and Fiscal Devices to Encourage the Development of Training: A Case Study of France." Mimeo.

Bicchieri, C. 1993. *Rationality and Coordination.* New York, Cambridge University Press.

Bluhm, K. 1999. *Zwischen Markt und Politik: Probleme und Praxis von Unternehmenskooperation in der Transformationsökonomie.* Opladen, Germany, Leske and Budrich.

BMBW (Bundesministerium für Bildung, Wissenschaft, Forschung und Technologie). 1993. *Berufsbildungsbericht 1993.* Bad Honnef, K. H. Bock Verlag.

——. 1994. *Berufsbildungsbericht 1994.* Bad Honnef, K. H. Bock Verlag.

——. 1995. *Berufsbildungsbericht 1995.* Bad Honnef, K. H. Bock Verlag.

——. 1996. *Berufsbildungsbericht 1996.* Rheinback, Druckpartner Moser.

——. 1997. *Berufsbildungsbericht 1997.* Rheinback, Druckpartner Moser.

——. 1998. *Berufsbildungsbericht 1998.* Magdeburg, Gebr. Garloff.

——. 1999. *Berufsbildungsbericht 1999.* Bonn, Bonn University Press.

Boix, C. 1998. *Political Parties, Growth, and Equality.* New York, Cambridge University Press.

Booth, A., and D. Snower. 1996. *Acquiring Skills: Market Failures, Their Symptoms and Policy Responses.* New York, Cambridge University Press.

Bouyx, B. 1997. *L'enseignement technologique et professionnel.* Paris, La Documentation française.

Boyer, R. 1995. "Wage Austerity and/or an Education Push: The French Dilemma." *Labour* (spec. issue): 519–66.

Brochier, D., L. Causse, A. Richard, and E. Verdier. 1994. *L'apprentissage coopératif en Rhône-Alpes: Portée et limites d'une politique novatrice (1988–1993).* CEREQ study 66. Marseille.

——. eds. 1995. *Les Unités de formation par alternance (UFA): Une coopération Éducation nationale-professions dans la région Rhône-Alpes (1988–1993).* CEREQ documents 102, Marseille.

Brown, R. 1988. *Group Processes: Dynamics within and between Groups.* New York, Basil Blackwell.

Bunel, J. 1995. *La Transformation de la représentation patronale en France: CNPF et CGPME.* Paris, Commissariat Général du Plan.

Burnstein, E., and A. Vinokur. 1977. "Persuasive Argumentation and Social Comparison as Determinants of Attitude Polarization." *Journal of Experimental Social Psychology* 13: 315–32.

Calvert, R. 1995. "The Rational Choice Theory of Social Institutions: Cooperation, Coordination, and Communication." In *Modern Political Economy,* edited by J. Banks and E. Hanushek, 216–67. New York, Cambridge University Press.

Cappelli, P., D. Shapiro, and N. Shumanis. 1998. "Employer Participation in School-to-Work Programs." *Annals of the American Academy of Political and Social Science* no. 559: 109–24.

Carlin, W., and C. Mayer. 1995. "Structure and Ownership of East German Enterprises." Working Paper FS1 95-305, Wissenschaftszentrum Berlin für Sozialforschung.

Carlin, W., and D. Soskice. 1997. "Shocks to the System: The German Political Economy under Stress." *National Institute Economic Review* no. 159: 57–76.

Casella, P., and J. Freyssinet. 1999. "Les acteurs économiques et sociaux face aux nouvelles responsabilités des régions en matière de formation profession-nelle." Report produced for the Comité de coordination by the IRES and Travail et Mobilité research centers, Paris, July 1999.

CBP (Chesapeake Bay Program). 1994. "Achieving the Chesapeake Bay Nutri-ent Goals: A Synthesis of Tributary Strategies for the Bay's Ten Watersheds." Report of the CBP, Annapolis.

Charpail, C., and S. Zilberman, 1998. "Diplôme et insertion professionnelle après un contrat de qualification." In *Bilan de la Élitique de L'Emploi 1997*, Direc-tion de l'animation de la Recherche, des Études et des Statistiques (DARES), 187–93. Paris, DARES.

Charraud, A. 1995. "Reconnaissance de la qualification: Contrats de qualifica-tion et évolution des règles." *Formation Emploi* 52: 113–32.

Charraud, A., E. Personnaz, and P. Venau. 1996. "Les certificats de qualification professionnelle (CQP): Construction des référentiels et mise en œuvre dans la métallurgie, l'agro-alimentaire, et la plasturgie." Collection CPC document, no. 8, Direction des Lycées et Collèges, Paris.

Chwe, M. S.-Y. 1999. "Structure and Strategy in Collective Action." *American Journal of Sociology* 105(1): 128–56.

Cohen, J. 1997. "Deliberation and Democratic Legitimacy." In *Deliberative Democ-racy*, edited by J. Bohman and W. Rehg, 67–91. Cambridge, Mass.: MIT Press.

———. 1998. "Democracy and Liberty." In *Deliberative Democracy*, edited by J. Elster, 185–231. New York: Cambridge University Press.

Cohen, J., and J. Rogers. 1992. "Secondary Associations and Democratic Governance." *Politics and Society* 20(4): 393–472.

Coleman, J. S. 1990. *Foundations of Social Theory*. Cambridge, Mass.: Harvard University Press.

Collier, I. 1993. "German Economic Integration: The Case for Optimism." In *From Bundesrepublik to Deutschland: German Politics after Unification*, edited by M. Huelshoff, A. Markovits, and S. Reich, 93–114. Ann Arbor, University of Michigan Press.

Comité de coordination. 1996a. *L'Apprentissage en France*. Report published by the Comité de coordination des programmes régionaux d'apprentissage et de formation professionnelle continue, Paris.

———. 1996b. *Évaluation des politiques régionales de formation professionnelle*. Report published by the Comité de coordination des programmes régionaux d'apprentissage et de formation professionnelle continue, Paris.

———. 1996c. *Innovations régionales et formation professionnelle*. Report published by the Comité de coordination des programmes régionaux d'apprentissage et de formation rpofessionnelle continue, Paris.

———. 1999. *Évaluation des politiques régionales de formation professionnelle*. Report published by the Comité de coordination des programmes régionaux d'ap-prentissage et de formation professionnelle continue, Paris.

Cooke, P., and K. Morgan. 1998. *The Associational Economy*. New York, Oxford University Press.

CRA (Conseil Régional d'Alsace). 1993. "Schéma prévisionnel des formations en Alsace." Government Document.

Cramer, G., and K. Müller. 1994. "Nutzen der betrieblichen Berufsausbildung." *Beiträge des Instituts der deutschen Wirtschaft und Gesellschafts- und Bildungspolitik*, no. 195(5): 1–13. Cologne.

Crossan, M., H. Lane, and R. White. 1999. "An Organizational Learning Framework: From Intuition to Institution." *The Academy of Management Review*, 24(3): 522–37.

Crouch, C., D. Finegold, and M. Sako. 1999. *Are Skills the Answer? The Political Economy of Skill Creation in the Advanced Industrial Countries.* New York, Oxford University Press.

Culpepper, P. D. 1999. "Individual Choice, Collective Action, and the Problem of Training Reform: Insights from France and Eastern Germany." In *The German Skills Machine: Sustaining Comparative Advantage in a Global Economy*, edited by P. D. Culpepper and D. Finegold, 269–325. New York, Berghahn Books.

Culpepper, P. D., and D. Finegold, eds. 1999. *The German Skills Machine: Sustaining Comparative Advantage in a Global Economy.* New York, Berghahn Books.

Cuminal, V. 1998. "Le C2T du Vimeu." In *Chronique De L'Industrie Française du Décolletage*, edited by P. Guichonnet 251–54. La Roche sur Foron, France, Chevalier and Associates.

Cusack, T. 1997. "Social Capital, Institutional Structures, and Democratic Performance: A Comparative Study of German Local Governments." Working Paper FS 3 97–201, Wissenschaftszentrum Berlin für Sozialforschung.

Davison, S. J. Merwin, J. Capper, G. Power, and F. Shivers. 1997. *Chesapeake Waters* 2d ed. Centreville, Md., Tidewater.

De Bernardy, M. 1991. "Dans la vallée de l'Arve, le CTDEC." Mimeo.

Deeg, R. 1999. *Finance Capitalism Unveiled.* Ann Arbor, University of Michigan Press.

Dewatripont, M., and G. Roland. 1995. "The Design of Reform Packages under Uncertainty." *American Economic Review* 85(5): 1207–23.

D'Iribarne, A., and A. Lemaître. 1987. *Le role des partenaires sociaux dans la formation professionnelle en France.* Brussels, CEDEFOP.

Donahue, J., and J. Nye. 2001. *Governance amid Bigger, Better Markets.* Washington, D.C., Brookings Institution.

Dresser, L., J. Rogers, and S. Zdrazil. 2001. "Wisconsin Regional Training Partnership." Mimeo.

Dubar, C. 1995. *La Formation Professionnelle Continue.* Paris, La Découverte.

Ebbinghaus, B., and A. Hassel. 2000. "Striking Deals: Concertation in the Reform of Continental European Welfare States." *Journal of European Public Policy* 7(1): 44–62.

Eckstein, H., and T. Gurr. 1975. *Patterns of Authority: A Structural Basis for Political Inquiry.* New York, John Wiley and Sons.

Ergas, H. 1987. "The Importance of Technology Policy." In *Economic Policy and Technological Performance*, edited by P. Dasgupta and P. Stoneman, 51–96. New York: Cambridge University Press.

Estevez-Abe, M., T. Iversen, and D. Soskice. 2001. "Social Protection and the Formation of Skills: A Reinterpretation of the Welfare State." In *Varieties of*

Capitalism: The Institutional Foundations of Comparative Advantage, edited by P. A. Hall and D. Soskice, 145–83. New York, Oxford University Press.

Ettl, W. 1995. "Arbeitgeberverbände als Transformationsakteure: Organisationsentwicklung und Tarifpolitik im Dilemma von Funktionalität und Repräsentitativität." In *Einheit als Interessenpolitik*, edited by H. Wiesenthal, 34–94. Frankfurt, Campus.

Ettl, W., and A. Heikenroth. 1995. "Strukturwandel, Verbandsabstinenz, Tarifflucht: Zur Lage ostdeutscher Unternehmen und Arbeitgeberverbände." Working Paper, Max Planck Gesellschaft, Arbeitsgruppe Transformationsprozesse in den neuen Bundesländern.

Evans, P. 1995. *Embedded Autonomy*. Princeton, Princeton University Press.

Fearon, J. 1998. "Deliberation as Discussion." In *Deliberative Democracy*, edited by J. Elster, 44–68. New York, Cambridge University Press.

Fearon, J., and D. Laitin. 2000. "Violence and the Social Construction of Ethnic Identity." *International Organization* 54(4): 845–77.

Fearon, J., and A. Wendt. 2002. "Rationalism versus Constructivism: A Skeptical View." In *Handbook of International Relations*, edited by W. Carlsanes,T. Risse, and B. Simmons, 52–72. London, Sage Publications.

Fenby, J. 1999. *France on the Brink*. New York, Arcade Publishing.

Fernandez, R., and D. Rodrik. 1991. "Resistance to Reform: Status Quo Bias in the Presence of Individual-Specific Uncertainty." *American Economic Review* 81(5): 1146–55.

Fichter, M. 1993. "A House Divided: A View of German Unification as it has Affected Organized Labour." *German Politics* 2(1): 21–39.

———. 1997. "Unions in the New Länder: Evidence for the Urgency of Reform." In *Negotiating the New Germany*, edited by L. Turner, 87–112. Ithaca, Cornell University Press.

Fierke, K. M., and M. Nicholson. 2001. "Divided by a Common Language: Formal and Constructivist Approaches to Games." *Global Society* 15(1): 7–25.

Finegold, D., and D. Soskice. 1988. "The Failure of Training in Britain." *Oxford Review of Economic Policy* 4(3): 36–61.

Finegold, D. and K. Wagner. 1999. "The German Skill Creation System and Team-Based Production: Competitive Asset or Liability?" In *The German Skills Machine: Sustaining Comparative Advantage in a Global Economy*, edited by P. D. Culpepper and D. Finegold, 115–55. New York, Berghahn Books.

Finnemore, M., and K. Sikkink. 2001. "Taking Stock: The Constructivist Research Program in International Relations and Comparative Politics." *Annual Review of Political Science* 4: 391–416.

Fukuyama, F. 1995. *Trust: The Social Virtues and the Creation of Prosperity*. New York, Free Press.

Garrett, G. 1997. *Partisan Politics in the Global Economy*. New York, Cambridge University Press.

Garrett, G., and P. Lange. 1991. "Political Responses to Interdependence: What's Left for the Left?" *International Organization* 45(4): 539–64.

Gehin, J.-P., and P. Méhaut. 1993. *Apprentissage ou formation continue?* Paris, Harmattan.

Glazer, A., and L. S. Rothenberg. 2001. *Why Government Succeeds and Why It Fails.* Cambridge, Mass., Harvard University Press.

Goasguen, C. R. 1994. "Rapport de la Commision d'Enquête sur l'utilisation des fonds affectés à la formation professionnelle." Assemblée nationale, 2 vols. Parliamentory Report, Paris.

Goetz, K. 1993. "Rebuilding Public Administration in the New German Laender: Transfer and Differentiation." *West European Politics* 16(4): 447–69.

Goldthorpe, J., ed. 1984. *Order and Conflict in Contemporary Capitalism.* New York, Oxford University Press.

Granovetter, M. 1978. "Threshold Models of Collective Behavior." *American Journal of Sociology* 83(6): 1420–43.

——. 1985. "Economic Action and Social Structure: The Problem of 'Embeddedness.'" *American Journal of Sociology* 91: 481–510.

Grézard, C. 1993. "L'Apprentissage en 1992." In *Bilan de la politique de l'emploi en 1992*, 49–53. Paris, Ministry of Work, Employment and Professional Training.

Guichonnet, P. 1998. *Chronique de l'industrie française du décolletage.* La Roche sur Foron, France, Chevalier and Associates.

Hall, P. 1994. "Central Bank Independence and Coordinated Wage Bargaining: Their Interaction in Germany and Europe." *German Politics and Society* 31: 1–23.

——. 1999. "The Political Economy of Europe in an Era of Interdependence." In *Change and Continuity in Contemporary Capitalism*, edited by H. Kitschelt, P. Lange, G. Marks, and J. Stephens, 135–63. New York, Cambridge University Press.

Hall, P. A., and D. Soskice. 2001. "An Introduction to Varieties of Capitalism." In *Varieties of Capitalism: The Institutional Foundations of Comparative Advantage*, edited by P. A. Hall and D. Soskice, 1–68. New York, Oxford University Press.

Hancké, B. 2001. "Revisiting the French Model: Coordination and Restructuring in French Industry." In *Varieties of Capitalism: The Institutional Foundations of Comparative Advantage*, edited by P. A. Hall and D. Soskice, 307–34. New York, Oxford University Press.

Hardin, G. 1968. "The Tragedy of the Commons." *Science* 162: 1243–48.

Harhoff, D., and T. Kane. 1997. "Is the German Apprenticeship System a Panacea for the US Labour Market?" *Journal of Population Economics* 10(2): 171–96.

Hassel, A., and B. Ebbinghaus. 2000. "Concerted Reforms: Linking Wage Formation and Social Policy in Europe." Paper prepared for the Twelfth International Conference of Europeanists, 30 March–1 April 2000, Chicago.

Heckathorn, D. 1996. "The Dynamics and Dilemmas of Collective Action." *American Sociological Review* 61: 250–77.

Heclo, H. 1974. *Modern Social Politics in Britain and Sweden: From Relief to Income Maintenance.* New Haven, Yale University Press.

Helliwell, J., and R. Putnam. 1995. "Economic Growth and Social Capital in Italy." *Eastern Economic Journal* 21(3): 295–307.

Henderson, D. 2000. "EU Regional Innovation Strategies." *European Urban and Regional Studies* 7(4): 347–58.

Henneberger, F. 1993. "Transferstart: Organisationsdynamik und Strukturkon-servatismus westdeutscher Unternehmerverbände-Aktuelle Entwicklungen unter besonderer Berücksichtigung des Aufbauprozesses in Sachsen und Thüringen." *Politische Vierteljahresschrift* 34(4): 640–73.

Herrigel, G. 1996. *Industrial Constructions: The Sources of German Industrial Power.* New York, Cambridge University Press.

Hicks, A., and L. Kenworthy. 1998. "Cooperation and Political Economic Per-formance in Affluent Democratic Capitalism." *American Journal of Sociology* 103(6): 1631–72.

Hitchens, D., K. Wagner, and E. Birnie. 1993. *East German Productivity and the Transition to the Market Economy.* Aldershot, Avebury.

Hjern, B., and C. Hull. 1982. "Implementation Research as Empirical Consti-tutionalism." *European Journal of Political Research* 10: 105–15.

Hjern, B., and D. O. Porter. 1981. "Implementation Structures: A New Unit of Administrative Analysis." *Organization Studies* 1(3): 211–27.

Hoppenstedt. 1993, 1994. *Firmen in den Neuen Bundesländer.* Darmstadt, Hoppenstedt Verlag.

Howell, C. 1992. *Regulating Labor: The State and Industrial Relations in Post-War France.* Princeton, Princeton University Press.

Hudson, K. 1995. "Restoring the Chesapeake: Bottom-up approach is winning pollution battle." *The American City & County* 110(7): 30–39.

Hull, C., and B. Hjern. 1987. *Helping Small Firms Grow.* New York, Croom Helm.

Huré, F., C. Dufour, J-J. Sanvert, and P. de Rivoire. 1995. "L'apprentissage relevant des chambres consulaires," Report of the Inspection générale de l'industrie et de commerce, Paris.

Hyman, R. 1996. "Institutional Transfer: Industrial Relations in Eastern Germany." Working Paper FS1 96-305, Wissenschaftszentrum. Berlin Für Sozialforschung.

Iida, K. 1993. "Analytic Uncertainty and International Cooperation: Theory and Application to International Economic Policy Coordination." *International Studies Quarterly* 37(4): 431–57.

INSEE (Institute national des statistiques et des études économiques). 1998. *Atlas des zones d'emploi.* Paris, INSEE.

Isenberg, D. J. 1986. "Group Polarization: A Critical Review and Meta-Analysis." *Journal of Personality and Social Psychology* 50(6): 1141–51.

Iversen, T. 1999. *Contested Economic Institutions: The Politics of Macroeconomic and Wage Bargaining.* New York, Cambridge University Press.

Iversen, T., and D. Soskice. 2001. "An Asset Theory of Social Policy Preferences." *American Political Science Review* 95(4): 875–93.

Jobert, A., and M. Tallard. 1995. "Diplômes et Certification des branches dans les conventions collectives." *Formation Emploi* 52: 133–50.

Johnson, C. 1995. "Die Rolle intermediärer Organisationen beim Wandel des Berufsbildungssystems." In *Einheit als Interessenpolitik: Studien zur sektoralen Transformation Ostdeutschlands,* edited by H. Wiesenthal, 126–59. Frankfurt. Campus.

Kahneman, D., and A. Tversky. 1979. "Prospect Theory: An Analysis of Decision under Risk." *Econometrica* 47(2): 263–91.

Katzenstein, P. J. 1987. *Policy and Politics in West Germany: The Growth of a Semi-sovereign State.* Philadelphia, Temple University Press.

——. ed. 1989. *Industry and Politics in West Germany.* Ithaca, Cornell University Press.

Katzenstein, P. J., R. Keohane, and S. Krasner. 1998. "International Organization and the Study of World Politics." *International Organization* 52(4): 645–85.

Kaufman, H. 1960. *The Forest Ranger.* Baltimore, Johns Hopkins Press.

Keeler, J. T. S. 1987. *The Politics of Neocorporatism in France.* New York, Oxford University Press.

Keohane, R. 1984. *After Hegemony: Cooperation and Discord in the World Political Economy.* Princeton, Princeton University Press.

King, G., R. Keohane, and S. Verba. 1994. *Designing Social Inquiry: Scientific Inference in Qualitative Research.* Princeton, Princeton University Press.

Kingdon, J. W. 1984. *Agendas, Alternative, and Public Policies.* New York, Harper Collins.

Kitschelt, H., P. Lange, G. Marks, and J. Stephens, eds. 1999. *Continuity and Change in Contemporary Capitalism.* New York, Cambridge University Press.

Kleiner, H., and C. Bretz 1995. Joint letter from the UVB and the DGB-Berlin-Brandenburg to Eberhard Diepgen, Mayor of Berlin, 3 May 1995.

Klimecki, R., and H. Lassleben. 1998. "Modes of organizational learning: Indications from an empirical study." *Management Learning* 29(4): 405–30.

Kreps, D. 1990. "Corporate Culture and Economic Theory." In *Perspectives on Positive Political Economy,* edited by J. Alt and K. Shepsle, 90–143. New York, Cambridge University Press.

Kreps, D., P. Milgrom, J. Roberts, and R. Wilson. 1982. "Rational Cooperation in the Finitely Repeated Prisoners' Dilemma." *Journal of Economic Theory* 27: 245–52.

Laitin, D. 1998. *Identity in Formation.* Ithaca, Cornell University Press.

Lamm, H., and D. G. Myers. 1978. "Group-induced polarization of attitudes and behavior." *Advances in Experimental Psychology.* 11: 145–95.

Lange, T., and G. Pugh. 1998. *The Economics of German Unification.* Aldershot, Edward Elgar.

Lange, T., and J. R. Shackleton. 1998. *The Political Economy of German Unification.* Providence, Berghahn Books.

Lefebvre, P. 1992. "Le Vimeu: terre du métal travaillé." *Annales des Mines* (spec. issue, November): 24–26.

Levy, J. 1992. "An Introduction to Prospect Theory." *Political Psychology* 13(2): 171–86.

——. 1994. "Learning and Foreign Policy: Sweeping a Conceptual Minefield." *International Organization* 48(2): 279–312.

——. 1996. "Loss Aversion, Framing, and Bargaining: The Implications of Prospect Theory for International Conflict." *International Political Science Review* 17(2): 179–95.

Levy, J. D. 1999. *Tocqueville's Revenge: State, Society, and Economy in Contemporary France.* Cambridge, Mass., Harvard University Press.

Lhotel, H., and A. Monaco. 1993. "Regards croisés sur l'apprentissage et les contrats de qualification." *Formation Emploi* 42: 32–45.

Lichtenberger, Y. 1993. "La décentralisation de la formation professionnelle: Transfert de compétence et innovation." In *La Décentralisation de la formation: Marché du travail, institutions, acteurs*, Collection des Études no. 64, 9–26. Marseille, CEREQ.

Locke, R. 1995. *Remaking the Italian Economy*. Ithaca, Cornell University Press.

Locke, R. and W. Jacoby (1997). "The Dilemmas of Diffusion: Institutional Transfer and the Remaking of Vocational Training Practices in Eastern Germany." In *Negotiating the New Germany*, edited by L. Turner, 33–68. Ithaca, Cornell University Press.

Lohmann, S. 1994. "Dynamics of Informational Cascades: The Monday Demonstrations in Leipzig, East Germany, 1989–91." *World Politics* 47(1): 42–101.

Lutz, B., and H. Grünert. 1999. *Evaluierung der Vorhaben zur Förderung der beruflichen Erstausbildung*. Magdeburg, Ministerium für Arbeit, Frauen, Gesundheit und Soziales des Landes Sachsen-Anhalt.

Lynch, L., ed. 1994. *Training and the Private Sector*. Chicago, University of Chicago Press.

Macdonald, A. 1997. "Bay Watch: Safer, but Still Not Saved." *Washington Post* 23 February 1997, C3.

Macy, M. 1991. "Learning to Cooperate: Stochastic and Tacit Collusion in Social Exchange." *American Journal of Sociology* 97(3): 808–43.

Mansbridge, J. J. 1992. "A Deliberative Theory of Interest Representation." In *The Politics of Interests: Interest Groups Transformed*, edited by M. P. Petracca, 32–57. Boulder, Westview Press.

March, J., and J. Olsen. 1989. *Rediscovering Institutions: The Organizational Basis of Politics*. New York, Free Press.

Margirier, G., and A. Richard. 1995. *La formation professionnelle des jeunes en Rhône-Alpes*. CEREQ documents 103, Marseille.

Marwell, G., and P. Oliver. 1993. *The Critical Mass in Collective Action: A Micro-Social Theory*. Cambridge, UK, Cambridge University Press.

Matuszeski, W. 1995. "The Chesapeake Bay Program." *Ekistics* 62(370): 48–55.

Maurice, M., F. Sellier, and J. Silvestre. 1986. *The Social Foundations of Industrial Power*. Trans. A. Goldhammer. Cambridge, Mass., Cambridge University Press.

Mayntz, R., ed. 1983. *Implementation Politischer Programme II: Anzätze zur Theoriebildung*. Opladen, Germany, Westdeutscher Verlag.

Mazmanian, D. A., and M. E. Kraft. 1999. *Toward Sustainable Communities*. Cambridge, Mass., MIT Press.

Mazmanian, D. A., and P. Sabatier. 1983. *Implementation and Public Policy*. Palo Alto, Scott Foresman and Co.

McCubbins, M. D., and T. D. Schwartz. 1984. "Congressional Oversight Overlooked: Police Patrols versus Fire Alarms." *American Journal of Political Science* 2(1): 165–79.

Mériaux, O. 1999. "L'action publique partagée: Formes et dynamiques institutionnelles de la régulation politique du régime français de formation professionnelle continue." Ph.D. diss., Institut d'Études Politiques, Université Grenoble II.

Möbus, M. 1996. "Politiques de branche et stratégies des entreprises: état des lieux." In *L'alternance: Enjeux et débats*, 19–32. Paris, La Documentation Française.

Morgan, K. 1997. "The Learning Region: Institutions, Innovations and Regional Renewal." *Regional Studies* 31(5): 491–503.

Münch, J. 1991. *Vocational Training in the Federal Republic of Germany*. 3rd ed. Berlin, CEDEFOP.

North, D. 1990. *Institutions, Institutional Change, and Economic Performance*. New York, Cambridge University Press.

——. 1995. "Five Propositions about Institutional Change." In *Explaining Institutional Change*, edited by J. Knight and I. Sened, 15–26. Ann Arbor, University of Michigan Press.

OECD (Organization for Economic Cooperation and Development). 1994. *Apprenticeship: Which Way Forward?* Paris, OECD.

Offe, C. 1997. *Varieties of Transition: The East European and East German Experience*. Cambridge, Mass, MIT Press.

OIP (Observatoire Interrégional du Politique). 1990–1993. OIP Surveys. Paris, OIP.

Olson, M. 1965. *The Logic of Collective Action*. Cambridge, Mass., Harvard University Press.

Osborne, D., and T. Gaebler. 1992. *Reinventing Government: How the Entrepreneurial Spirit is Transforming the Public Sector*. Reading, Mass., Addison-Wesley.

Ostrom, E. 1990. *Governing the Commons: The Evolution of Institutions for Collective Action*. New York, Cambridge University Press.

——. 1998. "A Behavioral Approach to the Rational Choice Theory of Collective Action." *American Political Science Review* 92(1): 1–22.

Ostrom, E., R. Gardner, and J. Walker. 1994. *Rules, Games, and Common Pool Resources*. Ann Arbor, University of Michigan Press.

Padgett, S. 1999. *Organizing Democracy in Eastern Germany: Interest Groups in Post-Communist Society*. Cambridge, UK: Cambridge University Press.

Paolisso, M., and R. S. Maloney. 2000. "Recognizing Farmer Environmentalism: Nutrient Runoff and Toxic Dinoflagellate Blooms in the Chesapeake Bay Region." *Human Organization* 59(2): 209–21.

Parker, E., and J. Rogers. 1999. "Sectoral Training Initiatives in the U.S.: Building Blocks of a New Workforce Preparation System?" In *The German Skills Machine*, edited by P. D. Culpepper and D. Finegold, 326–62. New York, Berghahn Books.

Pascaud, E. 1991. "Décentralisation de la formation professionnelle: Réalisations, difficultés, et propositions." Mimeo.

Peterson, M., and J. Walker. 1991. "Interest Groups and the Reagan Presidency." In *Mobilizing Interest Groups in America*, edited by J. Walker, 141–56. Ann Arbor, University of Michigan Press.

Pfeiffer, B. 1997. "Das Ausbildungsangebot der westdeutschen Betriebe 1995—Ergebnisse des IAB-Betribspanels." *Berufsbildung in Wissenschaft und Praxis* 26(2): 10–16.

Piore, M. J., and C. F. Sabel. 1984. *The Second Industrial Divide*. New York, Basic Books.

Poleyn, J. 1996. "L'industrie du décolletage: au fil de l'Arve." *Les 4 Pages des statistiques industrielles*, 1–4. French Ministry for Industry, Paris.

Porter, M. E. 1998. *On Competition*. Cambridge, Mass., Harvard Business School.

Pressman, J. L., and A. Wildavsky. 1973. *Implementation*. Berkeley, University of California Press.

Przeworski, A. 1998. "Deliberation and Ideological Domination." In *Deliberative Democracy*, edited by J. Elster, 140–60. New York, Cambridge University Press.

Putnam, R. D. 1993. *Making Democracy Work*. Princeton, Princeton University Press.

———. 2000. *Bowling Alone: The Collapse and Revival of American Community*. New York, Simon and Schuster.

Regini, M. 1995. "Firms and Institutions: The Demand for Skills and their Social Production in Europe." *European Journal of Industrial Relations* 1(2).

———. 1997a. "Different Responses to Common Demands: Firms, Institutions, and Training in Europe." *European Sociological Review* 13(3): 267–82.

———. 1997b. "Still Engaging in Corporatism? Recent Italian Experience in Comparative Perspective." *European Journal of Industrial Relations* 3(3): 259–78.

Rhodes, M. 1998. "Globalization, Labour Markets, and Welfare States: A Future of Competitive Corporatism." In *The Future of European Welfare*, edited by M. Rhodes and Y. Mény, 178–203. New York, St. Martin's Press.

Riker, W., and D. Weimer. 1995. "The Political Economy of Transformation." In *Modern Political Economy*, edited by J. Banks and E. Hanushek, 80–107. New York, Cambridge University Press.

Rodrik, D. 1996. "Understanding Economic Policy Reform." *Journal of Economic Literature* 34: 9–41.

Rüttgers, J. 1995. Letter to Gesamtmetall, 31 March, 1995.

Sabel, C. 1991. "Moebius-Strip Organizations and Open Labor Markets: Some Consequences of the Reintegration of Conception and Execution in a Volatile Economy." In *Social Theory for a Changing Society*, edited by J. Coleman and P. Bourdieu, 23–63. Boulder, Westview Press.

———. 1994. "Learning by Monitoring: The Institutions of Economic Development." In *The Handbook of Economic Sociology*, edited by N. Smelser and R. Swedberg, 137–65. Princeton, Princeton University Press.

———. 1995. "Bootstrapping Reform: Rebuilding Firms, the Welfare State, and Unions." *Politics and Society* 23(1): 5–48.

Sabel, C., A. Fung, and B. Karkkainen. 1999. "Beyond Backyard Environmentalism: How Communities Are Quietly Refashioning Environmental Regulation." *Boston Review* 24(5): 4–11.

Sanchez, R. 1997. "Formation et insertion des jeunes: l'essor de l'alternance se poursuite en 1997." *Bilan de la Politique de L'emploi en 1997*, 43–55. Paris, Ministry of Work, Employment and Professional Training.

Saxenian, A. 1994. *Regional Advantage: Culture and Competition in Silicon Valley and Route 128*. Cambridge, Mass., Harvard University Press.

Scharpf, F. 1983. "Interessenanlage der Adressaten und Spielräume der Implementation bei Anreizprogrammen." In *Implementation Politischer Programme II*, edited by R. Mayntz, 99–116. Opladen, Germany, Westdeutscher Verlag.

——. 1991. *Crisis and Choice in European Social Democracy*. Ithaca, Cornell University Press.

——. 1997. *Games Real Actors Play*. Boulder, Westview Press.

Schelling, T. C. 1960. *The Strategy of Conflict*. Cambridge, Harvard University Press.

——. 1978. *Micromotives and Macrobehavior*. New York, W.W. Norton.

Schmitter, P. 1974. "Still the Century of Corporatism?" *The Review of Politics* 36(1): 85–131.

Schmitter, P., and G. Lehmbruch, eds. 1979. *Trends toward Corporatist Intermediation*. Beverly Hills, Sage.

Schober, K. 1994. "Der schwierige Übergang zum dualen System." *Materialen aus dem Arbeitsmarkt- und Berufsforschung*. 3: 1–23.

Schober, K., and A. Rauch. 1995. "Gute Noten trotz schwiegier Arbeitsmarktlage." *IAB Kurzbericht* no. 8.

Scholz, J., and W. B. Gray. 1997. "Can Government Facilitate Cooperation? An Informational Model of OSHA Enforcement." *American Journal of Political Science* 41(3): 693–717.

Schramedei, H. 1995. "Ungünstige politische Rahmenbedingungen für die Wirtschaftsentwicklung in Sachsen-Anhalt." *VME Sachsen-Anhalt Newsletter* 5: 1–2.

Schweikert, K. 1999. *Aus einem Holz? Lehrlinge in Deutschland*. Bielefeld, Germany: Bertelsmann Verlag.

Scott, J. C. 1998. *Seeing like a State: How Certain Schemes to Improve the Human Condition Have Failed*. New Haven, Yale University Press.

Shonfield, A. 1965. *Modern Capitalism*. Oxford, Oxford University Press.

Silvia, S. 1997. "German Unification and Emerging Divisions with German Employers' Associations: Cause or Catalyst?" *Comparative Politics* 29(2): 187–208.

Skocpol, T. 1999. "How Americans Became Civic." In *Civic Engagement in American Democracy*, edited by T. Skocpol and M. Fiorina. 27–80. Washington, D.C., Brookings Institution.

Skocpol, T., and M. Fiorina, eds. 1999. *Civic Engagement in American Democracy*. Washington D.C., Brookings Institution.

Soskice, D. 1990a. "Reinterpreting Corporatism and Explaining Unemployment." In *Labour Relations and Economic Performance*, edited by R. Brunetta and C. Dell'Aringa, 170–214 New York, New York University Press.

——. 1990b. "Wage Determination: The Changing Role of Institutions in Advanced Industrialized Countries." *Oxford Review of Economic Policy* 6(4): 36–61.

——. 1994. "Reconciling Markets and Institutions: The German Apprenticeship System." In *Training and the Private Sector: International Comparisons*, edited by L. Lynch. 25–60. Chicago, University of Chicago Press.

——. 1999. "Divergent Production Regimes: Coordinated and Uncoordinated Market Economies in the 1980s and 1990s." In *Continuity and Change in Contemporary Capitalism*, edited by H. Kitschelt, P. Lange, G. Marks, and J. Stephens, 101–34. New York, Cambridge University Press.

SSWA (Sächsisches Staatsministerium für Wirtschaft und Arbeit). 1994. Minutes from meeting of the Working Group "Lehrstellenoffensive," Sächsisches Staatsministerium für Wirtschaft und Arbeit, 25 July 1994, Dresden.

———. 1995. "Lehrstellen: Sächsische Lösung Steht." Press Release, 5 September 1995, Dresden.

Stark, D., and L. Bruszt. 1998. *Postsocialist Pathways: Transforming Politics and Property in East Central Europe.* New York, Cambridge University Press.

Stokey, E., and R. Zeckhauser. 1978. *A Primer for Policy Analysis.* New York, Norton.

Stoner, J. 1961. "A comparison of individual and group decisions including risk." Ph.D. diss., School of Management, Massachusetts Institute of Technology.

Stranahan, S. 1993. *Susquehanna, River of Dreams.* Baltimore, Johns Hopkins University Press.

Streeck, W. 1992. *Social Institutions and Economic Performance.* Newbury Park, Sage.

———. 1997. "German Capitalism: Does It Exist? Can It Survive?" In *Political Economy of Modern Capitalism: Mapping Convergence and Diversity,* edited by C. Crouch and W. Streeck, 33–54. London, Sage.

Streeck, W., J. Hilbert, K. Kevelaer, F. Maier, and H. Weber. 1987. *The Role of the Social Partners in Vocational Training and Further Training in the Federal Republic of Germany,* Berlin, CEDEFOP.

Streeck, W., and P. Schmitter. 1985. "Community, Market, State—and Associations?" *European Sociological Review* 1: 119–38.

Sunstein, C. R., D. Kahneman, and D. Schkade. 1998. "Assessing Punitive Damages (with Notes on Cognition and Valuation in Law)." *Yale Law Journal* 107(7): 2071–153.

Swank, D., and C. J. Martin. 2001. "Employers and the Welfare State: The Political Economic Organization of Firms and Social Policy in Contemporary Capitalist Democracies." *Comparative Political Studies* 34(8): 889–923.

Thelen, K. 1991. *Union of Parts: Labor Politics in Postwar Germany.* Ithaca, Cornell University Press.

Thomas, K. 2000. "Creating Regional Cultures of Innovation? The Regional Innovation Strategies in England and Scotland." *Regional Studies* 34(2): 190–98.

Trib Team Monitor. 1997. "Chesapeake Bay Trust: Potential Funding for Trib Team Projects." Winter 1997, 1(3): 1–3. Available at http://www.dnr.state.md.us/bay/tribstrat/monitor/.

UIMM (Union des industries minières et métallurgiques). 1997. *Certificats de qualification professionnelle de la métallurgie.* Paris, UIMM.

Ulrich, J. G. 1995. "Außerbetriebliche Ausbildung für marktbenachteiligte Jugendliche." *Berufsbildung in Wissenschaft and Praxis* 24(4): 24–28.

Verdier, E. 1995. "L'accord fondateur d'une politique régionale: une ambiguité créatrice?" In *La stratégie des acteurs locaux dans les politiques de formation,* edited by A. Larceneux and E. Kabantchenko, 96–110. CEREQ documents 111, Marseille.

Vialla, A. 1997. "Apprentissage: ruptures, enchaînements de contrats et accès à l'emploi." *Note d'Information, Ministère de l'Education Nationale* 97(22): 1–4.

Visser, J. and A. Hemerijck. 1997. *"A Dutch Miracle": Job Growth, Welfare Reform and Corporatism in the Netherlands.* Amsterdam, Amsterdam University Press.

VME (Verband der Metall- und Elektroindustrie in Berlin und Brandenburg). 1995. "Ausbildungsverbund." Summary of expert joint commission on vocational training of IG Metall and Gesamtmetall. Dresden.

von Bardeleben, R. 1993. "Probleme der Berufsausbildung in der neuen Bundesländern aus der Sicht nichtausbildender Betriebe." In *Berufsbildung im Übergang,* edited by U. Degen, 45–54. Berlin, Bundesingtitut für Berufsbildung.

——. 1995. "Gründe für die Ausbildungsabstinenz." In *Berufsausbildung in den neuen Bundesländern: Daten, Analysen, Perspektiven,* edited by U. Degen, G. Walden, and K. Berger, 82–87. Bielefeld, Bertelsmann.

von Bardeleben, R., U. Beicht, and K. Fehér 1995. "Cost and benefit of in-house professional and vocational training." Mimeo.

VSME (Verband der Sächsischen Metall- und Elektroindustrie). 1995. *Geschäftsbericht 1994/95.* Dresden, Verband der Sächsischen Metall- und Elektroindustrie.

Wagner, K. 1999. "The German Apprenticeship System under Strain." In *The German Skills Machine,* edited by P. D. Culpepper and D. Finegold, 37–76. New York, Berghahn Books.

Wallach, M. A., N. Kogan, and D. J. Bem. 1962. "Group Influence on Individual Risk Taking." *Journal of Abnormal and Social Psychology* 25: 75–86.

Wendt, A. 1999. *Social Theory of International Politics.* New York, Cambridge University Press.

Wiesenthal, H., ed. 1995. *Einheit als Interessenpolitik: Studien zur sektoralen Transformation Ostdeutschlands.* Frankfurt, Campus.

Williamson, O. E. 1985. *The Economic Institutions of Capitalism.* New York, The Free Press.

Wonneberger, B. 1994. *Fehlende Lehrstellen und Fehlqualifizierung als Probleme des dualen Systems sowie deren berufbildungspolitische Behandlung durch Staat, Arbeitgeber und Gewerkschaften in den Jahren 1978 bis 1986.* Berlin, Peter Lang.

Wood, S. 1997. "Capitalist Constitutions: Supply Side Reforms in Britain and West Germany, 1960–1990." Ph.D. diss., Department of Government, Harvard University.

——. 2001. "Business, Government, and Patterns of Labor Market Policy in Britain and the Federal Republic of Germany." In *Varieties of Capitalism: The Institutional Foundations of Comparative Advantage,* edited by P. A. Hall and D. Soskice, 247–74. New York, Oxford University Press.

Yakubovich, C. 1998. "Malgré Les Restructurations, La Part des Ouvriers et des Cadres Démeure Plus Forte en Allemagne qu'en France dans L'Industrie." *Premières Informations et Premières Synthèses* 14(1): 1–6.

Ziegler, N. 1997. *Governing Ideas: Strategies for Innovation in France and Germany.* Ithaca, Cornell University Press.

Index